MEDIUM ÆVUM MONOGRAPHS

NEW SERIES XII

I0224829

A DESCRIPTIVE GUIDE
TO THE MANUSCRIPTS OF THE
PRICK OF CONSCIENCE

ROBERT E. LEWIS
and
ANGUS McINTOSH

The Society for the Study of
Mediæval Languages and Literature
Oxford
1982

THE SOCIETY FOR THE STUDY OF
MEDIEVAL LANGUAGES AND
LITERATURE

http://mediumaevum.modhist.ox.ac.uk

British Library Cataloguing in Publication Data
A catalogue record for this book is available
from the British Library

ISBN-13: 978-0-907570-02-8 (pb)

Reprinted 2016

PREFACE

Our aim in what follows is to provide a guide to the manuscripts, versions, and texts of the popular Middle English poem the *Prick of Conscience*. We have chosen the word 'guide' (rather than 'catalogue') intentionally to emphasize our view of its purpose: to provide basic bibliographical information and suggest leads to be pursued in such a way as to be of direct practical value to anyone studying the poem itself as well as to stimulate and facilitate research into some of the important broader questions connected with it, such as its genre, the reasons for its popularity, its audience, and its influence in Britain in the later Middle Ages. In preparing the guide we have each undertaken specific tasks, though we have of course read and discussed each other's work and have each played our part in making the overall inventory of manuscripts as full and as accurate as possible. Lewis is responsible for categories 1–4 and 6 of the guide, the corresponding parts of the introduction, and the bibliography. McIntosh is responsible for category 5, the corresponding part of the introduction, and the appendix; he has also contributed notes on a number of hands for category 1. We are jointly responsible for category 7 and the corresponding part of the introduction.

The idea for this guide began to take shape during 1973–74, when Lewis was a visiting research fellow at the Institute for Advanced Studies in the Humanities at the University of Edinburgh, and he is indebted to the Institute and its former director, Professor William Beattie, both for the fellowship and for the congenial setting for research. He is also indebted to the American Council of Learned Societies and to Indiana University for research grants during the same period and to the American Philosophical Society for a research grant (Penrose fund No. 7622) during the summer of 1976. We both gratefully acknowledge publication subsidies from the Carnegie Trust for the Universities of Scotland and the President's Council on the Humanities at Indiana University.

Our work has been very greatly facilitated by the availability of an almost complete collection of microfilms of the manuscripts of the poem, housed in the library of Edinburgh University

and forming part of the collection of material built up over the
last thirty years for the Middle English Dialect Project. We grate-
fully acknowledge the assistance we have received from Mr
J. T. D. Hall, Miss Marjorie Robertson, and their predecessors,
and in particular the unstinting help over many years of Mr C. P.
Finlayson. Other libraries have generously provided supplemental
microfilms, and many librarians have patiently answered our ques-
tions. The list would be too long if we mentioned all the librarians
by name, but we must thank the following for help beyond
the ordinary and expected: Mrs Consuelo Wager Dutschke, Miss
Joan Gibbs, Miss G. J. Groocock, Mr Daniel Huws, Miss G. A.
Matheson, Miss Eleanor L. Nicholes, Mr William O'Sullivan, Mr
A. E. B. Owen, Mr Stephen R. Parks, Dr John Martin Robinson,
Mrs Sara Rodger, Miss Anne C. Snape, and Dr Frank Taylor.

For giving us the benefit of their knowledge, experience, and
time we particularly wish to thank Mrs Ginny Barnes, Mr Ronald
Batty, Dr Nita Scudder Baugh, Dr Richard Beadle, Mr Michael
Benskin, Mr Derek Britton, Mrs Joan Bryant, Dr Curt F. Bühler,
Mr Peter Buneman, Professor A. S. G. Edwards, Miss Christina
Foyle, Dr W. O. Hassall, Dr Anne Hudson, Professor Jeanne
Krochalis, Miss Jean Preston, Professor Paul Saenger, Dr Kath-
leen L. Scott, and Professor Stacy Waters.

We owe special thanks to Mr George Leslie for preparing the
maps printed in the appendix; to Dr N. R. Ker for his encourage-
ment, notes on manuscripts, and other kindnesses over the
years; to Dr A. I. Doyle for so generously putting at our dispo-
sal a great amount of information bearing both directly and in-
directly on the subject of this guide; and above all to Professor
M. L. Samuels, to whom we owe the suggested scribal origins
of almost all the texts of the Southern Recension and of all the
texts of the Main Version from the south and the south Midlands.

After the guide was completed, Mr M. B. Parkes kindly called
to our attention the existence of a fragmentary copy of the
poem at Hatfield House, and Mr R. H. Harcourt Williams subse-
quently provided fuller information about it. To have inserted
this manuscript at its proper place in our alphabetical system
would have necessitated a renumbering of over half the manu-
scripts in the guide, and we decided instead, since our categories
are open-ended, to add it at the end of the appropriate category
(the Main Version). If any further manuscripts of the poem are
discovered, they can be added in the same way.

CONTENTS

BIBLIOGRAPHICAL ABBREVIATIONS

The following books, articles, and series are cited by abbreviation in at least two different places in the guide. For items cited only once full bibliographical details will be found in the notes to the introduction or in category 6 of the entries in the body of the guide.

Abbott	Abbott, T. K., *Catalogue of the Manuscripts in the Library of Trinity College, Dublin to Which Is Added a List of the Fagel Collection of Maps in the Same Library* (Dublin: Hodges, Figgis, and Co., Ltd., 1900)
Additional Cat. 1877	*Catalogue of Additions to the Manuscripts in the British Museum in the Years MDCCCLIV–MDCCCLXXV*, Volume II (London: Trustees of the British Museum, 1877)
Additional Cat. 1907	*Catalogue of Additions to the Manuscripts in the British Museum in the Years MDCCCC–MDCCCCV* (London: Trustees of the British Museum, 1907)
Allen, 'Authorship'	Allen, Hope Emily, 'The Authorship of the *Prick of Conscience*', *Studies in English and Comparative Literature*, Radcliffe College Monographs, 15 (Boston: Ginn and Co., 1910), pp. 115-70
Allen, '*SV*'	——, 'The *Speculum Vitae*: Addendum', *PMLA*, 32 (1917), 133-62
Allen, 'Two'	——, 'Two Middle-English Translations from the Anglo-Norman', *Modern Philology*, 13 (1916), 744-45
Allen, *Writings*	——, *Writings Ascribed to Richard Rolle Hermit of Hampole and Materials for His Biography*, Monograph Series, Modern Language Association of

America (New York: D. C. Heath and Co., 1927)

Andreae — Andreae, Percy, *Die Handschriften des Pricke of Conscience von Richard Rolle de Hampole im Britischen Museum* (Berlin: G. Bernstein, 1888)

Art — *The Art of Writing 2800 B.C. to 1930 A.D.* (London: Maggs Bros., 1930)

Ashmole Cat. — Black, William Henry, *A Descriptive, Analytical, and Critical Catalogue of the Manuscripts Bequeathed unto the University of Oxford by Elias Ashmole, Esq., M.D., F.R.S., Windsor Herald* . . . (Oxford: Oxford University Press, 1845)

Ayscough — Ayscough, Samuel, *A Catalogue of the Manuscripts Preserved in the British Museum Hitherto Undescribed*, 2 vols (London: S. Ayscough, 1782)

Bale — Bale, John, *Index Britanniae Scriptorum* (1550s), ed. R. L. Poole and Mary Bateson, *Anecdota Oxoniensia,* Mediaeval and Modern Series, Part IX (Oxford: Clarendon Press, 1902)

Baugh — Baugh, Nita Scudder, *A Worcestershire Miscellany, Compiled by John Northwood, c. 1400, Edited from British Museum MS. Add. 37,787* (Philadelphia: privately printed, 1956)

Benedikz — Benedikz, B. S., *Lichfield Cathedral Library: A Catalogue of the Cathedral Library Manuscripts*, revised version (Birmingham: University Library, 1978)

Benskin and Laing — Benskin, Michael, and Margaret Laing, 'Translations and *Mischsprachen* in Middle English Manuscripts', in *So Meny People Longages and Tonges: Philological Essays on Scots and Mediaeval English Presented to Angus McIntosh*, ed. Michael Benskin and

M. L. Samuels (Edinburgh, 1981), 55–106

Britton   Britton, Derek, 'Unnoticed Fragments of the *Prick of Conscience*', *Neuphilologische Mitteilungen*, 80 (1979), 327–34

Bülbring, *Archiv*   Bülbring, Karl D., 'Über die Handschrift Nr. 491 der Lambeth-Bibliothek', *Archiv für das Studium der neueren Sprachen und Litteraturen*, 86 (1891), 383–92

Bülbring, *ES*   ——, 'Zu den Handschriften von Richard Rolle's "Prick of Conscience" ', *Englische Studien*, 23 (1897), 1–30

Bülbring, *Trans.*   ——, 'On Twenty-five MSS. of Richard Rolle's "Pricke of Conscience", Eighteen of Them in the British Museum, Four in the Library of Trinity College, Dublin, the Corser MS., and Two in Lichfield Cathedral Library', *Transactions of the Philological Society, 1888–90* (1891), 261–83

Campbell   Campbell, Killis, 'A Neglected Manuscript of *The Prick of Conscience*', *Modern Language Notes*, 20 (1905), 210–11

Census   DeRicci, Seymour J., and W. J. Wilson, *Census of Medieval and Renaissance Manuscripts in the United States and Canada*, 3 vols (New York: H. W. Wilson Co., 1935–40)

Cotton Cat.   *A Catalogue of the Manuscripts in the Cottonian Library Deposited in the British Museum* (London: L. Hansard, 1802)

Coxe   Coxe, H. O., *Catalogus Codicum MSS. Qui in Collegiis Aulisque Oxoniensibus Hodie Adservantur*, 2 vols (Oxford: Oxford University Press, 1852). For vol. I we have used the reprint made from the annotated copy at the Bodleian Library, with introduction by K. W. Humphreys (East Ardsley, Wakefield, Yorks.: EP Publishing Ltd., 1972)

CUL Cat.   *A Catalogue of the Manuscripts Preserved in the Library of the University of Cambridge*, 6 vols (Cambridge: Cambridge University Press, 1856–67)

Dareau and McIntosh Dareau, Margaret G., and Angus McIntosh, 'A Dialect Word in Some West Midland Manuscripts of the *Prick of Conscience*', in *Edinburgh Studies in English and Scots*, ed. A. J. Aitken, A. McIntosh, and H. Pálsson (London: Longman, 1971), 20–26

D'Evelyn   D'Evelyn, Charlotte, 'An East Midland Recension of *The Pricke of Conscience*', *PMLA*, 45 (1930), 180–200

Digby Cat.   Macray, Gulielmus D., *Catalogi Codicum Manuscriptorum Bibliothecae Bodleianae Pars Nona, Codices a Viro Clarissimo Kenelm Digby, Eq. Aur., Anno 1634 Donatos, Complectens* (Oxford: Clarendon Press, 1883)

Doyle, 'Shaping'   Doyle, A. I., 'The Shaping of the Vernon and Simeon Manuscripts', in *Chaucer and Middle English Studies in Honour of Rossell Hope Robbins*, ed. Beryl Rowland (Kent, Ohio: Kent State University Press, 1974), 328–41

Doyle, 'Survey'   ——, 'A Survey of the Origins and Circulation of Theological Writings in English in the 14th, 15th, and Early 16th Centuries with Special Consideration of the Part of the Clergy Therein', 2 vols (unpublished Ph.D. thesis, Cambridge University, 1953)

EETS os   Early English Text Society, original series

Faye and Bond   Faye, C. U., and W. H. Bond, *Supplement*

	to the *Census of Medieval and Renaissance Manuscripts in the United States and Canada* (New York: The Bibliographical Society of America, 1962)
Furnivall	Furnivall, Frederick J., ed., *Ballads from Manuscripts*, I (London: The Ballad Society, 1868-72)
Halliwell	Halliwell, James Orchard, ed., *The Thornton Romances* (London: Camden Society, 1844)
Harley Cat.	*A Catalogue of the Harleian Manuscripts in the British Museum*, 4 vols (London: G. Eyre and A. Strahan, 1808-12)
Hood	Hood, Eu. (=Joseph Haslewood), 'Stimulus Conscientie', *The Gentleman's Magazine and Historical Chronicle*, 97, 2 (1827), 216-20
Horstman	Horstman, Carl, ed., *Yorkshire Writers: Richard Rolle of Hampole an English Father of the Church and His Followers*, 2 vols (London: Swan Sonnenschein and Co., 1895-96)
Humphreys and Lightbown	Humphreys, K. W., and J. Lightbown, 'Two Manuscripts of the *Pricke of Conscience* in the Brotherton Collection, University of Leeds', *Leeds Studies in English and Kindred Languages*, 7-8 (1952), 29-38
IMEV	Brown, Carleton, and Rossell Hope Robbins, *The Index of Middle English Verse* (New York: Columbia University Press, for The Index Society, 1943). *Supplement to the Index of Middle English Verse*, by Robbins and John L. Cutler (Lexington: University of Kentucky Press, 1965)
Kaiser	Kaiser, Rolf, ed., *Medieval English*, 3rd edn (West Berlin: Rolf Kaiser, 1958);

	the selections from the *Prick of Conscience* are also in the first and second German editions
Ker	Ker, Neil R., unpublished notes for *MMBL*, III
Lambeth Cat.	James, M. R., and Claude Jenkins, *A Descriptive Catalogue of the Manuscripts in the Library of Lambeth Palace*, 5 parts (Cambridge: Cambridge University Press, 1930–32)
Laud Cat.	Coxe, H. O., *Catalogi Codicum Manuscriptorum Bibliothecae Bodleianae: Pars Secunda Codices Latinos et Miscellaneos Laudianos Complectens*, 2 fascicles (Oxford: Oxford University Press, 1858–85)
Lewis, 'Editorial'	Lewis, Robert E., 'Editorial Technique in the *Index of Middle English Prose*', in *Middle English Prose: Essays on Bibliographical Problems*, ed. A. S. G. Edwards and Derek Pearsall (New York: Garland Publishing, Inc., 1981), 43–64
Lewis, 'Relationship'	——, 'The Relationship of the Vernon and Simeon Texts of the *Pricke of Conscience*', in *So Meny People Longages and Tonges: Philological Essays on Scots and Mediaeval English Presented to Angus McIntosh*, ed. Michael Benskin and M. L. Samuels (Edinburgh, 1981), 251–64
Lightbown	Lightbown, J., '*The Pricke of Conscience*: A Collation of MSS. Galba E IX and Harley 4196', *Leeds Studies in English and Kindred Languages*, 4 (1935), 58–61
List	*List of Additions to the Manuscripts in the British Museum in the Years MDCCCXXXVI–MDCCCXL* (London: Trustees of the British Museum, 1843)

Magdalene Cat. - James, M. R., *A Descriptive Catalogue of the Manuscripts in the College Library of Magdalene College Cambridge* (Cambridge: Cambridge University Press, 1909)

McIntosh, 'Scribal' - McIntosh, Angus, 'Scribal Profiles from Middle English Texts', *Neuphilologische Mitteilungen*, 76 (1975), 218–35

McIntosh, 'Two' - ——, 'Two Unnoticed Interpolations in Four Manuscripts of the *Prick of Conscience*', *Neuphilologische Mitteilungen*, 77 (1976), 63–78

MLGB - Ker, N. R., *Medieval Libraries of Great Britain: A List of Surviving Books*, 2nd edn (London: Royal Historical Society, 1964)

MMBL - Ker, N. R., *Medieval Manuscripts in British Libraries, I: London* and *II: Abbotsford-Keele* (Oxford: Clarendon Press, 1969, 1977)

Morris - Morris, Richard, ed., *The Pricke of Conscience (Stimulus Conscientiae) a Northumbrian Poem by Richard Rolle de Hampole*, Philological Society (Berlin: A. Asher & Co., 1863; rptd New York: AMS Press, 1973)

M.R. - R., M., 'Hampole's Works', *Notes and Queries*, 3rd Series, 2 (1862), 386a

Oudin - Oudin, Casimir, *Commentarius de Scriptoribus Ecclesiae Antiquis Illorumque Scriptis Tam Impressis Quam Manuscriptis . . .* , III (Frankfurt am Main and Leipzig, 1722)

Pembroke Cat. - James, M. R., *A Descriptive Catalogue of the Manuscripts in the Library of Pembroke College, Cambridge* (Cambridge: Cambridge University Press, 1905)

Pink - Pink, H. L., unpublished descriptions, based on those of M. R. James, of selected manuscripts at Cambridge University Library

Pits   Pits, John, *Relationum Historicarum de Rebus Anglicis*, I (Paris: R. Thierry and S. Cramoisy, 1619)

Rawlinson Cat.   Macray, Gulielmus D., *Catalogi Codicum Manuscriptorum Bibliothecae Bodleianae Partis Quintae . . . Viri Munificentissimi Ricardi Rawlinson . . .* (Oxford: Oxford University Press, 1862–1900)

Ritson   Ritson, Joseph, *Bibliographica Poetica: A Catalogue of Engleish Poets of the Twelfth, Thirteenth, Fourteenth, Fifteenth and Sixteenth, Centurys . . .* (London: G. and W. Nicol, 1802)

Robbins   Robbins, Rossell Hope, 'The Gurney Series of Religious Lyrics', *PMLA*, 54 (1939), 369–90

Royal Cat.   Warner, Sir George F., and Julius P. Gilson, *Catalogue of Western Manuscripts in the Old Royal and King's Collections*, 4 vols (London: Oxford University Press, 1921)

Saenger   Saenger, Paul, unpublished notes for a forthcoming catalogue of the pre-1500 manuscripts at the Newberry Library, Chicago

Sajavaara   Sajavaara, Kari, 'The Relationship of the Vernon and Simeon Manuscripts', *Neuphilologische Mitteilungen*, 68 (1967), 428–40

SC   Hunt, R. W., F. Madan, H. H. E. Craster, N. Denholm-Young, and P. D. Record, *A Summary Catalogue of Western Manuscripts in the Bodleian Library at Oxford Which Have Not Hitherto Been Catalogued in the Quarto Series with References to the Oriental and Other Manuscripts*, 7 vols in 8 (Oxford: Clarendon Press, 1895–1953)

Schulz, *HLQ*	Schulz, H. C., 'A Middle English Manuscript Used as Printer's Copy', *The Huntington Library Quarterly*, 29 (1966), 325-36
Schulz, *Library*	——, 'Manuscript Printer's Copy for a Lost Early English Book', *The Library*, 4th Series, 22 (1942), 138-44
St John's Cat.	James, M. R., *A Descriptive Catalogue of the Manuscripts in the Library of St John's College Cambridge* (Cambridge: Cambridge University Press, 1913)
Tanner	Tanner, Thomas, *Bibliotheca Britannico-Hibernica* . . . (London: Societas ad Literas Promovendas, 1748)
Tyson	Tyson, Moses, 'Hand-List of the Collection of English Manuscripts in the John Rylands Library, 1928', *Bulletin of the John Rylands Library Manchester*, 13 (1929), 152-219
Warton-Hazlitt	Warton, Thomas, *History of English Poetry from the Twelfth to the Close of the Sixteenth Century*, edited by W. Carew Hazlitt (London: Reeves and Turner, 1871), II; all references to the 1824 edition (see next item) are also in the 1871 edition unless noted; all references to the 1871 edition are to material new to this edition
Warton-Price	——, *The History of English Poetry from the Close of the Eleventh to the Commencement of the Eighteenth Century*, new edition by Richard Price (London: Thomas Tegg, 1824), II; this edition includes Warton's original text with notes by Price and others; the *Prick of Conscience* material was originally in Warton's Vol. I (1774)
Waters	Waters, Stacy, '*The Pricke of Conscience*:

The Southern Recension, Book **V'**
(unpublished Ph.D. thesis, University
of Edinburgh, 1976)

Wells   Wells, John Edwin, *A Manual of the
Writings in Middle English 1050–
1400*, with nine supplements to 1945
(New Haven: Connecticut Academy
of Arts and Sciences, 1916–1951)

Wright   Wright, Cyril Ernest, *Fontes Harleiani:
A Study of the Sources of the Har-
leian Collection of Manuscripts
Preserved in the Department of
Manuscripts in the British Museum*
(London: The Trustees of the British
Museum, 1972)

Yates   Yates, Joseph Brooks, 'An Account of
an Unprinted English Poem, Written
in the Early Part of the Fourteenth
Century, by Richard de Hampole,
and Entitled "Stimulus Conscien-
tiae", or "The Prick of Conscience" ',
Archaeologia, 19 (1821), 314–35

Zacour and Hirsch   Zacour, Norman P., and Rudolf Hirsch,
*Catalogue of the Manuscripts in the
Libraries of the University of Penn-
sylvania to 1800* (Philadelphia: Uni-
versity of Pennsylvania Press, 1965)

INTRODUCTION

i

The *Prick of Conscience*: Its Nature, Popularity, and Circulation

The *Prick of Conscience*, to judge from the number of known manuscripts (115), was the most popular English poem of the Middle Ages, surpassing such popular poems as Chaucer's *Canterbury Tales* (its nearest competitor with sixty-four manuscripts), *Piers Plowman* (with fifty-four), and Gower's *Confessio Amantis* (with fifty-one), and far surpassing such related works as Robert Mannyng's *Handlyng Synne* (with six) and Dan Michel of Northgate's *Ayenbite of Inwyt* (with only one).[1] It is an important poem and worth studying for a number of reasons and from a variety of points of view. Because of its popularity, for example, a careful study of its contents can tell us a great deal about reading and listening tastes and interests in Britain in the late Middle Ages. It is of interest to dialectologists because of the geographical distribution of the manuscripts: nearly four fifths of the counties in England can claim at least one copy of the poem, and some have more than one. The variety of ways and versions in which it circulated and the extent to which it was

---

[1] The figures for the verse texts are from the Supplement to *The Index of Middle English Verse* (*IMEV*). We have arrived at 115 for the *Prick of Conscience* in the same way as *IMEV* arrived at sixty-four for the *Canterbury Tales*, viz., by counting complete, incomplete, and fragmentary copies but not extracts circulating separately. See further, on the *Canterbury Tales*, Daniel S. Silvia, 'Some Fifteenth-Century Manuscripts of the *Canterbury Tales*', in *Chaucer and Middle English Studies in Honour of Rossell Hope Robbins*, ed. Beryl Rowland (London: George Allen & Unwin, Ltd., 1974), pp. 153-63, who is in general agreement with the figure in *IMEV*; see especially p. 154, where he argues that the number to be used henceforth should be 'roughly sixty'.

The figure for the *Prick of Conscience* may in fact be 116, for in spite of our best efforts there is still one manuscript we have been unable to locate from the entries in *IMEV*: 3428.72, a fifteenth-century fragment of nine leaves from Book III formerly owned by J. O. Halliwell (Additional MS IV in Allen, *Writings*, p. 374); for a brief description see Sotheby's Sale Catalogue, 20-22 December 1920, Lot 515. See also note 31 below.

For *IMEV* and other bibliographical abbreviations used in the introduction and the guide see the list of abbreviations on pp. vi-xv; every item referred to in at least two different places will be found in the list.

quoted in Middle English literature provide a guide to the sub-
jects that medieval scribes and writers found most important in
religious writing. Notes of ownership and provenances in such a
large number of manuscripts of a single work, supplemented by
the nature of the contents, are a good starting point for a study
of the important question of the nature of the late medieval
audience. And because of the large number of sources on which
the poem is based, it provides a good testing ground for deter-
mining where a medieval religious writer got his source material,
in what form it reached him, and how he shaped it to his own
purposes.

Unfortunately, however, scholars have been hampered in
their study of these important issues—not to mention such
larger matters as the relationship of the poem to other works in
the same genre, its importance in the literary and intellectual
environment of the fourteenth century, the reasons for its popu-
larity, and its influence on later literature—for lack of basic
information about the manuscripts, versions, and texts of the
poem. There is only one edition, now over a hundred years old
and based on a study of only eleven manuscripts (ten at the
British Library and one in private hands),[2] and selections from
the poem seldom appear in anthologies;[3] the little scholarly
work that has been done on the manuscripts and versions (a
minuscule amount compared with that done on the *Canterbury
Tales* and *Piers Plowman*) is often buried in footnotes or appears
in inaccessible books and articles; indeed, there is not even a
reliable guide, with basic bibliographical, codicological, and tex-
tual information, to the manuscripts of the various versions.[4] It
is to correct this lack and thereby to provide a starting point for
further research on this important poem that we have prepared
the present guide.

The *Prick of Conscience* is a long poem (some 9624+ lines in

[2] By Richard Morris in 1863, reprinted in 1973. All line numbers for the *Prick of
Conscience*, and any references we make to the 'original' poem, both in the introduc-
tion and in the guide, are based on this edition.
[3] The exceptions among anthologies published since 1900 are A. Brandl and
O. Zippel, *Mittelenglische Sprach- und Literaturproben*, 2nd edn (Berlin: Weid-
mannsche Buchhandlung, 1927), pp. 159–63; Kaiser, pp. 234–42; and Celia and Ken-
neth Sisam, *The Oxford Book of Medieval Verse* (Oxford: Clarendon Press, 1970),
pp. 172–73 (very brief extract).
[4] Even *IMEV* is often unreliable on the two main versions of the poem, as the
first line of category 6 for a number of manuscripts in the guide reveals, though this
is not surprising, for Brown and Robbins were not engaged in detailed textual study.

Morris's edition), in rhyming couplets, containing a prologue; seven books which describe, in turn, the wretchedness of man's nature, the world and the various conditions thereof, death and the fear of death, purgatory, the day of judgment, the pains of hell, and the joys of heaven; and a short epilogue.[5] The poem has a great many sources—ultimately over twenty separate works, primarily Latin, including both well known ones like St Augustine's *De Civitate Dei*, Honorius of Autun's *Elucidarium*, and Bartholomeus Anglicus's *De Proprietatibus Rerum* and not so well known ones like Robert Grosseteste's *De Penis Purgatorii* (in its French version) and the *Compendium Theologice Veritatis* by Hugh Ripelin of Strasbourg.[6] The poem is often put in the same general class as *Handlyng Synne* and the *Ayenbite of Inwyt*,[7] but those works deal largely with the Seven Deadly Sins, whereas the *Prick of Conscience* treats a variety of topics and barely touches on the Sins; its closest companion is really the *Speculum Vite* attributed to William of Nassington, to which it is similar in 'dialect and manner',[8] though it treats different topics.

The *Prick of Conscience* is attributed five times in manuscripts to Richard Rolle of Hampole, who lived from 1300 to 1349, and three times to Robert Grosseteste, Bishop of Lincoln, who lived from *c.* 1170 to 1253.[9] The attribution to Rolle was the traditional one until it was persuasively disposed

[5] The Epilogue, unlike the Prologue, is never so designated in the manuscripts, but it is a convenient term for lines 9533-624 of the poem, has been used before (e.g., Allen, 'Authorship', pp. 122 and 138, and Allen, *Writings*, p. 386), and is used throughout this guide.

[6] For general studies of the sources see Reinhold Köhler, 'Quellennachweise zu Richard Rolle's von Hampole Gedicht *"The Pricke of Conscience"* ', *Jahrbuch für romanische und englische Literatur*, 6 (1865), 196-212, and Arnold Hahn, *Quellenuntersuchungen zu Richard Rolles englischen Schriften* (Dissertation, Halle a/S., 1900), pp. 16-40; Hahn's is the fuller of the two studies, though neither one does more than scratch the surface of this complex subject. See Robert J. Relihan, Jr., 'A Critical Edition of the Anglo-Norman and Latin Versions of *Les Peines de Purgatorie*' (unpublished Ph.D. dissertation, University of Iowa, 1978), pp. 71-86, for the evidence that the author is indebted to the French rather than the Latin version of Grosseteste's *De Penis Purgatorii*. See also note 10 below.

[7] e.g., by Wells, p. 447.

[8] Allen, *Writings*, p. 372.

[9] For Rolle, Main Version (MV) 6, 30, 46, 61 and Latin (L) 6 in the guide. Bale was apparently the first post-medieval writer to attribute the poem to Rolle (see Bale, p. 348, though he knew only of the Latin translation; see further note 32 below); at least one manuscript (MV 62) may have a post-medieval ascription to Rolle earlier than Bale. For Grosseteste, MV 25, 63, 72.

of on stylistic grounds by Hope Emily Allen in 1910 (Allen, 'Authorship') and again, with additional evidence, in 1927 (Allen, *Writings*, pp. 372-97); and Grosseteste can be disposed of on chronological grounds, having died before one of the main sources of the poem, the *Compendium Theologice Veritatis*, was written *c.* 1265-70.[10] Because of the similarities between the *Prick of Conscience* and the *Speculum Vite*, William of Nassington has also been suggested as the author,[11] but there is no proof for the suggestion, and, at least for the time being, one must call the poem anonymous. The traditional attribution to Rolle has also helped to provide the traditional date: towards the middle of the fourteenth century (that is, shortly before Rolle's death in 1349), and, though the reasons for this date are no longer valid, the date itself is probably correct. Manuscripts do not begin to appear until after 1350, but when they do appear, they do so in large numbers, which is usually a sign that the work in question was composed not many years before.[12] Many of these early manuscripts,[13] as well as those that are closest to the presumed original,[14] are in northern dialects, and scholars have been in agreement that the poem was written in the north of England, probably in Yorkshire.

[10] The *Compendium* is one of the few sources mentioned by the author (line 3951), though he attributes it to Thomas Aquinas. On the *Compendium* and its author see Georg Boner, 'Über den Dominikanertheologen Hugo von Strassburg', *Archivum Fratrum Praedicatorum*, 24 (1954), 269-86 (pp. 276-77 and 283).

[11] First by Allen, 'Authorship', pp. 163-70, basing her speculation on the findings of J. Ullmann, 'Studien zu Richard Rolle de Hampole I', *Englische Studien*, 7 (1884), 415-72 (pp. 419-22, 468-70). She later called his findings into question in '*SV*', especially pp. 133-36, but never rejected the possibility that Nassington may have been the author of the *Prick of Conscience*. See further Allen, *Writings*, pp. 371-72, and Britton, pp. 330-31, n. 12.

[12] Forty of the ninety-seven Main Version manuscripts are probably from the second half of the fourteenth century. MV 15 is the only manuscript recently and authoritatively dated in the middle of the fourteenth century (*MMBL*, II, 281: 's. xiv med.'); Campbell, following the *SC*, notes that MV 83 is 'about 1350' (p. 210), but Allen, following the best opinion at the Bodleian Library, refutes this (*Writings*, pp. 380-81, note 4 from p. 380); Wells says there are many manuscripts of *c.* 1350 (p. 447), but there is no evidence to support such a statement. If, as Morris points out (pp. 265-68, 269-72), the *Prick of Conscience* is indebted to the *Cursor Mundi*, and if that poem was written in the first quarter of the fourteenth century (see Wells, p. 340, who gives the accepted date), then *c.* 1325 is the *terminus a quo* for the *Prick of Conscience*, with the *terminus ad quem* 's. xiv med.' (MV 15). Cf. George R. Coffman, 'Old Age from Horace to Chaucer. Some Literary Affinities and Adventures of an Idea', *Speculum*, 9 (1934), 264-67, who believes that the *Cursor Mundi* was indebted to the *Prick of Conscience*, but this is unlikely.

[13] MV 5, 27, 34, 35, 41, 44, 62, 83, 93.

[14] MV 27, 34, 44, 83, 96, as based on the collations in Britton.

The popularity of the poem can be measured by the sheer number of manuscripts, by their dialectal distribution, by the extent of the poem's influence, by allusions to the poem in medieval wills and book lists,[15] and by the variety of ways in which the poem circulated. It is the last of these that has provided the organizational scheme for the present guide. We distinguish five versions in which the poem circulated and was read during the Middle Ages.

I

The Main Version

Though study of the exact nature and number of versions of the poem is far from complete—indeed, one of the purposes of the guide is to encourage such study—the general outlines are pretty clear. Two principal versions of the poem were in circulation: the original, or Main Version (MV), and a radically and thoroughly revised version, the Southern Recension. The Main Version, which exists in ninety-seven manuscripts (including complete, incomplete, and fragmentary copies), originated, as we have noted, in the north of England, probably in Yorkshire, but it is not confined to that county or even to the North as a whole and to the north Midlands, for, as map i in the appendix makes clear, copies can be found all over East Anglia, in the south west Midlands, and as far south as Sussex and Devon; there are even three copies in Hiberno-English. It is clear from what little work has been done on these ninety-seven manuscripts that subgroupings can be made on the basis of varying length of copies, rearrangement or addition of material, and line-by-line textual revision, but that, in comparison with the more radically and thoroughly revised Southern Recension, they are all, to a greater or lesser extent, variations of one and the same poem.

Some of these Main Version subgroupings call for further comment. As long ago as 1888 Percy Andreae made the first classification of manuscripts, using the eighteen he knew about at the British Library, and his groupings were followed and

---

[15] We know of seven, all but one from the fifteenth century; five of the seven record ownership by laity rather than clergy. For these seven see R. M. Wilson, *The Lost Literature of Medieval England*, 2nd edn (London: Methuen & Co. Ltd., 1970), p. 146; see also Allen, *Writings*, pp. 381, 386.

added to by subsequent scholars down to 1952.[16] Though much
more research is required before the relationships of the Main
Version manuscripts are completely understood, and though
contamination (as one would expect with such a large number
of manuscripts) often complicates the relationships, our investi-
gations have refined and corrected Andreae's groupings, and the
Main Version manuscripts now appear to divide themselves
tentatively into four groups.[17] The first (I) corresponds to
Andreae's Z and includes, among others, the manuscripts that
are closest to the presumed original (MV 27, 34, 44, 83, and 96).

The second (II), derived from I, corresponds to Andreae's C;
perhaps its most striking characteristic is a new sixteen-line pre-
face to Book IV, though it has many other readings that differ-
entiate it from the other three groups. Group II contains an
interesting subgroup that was first discussed by Allen (*Writings*,
pp. 387-94) as a Lollard subgroup. It consists of four manu-
scripts (MV 51, 56, 61, and 73), and, though the text exists in
somewhat different form in each, the subgroup itself can con-
veniently be characterized as having two interpolations and one
rearrangement (see category 3 in the specific entries in the guide
for more detailed information on the text in each). The first
interpolation consists of 440 lines of English verse and much
Latin prose incorporating an attack on the clergy, a common
subject in Lollard writings; it is inserted between lines 192 and
193 of the Prologue. The second interpolation consists of a long
series of Latin prose additions (the length varying from manu-
script to manuscript), interspersed with 563 lines of English
verse, also incorporating some anti-clerical sentiment; it is in-
serted in Book VI, between the end of the seventh pain of hell
(line 6894) and the beginning of the eighth (line 6895). The re-
arrangement involves transferring some text from Book V (112
lines corresponding to lines 6346-409) to the end of Book VII
(between lines 9474 and 9475, with a new eight-line link added

[16] The relevant studies, in chronological order, are Andreae (1888), Bülbring,
Trans. (1888-90), Bülbring, *Archiv* (1891), Bülbring, *ES* (1897), D'Evelyn (1930),
and Humphreys and Lightbown (1952). Andreae's test passages, also used in the five
subsequent studies, were lines 1836-927, 5126-204, and 9335-402.

[17] The following comments on the relationships of the Main Version manuscripts,
as well as the remarks in category 7 in the guide for each Main Version manuscript,
are based on our collations of lines 328-47, 644-97, 934-53, 1666-85, 2692-715,
3968-91, 4207-96, 6423-40, 7534-48, and 9575-601, correlated with the findings
in the items noted in note 16 above and in Britton. See the notes to the subgroups
below for further bibliography.

at the end of VII) to become a Book VIII, on the world after judgment day.[18]

The third group (III), derived ultimately from I, corresponds to nothing in Andreae (for he did not know about one of the British Library manuscripts in the group, MV 38, and the other two, MV 26 and 32, he put into a different group in his classification) or in any of the other scholars who have written on the manuscript relationships (for they did not classify any of the manuscripts in the group). The fourth group (IV), also derived ultimately from I, corresponds to Andreae's Xi. It is the largest of the four groups and contains at least three distinctive subgroups.

One involves the well known Vernon and Simeon manuscripts (MV 70 and 40 respectively). Though it is now clear that Simeon diverges from Vernon (although still part of Group IV) between lines 3784–4620, Vernon forms a tight subgroup with

[18] Our comments on the characteristics of this subgroup are based on the details in MV 56. We have not inquired very deeply into the origins of the two interpolations, but the first contains lines 1–26 and 33–64 from the Prologue to the *Cursor Mundi* (*IMEV* 2153) deploring the popularity of secular romances, and both the first and the second contain the 126 lines of a 'treatise in reproof of worldliness in the clergy' (*IMEV* 1425, extant as a separate poem in Bodleian Library MS. e Mus. 198, where it has been added in a late fourteenth-century hand on the end flyleaves, ff. 172–73v), lines 1–82 incorporated into the second interpolation and lines 83–126 reproduced in the first. For the *Cursor Mundi* see the edition by Richard Morris, EETS os 57 (London: N. Trübner & Co., 1874), pp. 8–13; see also Allen, *Writings*, pp. 389–90, and Bülbring, *ES*, p. 24. For *IMEV* 1425 (part of which is based on the *Cursor Mundi*), see the passages from MV 61 in Furnivall, pp. 63–64 (ll. 1–50), and Halliwell, pp. 260–61 (ll. 83–120); see also Allen, *Writings*, pp. 391–92.

It is interesting that one of these four manuscripts, MV 61, is also one of the five manuscripts that attribute the *Prick of Conscience* to Rolle, and the earliest of the five as well, having been written in the second half of the fourteenth century. Many works were attached to Rolle's name in the process of transmission, and it may be that the attribution of the *Prick of Conscience* to him originated with this so-called Lollard subgroup, his name having been added 'by a scribe who recognized that [it] would be a convenient protection for a text in which some Lollard matter was found' (Allen, *Writings*, p. 393). (There are also, by the way, two Lollard recensions of Rolle's *Psalter*.) It is probably significant, as Allen also points out (*Writings*, p. 388), that two of the four manuscripts have connections with counties (MV 56 and 73, Hertfordshire and Essex respectively) near where Lollardy apparently flourished. It is also interesting in this same connection that SR 8, which does not contain the interpolations, belonged to a Richard Reder, of Petersfield in Hampshire, who was apparently accused of heresy in 1473 (*Writings*, p. 387), and that a Richard Colins, who was a member of a family of heretics in Berkshire, 'was accused before the bishop of Lincoln [c. 1521] of having certain English books, among which was . . . the "Prick of Conscience" ' (*Writings*, p. 386). As Allen says, '. . . possibly the suspicions of the Church had been raised on the work in general' (*Writings*, pp. 387–88). See also Margaret Aston, 'Lollardy and Literacy', *History*, 62 (1977), 347–71 (pp. 362, 362, n. 71, 364–65, and 364, n. 83).

Simeon before and after—a subgroup that also includes, for all or part of the text, MV 18, 31, 36, 59, 77, and 82. This subgroup is characterized by the displacement (no doubt originally by mistake) of lines 950–1181 from Book II to a position between lines 585 and 586 in Book I, two titles to Book I at different places, a similar beginning to Book IV, and a number of other readings.[19]

The second of these subgroups exists in seven manuscripts (MV 23, 45, 54, 57, 68, 88, and 89, though MV 45 and 57 are defective at the beginning). All seven were written in the west Midlands, all but two (MV 68 and 88) coming from the Lichfield area in Staffordshire, and there is reason to believe that their ultimate exemplar may have been MV 31, which originated in Lichfield and in addition is a member of the Vernon-Simeon subgroup. This subgroup is characterized by ten new lines (expanded to twenty-two in MV 57 and 88) added to the beginning of the Prologue in which a title and an outline (neither of which exists at the beginning of the original poem) are given, as well as other readings that show an independent editor trying to make better sense of what he had in front of him.[20]

A third subgroup consists of four closely related manuscripts (MV 4, 24, 63, and 72) and is characterized by two additions in Book II, one of twenty lines and another of six lines. The ancestor of this subgroup appears to be the Vernon–Simeon subgroup, of which the probable original of the subgroup containing ten new lines at the beginning, MV 31, is also a member.[21] One can see with these three interrelated subgroups how a picture of the manuscript relationships of Main Version Group IV begins to emerge, though much more work is needed before the picture can become absolutely clear.

There are a number of other subgroups among the Main Version manuscripts that have not been studied as carefully as those already noted. For example, MV 11 and 14 from Group I are very closely related: both contain a considerably condensed (by over sixty per cent), paraphrastic text, though also with some expansion; both end, presumably by design, with a version

---

[19] Lewis, 'Relationship'; see also McIntosh, 'Two', pp. 69 and 69, n. 1. For detailed information on the text in each see category 3 in the specific entries in the guide.

[20] Dareau and McIntosh. This is the version that *IMEV* calls '*The Pricke of Conscience* with ten prefatory lines prefixed to the usual beginning', though the entry (1193) omits MV 45, 57, and 88.

[21] McIntosh, 'Two', especially pp. 64–69.

of line 9532 (or lines 9622-23).[22] A subgroup of Group II has as its title the 'Key of Knowyng' as well as a number of shared readings (MV 8, 33, 41, 58, 64, and 86).[23] One very closely related subgroup in Group III emerges from our collations (MV 6 and 76).[24] All of these subgroups need to be studied more thoroughly, and other new ones will doubtless come to light as scholars investigate the Main Version manuscript relationships further.

II
The Southern Recension

This version, which exists in eighteen manuscripts, deserves to be classified quite separately from the Main Version because it is a much more thorough revision than any of the groups or subgroups of the Main Version. The Southern Recension (SR) is in its various manifestations between seventy-four per cent and ninety-two per cent as long as the Main Version, has a different incipit and explicit,[25] expands certain sections and lines, compresses others, rearranges and re-words still others, changes many of the rhymes, and frequently has English subtitles. It originated somewhere far to the south of the original poem, perhaps in the Thames Valley, but as map ii in the appendix indicates, copies appear well to the north, both east and west, of the Thames Valley and also to the south. The Southern Recension has been studied in more detail than the Main Version: it corresponds to Andreae's Xii, the affiliations of which were tentatively worked out by Charlotte D'Evelyn in 1930 and,

[22] See also IV below, the manuscripts of the *Speculum Huius Vite*.

[23] The title to MV 33 appears only at line 9551, on leaves written in a sixteenth- or seventeenth-century hand, but the text of ff. 23–129 is similar to that in the other manuscripts of the subgroup; ff. 1-22v, however, appear to have a different exemplar. MV 86 has no title and no colophon and omits line 9551, but its text is similar to that in the other manuscripts. MV 92 also has 'The Key of Knowing' as the title, but in a twentieth-century hand; the text, however, which is fragmentary, appears to have some similarity to that in the other manuscripts. MV 8 has a conflated colophon, combining 'consciencie stimulus' with 'þe key of knowyng'.

[24] See especially lines 328, 332-38, 342, 942-45, 952, 1673-77, 1684, 2702, 2707-14, 3968-91. The relationship between the two manuscripts continues into Book V, but thereafter MV 6 becomes very paraphrastic. See further MV 6 and 76, category 7.

[25] The incipit is 'þe miȝt of þe fader of hevene', as in SR 1 (cf. the Main Version incipit from Morris: 'þe myght of þe Fader almyghty'); the explicit is 'þat for mannes love made al þinge', as in SR 1 (cf. the Main Version explicit from Morris: 'þat for us vouched safe on rode to hyng').

more thoroughly and accurately, by McIntosh and (for Book V)
by Stacy Waters.[26] The most likely source of the Southern
Recension was a manuscript of Main Version Group III.[27] The
Southern Recension manuscripts divide themselves into two
major subgroups, representing two stages of development: A
(SR 1, 2, 3, 4, 5, 10, 11, 12) and B, derived from A (SR 6, 7, 8,
9, 13, 14, 15, 16, 17, 18), with SR 3 and 12 (with an eight per
cent and a nine per cent reduction, respectively, from the origi-
nal poem) representing the earliest stage of development.[28]
Three of the Southern Recension manuscripts are conflations of
a Main Version text and a Southern Recension text: SR 6, 8,
and 15;[29] others show conflation of two or more Southern
Recension traditions;[30] and at least one (SR 18) has been cor-
rected from a manuscript of a different tradition.

III
Extracts

In addition to these two principal versions, extracts (E) from
the poem circulated separately, of which twelve are known in
eight manuscripts. Except for the one in E 4, they are all clearly
extracts from the Main Version rather than the Southern Recen-
sion, and even the one in E 4, which is quite different from the
text of Morris's edition, is related to a manuscript of Main Ver-
sion Group IV (MV 21). All of these are clearly extracts rather
than fragments of complete copies of the poem (cf. MV 37, 79,

---

[26] McIntosh collaborated with Peter Buneman and Neil Mitchison on a prelimi-
nary computer-based study of the stemmata of both the Southern Recension and the
Main Version and in addition directed Waters's work on Book V.

[27] Waters has pointed out for Book V (pp. 48–49) that the most likely candidate
would be a manuscript with a text like that in MV 16, 32, 67, 91—or possibly MV 1.

[28] See Waters, pp. 31–40, 62, 65a–68.

[29] See category 7 in the individual entries in the guide for specific details. One
subgroup of A identified by Waters (SR 2, 4, 5) has a table of contents before each
book, and it may be that the scribe of SR 15, which begins like a Main Version text,
combined these individual tables of contents into a single one for the whole poem
and put it at the beginning of his copy. See Morris, pp. xxxiv–xli, where this table of
contents is reproduced.

[30] e.g., SR 2, 10, 11, for which see Waters, pp. 31–40 passim. SR 11 and 14 have
an alternate title at line 9551: 'The floure of conscience' (as in SR 11), and MV 90 has
a Southern Recension explicit. Note also that in the work on the manuscript relation-
ships done before 1930 MV 26, 32, and 36 are placed, for a portion of text, in An-
dreae's Group Xii. In that year D'Evelyn dismissed MV 26 and 32 from Xii (p. 184),
though the earlier classification is retained in *IMEV* (1943); MV 36 was thought by
Andreae and Bülbring, *Trans.*, to shift relationships, and D'Evelyn essentially ignores it.

80, 84, and 97) because they either have a separate title or appear among a series of quotations from other works or else are set apart in some way from what precedes and follows.[31]

IV
The *Speculum Huius Vite*

The *Prick of Conscience* also appears in a highly abbreviated and altered version entitled *Speculum Huius Vite* (S), which exists in two manuscripts, both of the beginning of the fifteenth century. It contains only *c.* 3096 lines (as compared with the 9600+ lines of the original poem), with the abbreviation increasing as the poem progresses; in fact, this version has been reduced by more than two thirds, for approximately ten per cent of its lines are new material, both in English and in Latin. The alterations to the original made in the *Speculum* follow certain clear patterns: a number of organizational devices have been either changed or left out; virtually all *exempla* and all fine distinctions are omitted; not only are the Latin quotations of the original retained, however, but they and the lines before and after are rendered more faithfully than any other parts of the original; and the emphasis throughout is on the audience's *doing* something—forsaking sin, thinking on God, or thanking God for his blessings—in place of the *understanding* of the great variety of elements in God's universe that leads to self-knowledge, which is the main theme of the original poem. The *Speculum* may have been made from a manuscript of the version that appears in MV 11 and 14 (a subgroup of Main Version Group I, the one closest to and presumably including the original), for some of the added Latin quotations appear in both, the nine tokens of the day of judgment in MV 11 and MV 14 (reduced from the ten of the original) have been further reduced to eight in the *Speculum*, and there are other similarities (at least in Books II and III). But the exact relationship could only be determined after a thorough study of the two versions. Whatever the relationship, however, and in spite of its new title and extensive alterations, the *Speculum* follows the organization and controlling ideas of the original, and thus has been included in the present guide.

---

[31] It may be that the unlocated manuscript mentioned in note 1 above was an extract, perhaps not unlike E 5, because it begins with a subtitle similar to one that often appears in the manuscripts, especially those of Main Version Group III and the Southern Recension, between lines 1381 and 1382 in Book III: 'What manner thyng deth is'.

V
The Latin Translation

Finally, the poem is preserved in a Latin prose translation (L) that exists in five complete copies and in two extracts in a sixth. Before 1802 it was thought that this Latin version was the original, and that the English poem was a translation of it, but it appears from the title (or colophon) in three manuscripts that the Latin is a translation of the English: 'Iste tractatus vocatur stimulus consciencie qui ab Anglico in latinum a minus sciolo est translatus si quis igitur Sapiens in illo aliquos reperiat defectus deprecor ut eos corrigat mente pia et transactori imponat.'[32] The earliest manuscript is late fourteenth century (L 2), and the translation was probably made not long before. We have ourselves done very little work on this translation, but it deserves further study as part of the phenomenon of Latin translations of vernacular works which, as new evidence accumulates, we are discovering to be fairly common in the Middle Ages (e.g., the Latin translations of the English *Ancrene Riwle*, Rolle's *Form of Living*, and Walter Hilton's *Scale of Perfection*, and of the Anglo-Norman version of St Edmund's *Speculum Ecclesie*). There may also be connections between the Latin translation and the Latin prose in the margins of MV 4.

In addition to these five versions, the *Prick of Conscience* circulated in a variety of other ways and forms. For example, the poem was widely quoted in, and provided the inspiration for, a number of Middle English works. These range from two short poems in British Library MS Royal 17 B.xvii ('Of þo Flode of þo World' and 'þo Whele of Fortune') suggested by topics in

---

[32] As in the title to L 2, the oldest manuscript; cf. lines 9581–96 of the English. A nearly identical title is in L 3 and a nearly identical colophon in L 1; the title or colophon in the others is simply 'stimulus consciencie', without the added comment about translation from English. Bale (p. 348) was the first to list the Latin translation as Rolle's own work; he apparently knew of only one manuscript (L 6), which attributes it to 'hampole'. See also Pits (p. 466), Oudin (col. 928), and Tanner (p. 375, n. q), who follow Bale in the attribution (probably via Bale's *Scriptorum Illustrium Maioris Brytannie . . . Catalogus* printed in Basel in 1557, p. 432) but also give the English poem to Rolle. So far as we know, Thomas Warton in 1774 was the first to state that the English was a translation from the Latin (see Warton-Price, p. 99), but in 1802 Ritson (p. 37) noticed the title in L 2 and concluded that the Latin was a translation from the English, and that has been the accepted opinion since. See also Allen, *Writings*, p. 376.

the *Prick of Conscience*,[33] to the late fourteenth-century poem the *Stimulus Consciencie Minor* based on materials in the *Prick of Conscience* and probably St Edmund's *Speculum Ecclesie*,[34] to the fifteenth-century poem the *Desert of Religion* compiled from materials in the *Speculum Vite* and the *Prick of Conscience* adapted to the allegory of a forest.[35] There are also parallels between the *Prick of Conscience* and Chaucer's *Parson's Tale* that may indicate that even Chaucer was familiar with the poem.[36] Textually speaking, these quotations from the *Prick of Conscience* are quite different from the extracts noted earlier, for they modify the poem and adapt it to another context rather than preserve the text, as with the extracts, and have therefore not been listed in this guide to the versions of the poem; but they are no less interesting as examples of the poem's popularity.

Indeed, the popularity of the *Prick of Conscience* extended beyond literary uses: there is a stained-glass window of *c.* 1410 in the north aisle of All Saints Church, North Street, York, which illustrates, in fifteen panels, the Fifteen Signs Before Doomsday. The legend of the Fifteen Signs was well known, especially on the continent, where it often appeared in stained glass and painting; the interest of the York window is that underneath each of the fifteen representations is the appropriate line from Book V of the *Prick of Conscience*, where the subject is treated at length.[37] This is not the only example of the actual

[33] *IMEV* 1014 and 230 respectively; the former also appears as an insertion in one of the manuscripts of the whole *Prick of Conscience*, MV 42. Both poems are edited by Horstman, II, 67–71. See also Franz Kuhn, *Über die Verfasserschaft der in Horstmanns Library of Early English Writers Band I und II—R. Rolle de Hampole—enthaltenen lyrischen Gedichte* (Dissertation, Greifswald, 1900), pp. 62–63.

[34] *IMEV* 244; edited by Horstman, II, 36–45. This poem exists in eight manuscripts. The traditional title, which is from *IMEV*, is probably not the original title— the manuscript evidence would argue for another, the 'Markys of Meditacion'—but a form of the traditional title does appear in the colophon of one manuscript and would indicate that the *Prick of Conscience* was well enough known and widely enough read for someone to recognize that the subject matter of the two poems was similar. Lewis is in the process of editing this poem.

[35] *IMEV* 672; edited by Walter Hübner in *Archiv für das Studium der neueren Sprachen und Literaturen*, 126 (1911), 58–74. See also Hope Emily Allen, 'The Desert of Religion: Addendum', *Archiv für das Studium der neueren Sprachen und Literaturen*, 127 (1911), 388–90. The poem exists in three manuscripts, British Library MSS Cotton Faustina B. VI, Stowe 39, and Additional 37049, the last of which (E 7) contains three separate extracts from the *Prick of Conscience*.

[36] See Kate O. Petersen, *The Sources of the Parson's Tale*, Radcliffe College Monographs No. 12 (Boston: Ginn & Co., 1901), notes passim on pp. 2, 12–14, 30.

[37] The fullest description is by E. A. Gee, 'The Painted Glass of All Saints' Church, North Street, York', *Archaeologia*, 102 (1969), 158–62, with a good reproduction of

words of a Middle English poem working themselves into stained glass and painting,[38] but it is the most elaborate one we know of.

From the passages quoted in other Middle English works and in the York window and from the extracts that circulated separately, one can discover the kinds of subjects medieval readers and writers found most important and striking in the poem: the very colourful description of man at birth and at death from Book I, for example, the world as a place of exile from Book II, the nature of purgatory (and especially the description of the fifth pain, fire) from Book IV, the Fifteen Signs Before Doomsday from Book V, and the list of phrases that men use to describe the day of judgment from Book VI. These are standard subjects, of course, not really needing either general sources for the subjects themselves or specific sources for specific lines, and the fact that the lines are taken from the *Prick of Conscience* indicates that the poem was considered a storehouse of information to which a medieval reader could go for various kinds of religious lore and from which a medieval writer could borrow as he saw fit.

In addition, if the suggestion is correct, made on the basis of the evidence of the manuscripts themselves, especially those of the Main Version, the Southern Recension, and the Latin translation—that a number of the manuscripts were either definitely owned by or 'reflect the interests and preoccupations of the parish clergy'—then the *Prick of Conscience* would have been considered 'a compendium of knowledge which a priest, following the decrees of the Fourth Lateran Council and the Peckham *Constitutions*, would be expected to make known to his flock, or a handbook from which he could draw material for his sermons'.[39] Through such channels the influence of the *Prick of*

the whole window in Plate XXIII; good examples of five individual panels that show how the text is correlated with the glass can be found in Gee, Plate XXIV; Canon J. T. Fowler, 'The Fifteen Last Days of the World in Medieval Art and Literature', *The Yorkshire Archaeological Journal*, 23 (1915), Plate II; and Christopher Woodforde, *English Stained and Painted Glass* (Oxford: Clarendon Press, 1954), Plate 34. For the Fifteen Signs in general see William W. Heist, *The Fifteen Signs Before Doomsday* (East Lansing: Michigan State College Press, 1952), passim (pp. 131-33 for the *Prick of Conscience*), and in Middle English see Wells, pp. 328-29.

[38] See, e.g., *IMEV* 704 and 2464, fairly extensive remains of which appear(ed) in wall paintings; see also 'Wall verses', Supplement to *IMEV*, p. 550.

[39] R. E. Lewis, 'Medieval Popularity, Modern Neglect: The Case of the *Pricke of Conscience*', *Fourteenth-Century English Mystics Newsletter*, 2, 4 (1976), 6. Some of the most revealing manuscripts in this connection are MV 11, 43, 46 (especially the table of topics at the end), 47, 83; SR 14; E 5, 8; and L 3.

Conscience would have made itself felt among listeners as well as readers and writers and would thus have fulfilled the author's intention in writing his poem—that it should benefit *both* readers and listeners, especially the 'lewed' but also the 'lered' (Prologue, lines 328-47; Epilogue, lines 9454-48, 9581-99, 9613).

ii

Dialectal Distribution

Any estimate of the popularity of the *Prick of Conscience* should if possible take into account not only the number of manuscripts in which it has survived and the number of different forms in which all or parts of it are attested but also the areas over which, in its various forms, it appears to have been known. In the two maps in the appendix an attempt has been made to indicate the probable dialectal location of the scribes of as many texts as possible. It is not of course safe, even with a poem surviving—or partly surviving—in some 115 manuscripts, to assume that the distributions revealed by their mapping will accurately reflect the areas of dissemination of all the texts of it that once existed.[40] Nevertheless, the first map shows clearly the remarkably wide range of distribution of texts of the Main Version: it also shows, perhaps surprisingly in view of the various purposes for which they were made, that the extant extracts (all from the Main Version) seem to be geographically restricted in an interesting way. The second map very strongly suggests that the Southern Recension was probably very little if at all known beyond a much more restricted area.

The possibility, in what may seem a remarkable number of cases, of suggesting a fairly precise dialectal origin for the scribe of a *Prick of Conscience* manuscript rests in part on the fact that many scribes, when confronted with the task of copying a vernacular text, 'converted' it into their own form of written Middle English whatever the dialectal characteristics of the exemplar were. Orthographic conventions, whether they are of

---

[40] This caveat is especially necessary if a recent view is correct about the large number of manuscripts likely to have been lost for every one that has survived; see McIntosh, 'Two', pp. 73-75.

a kind which reflect some particular form of spoken Middle English or whether they are 'merely' alternative ways of symbolizing one and the same sound, differed remarkably between one place and another, even—in many areas—where these places are not very far apart. A further condition for localizing the dialectal characteristics of a scribe is that one should be in possession of a topographical framework which permits (or even demands) the association of a particular scribe's set of conventions with a certain area rather than any other. A crude framework of this sort has long existed, so that few would be at a loss if they were required to segregate what we here call fully northern texts from others from further south, or distinguish a Scots text from a northern English one, or a west Midland text from one whose scribe came from Kent, or either of these from the work of a Norfolk man.

The framework now available is essentially of the same kind as has been familiar for half a century but it has become much more finely and precisely structured.[41] As a result it has become possible to associate a large number of scribes with a particular county and indeed many of them with some much smaller area within one county.[42] One must not, of course, assume that a scribe by any means necessarily made his copy (or his contribution to a copy) of a text of the *Prick of Conscience* in the place where he learnt his craft. For it is evident from what we know of a volume like the Auchinleck manuscript that scribes (like two of those who contributed to that manuscript) sometimes worked far from their place of origin.[43] The dialectal notes on each English manuscript provided in category 5 of the guide

[41] See J. P. Oakden, *Alliterative Poetry in Middle English*, I: 'The Dialectal and Metrical Survey' (Manchester: Manchester University Press, 1930); S. Moore, S. B. Meech, and H. Whitehall, 'Middle English Dialect Characteristics and Dialect Boundaries', in *Essays and Studies in English and Comparative Literature* (University of Michigan Publications in Language and Literature), 13 (1935); *Middle English Dictionary*, ed. H. Kurath and S. M. Kuhn, I: 'Plan and Bibliography' (Ann Arbor: University of Michigan Press, 1954), 4–12. For a survey of more recent work see Michael Benskin, 'Local Archives and Middle English Dialects', *Journal of the Society of Archivists*, 5, no. 8 (1977), 500–14.
[42] See Margaret Laing, *Studies in the Dialect Material of Mediaeval Lincolnshire*, University of Edinburgh Ph.D. thesis 1978, two vols (unpublished but obtainable on microfilm).
[43] For further references to the composition of this manuscript, see A. McIntosh, 'The Middle English Poem *The Four Foes of Mankind*', *Neuphilologische Mitteilungen*, 79 (1978), 137, n. 1. Professor M. L. Samuels associates two of the hands dialectally with the west Midlands, one with Worcestershire, the other with Gloucestershire.

must therefore be interpreted in these terms, and there will be occasion to call attention to a small number of them on which two or more scribes collaborated and yet differ markedly (as in Auchinleck) in the kind of Middle English which they produce. In such cases it is evident that at most one of them could actually be working on his home ground. Nevertheless, even in instances of this kind, it is fairly rare to find that the collaborating scribes display such diverse dialectal characteristics as to require us to conclude that they came from widely different parts of the country; it is more usual—as indeed might be expected —to encounter situations in which the scribes working in some centre come themselves from somewhere not very far away. This being so, we may infer that when a single scribe copied an entire manuscript, he likewise did so, in the majority of instances, somewhere at least fairly near to where he learnt his craft.

In the case of the *Prick of Conscience*, the nature and purpose of the poem is such that copies of it must often have been made by local scribes (e.g., by parish priests) for edificatory use in their own district. We may presume that a copy was often thus produced in a form which, when read aloud, was immediately familiar to its hearers in the sense that it reflected quite closely, e.g., in its vocabulary and morphology and in the sound-system which it 'symbolized' the speech of the place where it was produced.[44] Because of this, there are, for example, few if any more important sources for our knowledge of the English of Devonshire in the later medieval period than MV 4 and MV 63; it is to be hoped that this kind of knowledge will more and more come to be recognized as embracing a proper understanding of the written-language conventions current in that (or any other) county and not involve merely the exploitation of these in a search for information about the spoken language. Indeed, it is not easy to see how the latter activity can be pursued in a profitable way without careful prior analysis and understanding of these conventions. At all events they cannot be set aside as

[44] One must qualify this slightly by noting that where the alteration of forms of any of these kinds would spoil rhymes or alliteration (and sometimes even rhythmical conventions) scribes quite often retain them. If such retained forms are at variance with a scribe's usual practice elsewhere, they should simply be discounted in making an inventory or 'profile' of his normal scribal habits. It may also be noted that these habits are sometimes only rather shakily exemplified in the first few folios of a scribe's work: there is not infrequently a noticeable 'settling down' period during which he has not fully adjusted himself to the task of conversion.

irrelevant by anyone seeking to add precision to our knowledge of the scribal provenance of Middle English manuscripts.[45]

The possibility of exploiting the complex of local pecularities which a given scribe may manifest depends of course on the degree of consistency with which he replaces whatever forms he finds in his exemplar by his own local usages; the questions that this problem raises have been touched upon elsewhere.[46] In the present context the central one is: what percentage of scribes who made or contributed to surviving copies of the *Prick of Conscience* have bequeathed to us text of sufficient dialect consistency for us to be able to say that it convincingly reflects the written-language conventions of some particular place or area, say Lichfield or south Lincolnshire or south west Yorkshire or Essex or Devon?

We may note that in principle any text satisfying these conditions may be produced by a process other than that of the scribe of the surviving version having imposed his own local characteristics on his exemplar. For if that (usually lost) exemplar itself satisfied these conditions and the scribe, even if it were in some dialect other than his own, was content to reproduce it *literatim*, then we should be unlikely ever to realize that its dialectal integrity was not of his own creation. In a sense this does not matter because the text will for most purposes be of equal value whether it results from the one procedure or the other; in the same way the dialectal value of a diplomatic transcript of a (say lost) Middle English manuscript with evidently Kentish characteristics in no way requires that the modern transcriber should have been brought up in Kent. In any case there is considerable evidence to suggest that this habit of *literatim* transcription by Middle English scribes of texts in dialects other than their own was exceptional. One good reason for believing this to be so is that if scribes did it at all frequently, then whenever two or

---

[45] In other words it is not enough to scrutinize texts for only those forms which probably reflect some regional *spoken*-language characteristic, e.g., *ho*: *sche*: *scho* for 'she' or *spekes*: *spekeþ* for 3rd sing. pres. ind. 'speaks' or *mony*: *many* for 'many'. It is also necessary to ask questions of a different order such as the following. Does the scribe make a visual distinction between the two symbols *y* and *þ* or not? Does he spell '-ly' as *-li* or as *-ly*? Does he write *-3t* or *-ght* or *-ht* or *-cht* in words like 'might'? Does he spell 'shall' as *schal* or *shal* or *schall* or *shall*? See A. McIntosh, 'Towards an Inventory of Middle English Scribes', *Neuphilologische Mitteilungen*, 75 (1974), 602-24.

[46] See A. McIntosh, 'Word Geography in the Lexicography of Medieval English', *Annals of the New York Academy of Sciences*, 211 (1973); 61-62.

more texts of diverse origin were copied by one scribe into a collection, one would expect that the different items in such a collection would often manifest different dialectal characteristics. In fact it is rather unusual to encounter this phenomenon;[47] when we do, we can still meaningfully ask the question posed earlier.

This question may most usefully and realistically be approached by considering it, to begin with, in relation to the ninety-seven texts (or parts of texts) of the Main Version of the *Prick of Conscience*. It should be noted that in by far the largest number of cases a text of the Main Version is the work of a single scribe; the same is true of versions of the Southern Recension. Such a scribe sets down in some instances no more than a text of the poem itself; in others he has produced a larger volume containing other material as well; in other cases the poem may appear in a manuscript to which further scribes have contributed the other (or some of the other) items. But it is only in a rather small minority of cases that two or more scribes have contributed to the production of a single text of any of the versions of the *Prick of Conscience* itself.

The problems raised by examples where they have done so need not be shirked; indeed, the existence of two or more hands in a single text, so long as the contribution of each is of a certain magnitude, usefully adds to the total inventory of Middle English scribes whose work is still accessible to us. But in an examination of the question of the scribal provenance of each of our ninety-seven texts it simply means that we are confronted with the investigation of a slightly larger number of separate problems than if each text had been written by only one scribe; the increase is only around thirteen per cent.[48] What is much more crucial is whether we can provide an answer to two main questions. How many of the scribes responsible for the Main Version texts can one regard—in the light of such information as is available about the ways of two or three thousand other scribes

---

[47] MV 65 provides an interesting example of this even within the bounds of the *Prick of Conscience*. This would suggest either that the scribe drew on three different exemplars in different parts of his text or that he made a literal copy of a manuscript that was the work of three scribes. The only other clear example of variation in the language of one scribe in the present material is provided by MV 69.

[48] In the Southern Recension twenty scribes (if we ignore short oddments) have a hand in the eighteen versions; the increase is therefore of a similar order here—around eleven per cent.

—as displaying sufficient internal consistency to allow us to conclude that they adequately exemplify a genuinely local set of scribal characteristics? Can these then be assigned to a particular place or area? A way of combining these questions is simply to ask: how many of our ninety-four English texts (the other three being of Irish provenance) would one with some confidence and with a reasonable standard of accuracy place somewhere on a map of England? The answer turns out to be rather encouraging, though the degree of precision of placing varies with the region to which one proposes to assign a particular manuscript. This itself is controlled mainly by two factors.

First, there are quite marked differences of degree of dialectal contrast within an area of (say) 1000 square miles in different parts of medieval England. The least heterogeneous region of the country, at least as far as we can deduce from the abundant surviving written material, is that to which we have assigned texts which we describe as 'fully northern'. This consists of the counties of Northumberland, Durham, Cumberland, Westmorland, and that part of Yorkshire which excludes the southwestern part of the county. The fully northern region corresponds roughly to the region north of the line marking the southern limit of the retention (at the appropriate date) of some form of unrounded vowel (normally spelt a) in·words descending from Old English and Old Norse $\bar{a}$. Within this area we have not attempted, in the present state of our knowledge, to assign specific positions to the thirteen texts which we list as fully northern. But this is not to say that it will remain impossible to do so. Elsewhere in England the problems of homogeneity over a large area are less severe. But the spread and influence of Wycliffite standard in the east Midlands and that of London English over a good part of the southern region and of the extreme south Midlands tends to dilute local dialect characteristics in texts from these areas by the date of most of our *Prick of Conscience* manuscripts and thus to reduce the sharpness of dialectal contrast between them. This is usually *not* the case, at the date in question, of texts from East Anglia, from the far north Midlands, or from the west Midlands.

The second important controlling factor is of a different kind, for it happens that for some regions which were probably far from homogeneous dialectally we have much less surviving information about the variations within them than we have for some others. For example Devon, Somerset, Dorset, and Wiltshire are much poorer in this respect than Worcestershire, Cheshire, Lincolnshire, or Norfolk.[49] If such evidence were totally lacking, instead of being just rather scanty, then it is obvious that one would not be able (except on external evidence) to assign any of our texts to one rather than another of any of a group of 'poor' counties, still less to an approximate position within one of them. But with the scrutiny of more and more material it should gradually become possible to associate further textual material with them, so that the 'poverty' problem in certain areas may be expected to lessen as time goes on. It is not to be expected, however, that those areas most influenced by one or other of the incipient standards from early in the fifteenth century onwards will ever be as adequately documented dialectally as those where this influence only made itself powerfully felt considerably later.

We may now consider the Main Version texts of English origin which were written by scribes from somewhere south of the fully northern region as it has been defined. Ignoring four fragments (79, 80, 84, and 97) which are altogether too short to assess adequately, there are seventy-seven such texts and account has been taken of the contribution of some eighty-four scribes. It is encouraging to report that about sixty-four (i.e., about seventy-six per cent) of these separate scribal contributions can be placed with some confidence well within an area no larger than the size of an average county and many of them can with some confidence be placed with considerably greater precision. This leaves us with twenty further scribal contributions to other texts which for one reason or another cannot be pinpointed in this sort of way. Some (perhaps most) are dialectally mixed. Some are in so nearly a standard form of the language that the few local forms they do display may be insufficient to allow us to hazard (at best) anything but a vague guess as to their origin; such texts as these are of course also a mixture, though of a special 'diluting' kind. Nevertheless, it is possible to make a broad but still useful assessment of about half of these twenty texts (i.e., of about a further twelve per cent of all the Main Version manuscripts). This leaves only another ten texts (i.e., a final

---

[49] For Lincolnshire see the reference in note 42. For Norfolk a descriptive list of literary manuscripts whose scribes were probably from that county is in course of preparation by McIntosh and Richard Beadle.

twelve per cent) about which, often (though not always) because
of their mixed composition, it would be imprudent to venture
anything but very cautious and imprecise suggestions.

If we look at the parallel though much smaller figures for the
Southern Recension, we find a remarkably similar proportion.
This time there are no fully northern texts and none of Irish ori-
gin. Of the twenty main hands involved in the eighteen manu-
scripts we may put the respective figures as 14 : 4 : 2, which in
percentages is 70 : 20 : 10. Even of the two most dialectally
problematic of these manuscripts (both hands of 6 and Hand 2
of 14) it is possible to say a good deal—enough, among other
things, to indicate that these do not lie beyond the interestingly
restricted area of dissemination of texts of the Recension as a
whole as it can at least roughly be defined by the totality of
locations assigned to the other eighteen.[50] If we add the cor-
responding figures for the *Speculum Huius Vite* and the extracts,
they tend to give the overall ratio an even more favourable
aspect; in percentages it is around 77 : 12 : 11.

About the texts in general it may also be noted that almost
all the more dialectally 'difficult' manuscripts merit much more
intensive analysis than it has been possible to subject them to.
Experience with other manuscripts which pose problems com-
parable to those which these present suggests that thorough
examination would in most cases yield much more precise infor-
mation about them;[51] furthermore, as our knowledge of Middle
English dialects increases, such information may be expected to
prove increasingly illuminating.

It will be evident from what has been said already that there
will often be a wide discrepancy between the value attached by
a dialectologist to a particular text of the *Prick of Conscience*
and a textual critic's assessment of its interest and merits. This
discrepancy will be particularly marked when the main con-
cern of the textual critic is to produce a text which lies as close
as possible to the author's original rather than to consider the
more general problems connected with the transmission of all

[50] For a comparably restricted area of dissemination of copies of a text see the
map indicating the distribution of surviving copies of Mirk's *Festial* in M. F. Wakelin,
'The Manuscripts of John Mirk's *Festial*', *Leeds Studies in English*, new series 1
(1967), 103.
[51] This is well illustrated by what emerges from the intensive analysis of some
dialectally difficult manuscripts in Chapter iv (especially pp. 262-339) of vol. i of the
work cited in note 42 above.

texts at all stages of their descent from that original. For such a person the more stages by which a version is separated from the holograph, the more likely is that version to have deviated in substance from it; successive stages down a line of descent are thus likely, in general, to be regarded by him as merely exemplifying an ever-worsening process of degeneration.

One should notice, however, that in certain circumstances of a rather special kind the textual critic may be driven to devote considerable attention to 'degenerate' versions. For several obvious reasons, for instance, readings of whatever surviving text or texts of the Main Version lie closest to the one (or perhaps more than one?) which furnished the underpinning for the Southern Recension are necessarily a matter of great interest to anyone concerned with the establishment of a text of that recension which is as near as possible to the holograph of its author. This has relevance to various other Middle English texts, e.g., to Rolle's *Commentary on the Psalter*, to *Piers Plowman*, and to the *Scale of Perfection*; it is difficult in all such cases to see how readings due to 'merely' dialectal considerations can be discounted or even be disassociated with any precision from substantive variations in the ordinary sense of that term.

The unenthusiastic reaction to what (textually speaking) is often a depressing process of decay down the chain of descent from one manuscript to the next is not normally shared by the dialectologist, for from his linguistic point of view there is not necessarily any degeneration at all, still less the menace of *progressive* degeneration. If a text is, dialectally speaking, rich and internally consistent, then it is for him relatively unimportant how many intermediate versions separate it from the original. If it is not, then his criteria for pronouncing it degenerate (if he used the word) would be based only on the degree to which it lacked these linguistic qualities. It would be easy, of course, to cite examples of texts which do lack them—texts which turn out to be a confusing hodge-podge consisting of two (or perhaps three or even four) layers of different kinds of Middle English all but one of which (at best) must have been carried over from antecedent versions about which we are likely to know nothing because in the vast majority of cases they themselves have not survived. MV 2, 17, 26, 32, and SR 6 provide (among others) good examples.

It is important to emphasize, however, that such *dialectal*

'degeneration' may be arrested and 'cancelled' at any point
down the chain of transmission in a way to which there is no
parallel in the case of textual degeneration, for whenever a
dialectally mixed text comes into the hands of a competent
scribe experienced in these matters whose intention is to con-
vert it into his own kind of Middle English, that text presents
him with problems scarcely greater than if he were faced with a
dialectally homogeneous text from some area other than his
own. So such a scribe, copying from a mixed text, will at one
stroke efface in his own copy the previous heterogeneity and
thus so to speak wipe the slate clean.

From the earlier discussion of ratios it will be evident that by
no means all dialectally mixed texts were thus 'purified', which
is no more than to say that some scribes were either not compe-
tent to achieve this or else not interested in doing so. The fact
that less than twenty-five per cent of the scribes contributing to
surviving texts of the *Prick of Conscience* produced texts which
were not fairly thoroughly purified gives us good reason to
believe that all *lost* manuscripts which likewise were not must
have existed in a similar proportion. Therefore, if all dialectally
mixed (M) texts in the total surviving *Prick of Conscience* corpus
are regarded as numbering around thirty (this generous estimate
being made to include some whose mixedness has not been
recognized),[52] it is important to observe that this total will not
be made up of an equal number of texts having two, three, four,
five, etc. ingredients (M_2, M_3, M_4, M_5), for three out of four
mixed texts at all stages will, on average, be 'purified' when
they are copied. Hence, only one M_2 text in four will become
an M_3 text when it is copied and similarly with the engendering
of higher orders of mixing. Our thirty texts will therefore be
made up of more M_2s than of M_3s, of more M_3s than of M_4s,
and so on, and the fall-off will be in the proportions: M_2: 64, M_3:
16, M_4: 4, M_5: 1. . . . This means that our thirty texts are likely
to consist of about twenty-one M_2s, six M_3s, at most two M_4s,
and probably none of any greater degrees of complexity. Since

---

[52] This is advisable for the following reason. If we encounter an M_2 text whose
two ingredients are markedly different in dialectal characteristics, say one being Lin-
colnshire and the other Essex (e.g., the first part of MV 69), then it is not usually
difficult to recognize that we are dealing with a mixture or to say something about
the nature of the two ingredients. But in an M_2 text where the two are closely simi-
lar we may fail altogether to recognize them for what they are and assume instead
that the text containing them genuinely represents a single dialect.

sufficiently close analysis of M_2 texts should ultimately enable us in the majority of cases to isolate and identify their two ingredients, it would only be the small remaining ten or so M_3 and M_4 (and very occasionally no doubt M_5) texts that would be likely, even after intensive investigation, to prove very difficult to unscramble.[53]

iii
Categories of the Guide

Our aim in the following guide is to record information (and only that information) that we believe will be of use to scholars in studying the text of the *Prick of Conscience* and the versions in which it circulated in the Middle Ages. Each manuscript has a separate entry, beginning with a line containing its version and number, the city and library in which it is located, its shelfmark (with the coexistent shelfmark or catalogue number added in parentheses where appropriate), the pages on which the *Prick of Conscience* (*PC*) is found, and the date of the MS (or of the part of the MS containing *PC* if two or more MSS are bound together, e.g., SR 12). Recto pages are indicated by a number alone (preceded by 'ff.' for folios or 'pp.' for pages) except in a few cases where, for clarity or contrast, an 'r' is used following the number; verso pages are indicated by a 'v' following the number except where a 'v' would cause confusion, in which case the word is printed in full (e.g., MV 81, category 4); 'a', 'b', and 'c' are used, respectively, for the first, second, and third columns on a page. Except where a more precise date is justified, our datings follow the abbreviations and usually the distinctions used by Ker in *MMBL* (see especially II, vii), with 's. xiv/xv' indicating the turn of the fourteenth to the fifteenth century, 's. xv

[53] It may be observed that if a detailed investigation were to be made of the dialectal characteristics of all the manuscripts of some text fairly similar to the *Prick of Conscience* in genre and in the conditions of its proliferation, these considerations would make possible certain predictions. We should expect (with due reservations of course about standard deviation) that of the approximately forty surviving copies of the *Speculum Vite*, around thirty of them would turn out to be reasonably pure dialectally; about ten would probably be mixed; all but about three of the ten would be M_2s and any degree of mixing beyond M_3 in these three would be rather unlikely. For a fuller and more formal treatment of this and related matters, see Benskin and Laing, pp. 79 ff. and note 22.

in.' the beginning of the fifteenth century (15th c.), 's. xv[1]' the
first half of the 15th c., 's. xv med.' around the middle of the
15th c., 's. xv[2]' the second half of the 15th c., 's. xv ex.' the end
of the 15th c., and 's. xv' by itself an undetermined date in the
15th c.

Following the first line, and for each MS in the guide, we
have divided the information into seven categories:

1. Brief codicological description, including material, number of
leaves and flyleaves, and size of the MS; nature of the hand-
writing, with notes on the number of scribes (e.g., MV 78);
peculiarities in the format of the MS (usually the omission of
leaves); collation if it contributes to an understanding of the
text of *PC*; number of columns per page and lines per page or
column (these refer to *PC* only unless otherwise noted); catch-
words or signatures if present; binding if medieval; and occa-
sional other information where appropriate.

Further comment on some of these items:

Material. We follow the practice of the Bodleian Library and
Ker in *MMBL* and use 'parchment' for both sheepskin and calf-
skin.

Leaves and flyleaves. We use lower-case Roman numerals for
beginning and end flyleaves and Arabic numerals for the leaves
of the MS (with the flyleaves and the leaves separated by a '+').
We have recorded, in so far as we are aware, only bona fide
flyleaves and not later binding leaves.

Size. We have given the measurements of all MSS in milli-
metres (mm.). When the size varies by more than five milli-
metres, we have given the actual figures; when less than five
millimetres, we have given 'circa' (*c.*) with the larger figure.

Handwriting. Our descriptions are brief, usually fairly general-
ized ones employing five terms used by M. B. Parkes in *English
Cursive Book Hands 1250–1500* (Oxford: Clarendon Press,
1969): anglicana, anglicana formata, bastard anglicana, secre-
tary, and textura. Most MSS of *PC* are written in anglicana for-
mata, as one would expect, but there are also a number written
in anglicana and a few in textura, perhaps more than one would
have expected for a vernacular text of the nature of *PC*. There
is often, however, a thin line between, especially, anglicana and
anglicana formata (e.g., MV 32), but also, though to a lesser
degree, between anglicana formata and bastard anglicana (e.g.,

MV 94) and between bastard anglicana and textura (cf. MV 12 with MV 67 Hand 1, and 71), and we have usually relied on the contrasts made, and the consistency employed, by a single scribe or between scribes rather than on a rigid set of ideal characteristics. Our primary aim has been to cut up the continuum from anglicana to anglicana formata to bastard anglicana to textura in a coherent and consistent way. It would have been desirable to attach a qualifier to 'anglicana' to avoid the confusion inherent in Parkes's terminology between the genus (the anglicana script itself) and the species (the less formal variety of that script, which he also calls 'anglicana'), but none of the qualifiers that have been suggested ('current', 'facilis', 'less formal', 'book hand', 'ordinary') is entirely satisfactory, and we have therefore retained 'anglicana', though with the caveat that it indicates the less formal variety of the anglicana script (in contrast with anglicana formata). We use 'bastard anglicana' to indicate a mixture of features from anglicana and textura, for, at least in the MSS of *PC*, one finds this mixture, varying in proportion according to the individual scribe, much more often than a full assimilation of the two scripts, which is the sense in which Parkes uses 'bastard anglicana'. Our 'bastard anglicana' is thus a range on the continuum between anglicana formata and textura, though, when a specific hand is very close to one of these two points, we have given it the designation for that point and have added appropriate qualifiers (e.g., MV 90). Our 'textura' covers a range from the most formal variety of the script, as used, e.g., for the Latin quotations in MV 12, to the near-textura of MV 71. We have not noted occasional secretary characteristics in a hand that is basically a variety of anglicana, for, as Parkes points out (pp. xxii–xxiv), secretary had an increasing influence on anglicana throughout the 15th c.

2. Contents of the MS. If a small number of items accompany *PC*, they are all listed by name. If the items are numerous, the total number is given, some of the important ones are listed, and the others are briefly characterized; a complete listing of the contents of such MSS will be found in the catalogue(s) listed in category 6. For all Middle English verse texts except the *Northern Homily Cycle* and the *South English Legendary*, which are too complex to be treated in such a way, we have given the *IMEV* numbers, and in nearly every case we have also

followed the practice of *IME V* with regard to titles. When *PC* is the only item in the MS, category 2 has been silently omitted.

Our reason for listing the contents of the MSS is to provide, in conjunction with the notes of ownership, provenances, and dialects in categories 4 and 5, a starting point for the study of the audience of *PC*. MSS in general reveal, through their contents, the tastes of the people who compiled them or for whom they were compiled, and, for works that were copied as often as *PC* and that therefore provide large amounts of data, the MSS can point the way to specific audiences, especially (as in the case of *PC*) through a correlation of contents and owners and through a comparison of the contents of MSS with owners (including non-*PC* MSS with similar contents) and the contents of MSS without owners.

3. Notes on the state of the text, including title and colophon if present; incipit and explicit; number of lines remaining, with brief comments on the nature of the text; specific omissions in the text; titles to books and subtitles if present; capitals or paragraph marks for subdivisions if present; marginalia and corrections if present; the page numbers on which each book of *PC* begins; and occasional other information where appropriate.

Further comment on some of these items:

Title and colophon. We are primarily interested in the medieval titles and colophons, but we have noted post-medieval titles when there are no medieval ones or when those that are post-medieval differ significantly from the medieval ones. If a MS has no title or colophon, and no further note appears, it is to be assumed that line 9551, if it appears in the MS, has some form or other of the title 'Prick of Conscience', for line 9551 is the only place *within* the poem where a specific title appears. We use the word 'colophon' to indicate any inscription at the end of a MS or an individual book of *PC* and thus distinguish it from 'explicit', which is the last line of the actual text of the MS or of an individual book.

Incipit (Inc) and explicit (expl) and other quotations from the MS, both here and in category 4. We have reproduced exactly what is in the MS except that we have ignored punctuation and have regularized *i* and *j* and *u* and *v* everywhere (with *i* and *u* for vowels and *j* and *v* for consonants) and *þ* and *y* for Middle English according to their modern English reflexes. We use square brackets surrounding three spaced periods ([. . .]) to indicate where the MS is damaged or the text is otherwise unreadable; occasionally, in place of the three spaced periods, we comment on the nature of the damage (e.g., MV 21). We also use square brackets to enclose anything supplied by us within a quotation, including the occasional addition of a capital letter at the beginning of a title, colophon, or incipit if the rubricator has neglected to add it. We have silently expanded abbreviations unless there was a question about their expansion, in which case we have italicized them. We have also italicized letters about whose transcription we had some doubt.

Number of lines remaining. Our figures are based on a comparison with the number of corresponding lines in Morris's text. For MV MSS we add a brief comment about the nature of the reduction or expansion, occasionally adding other comments about the nature of the text; for SR MSS, where we are dealing with a recension of the MV, we let the line numbers stand by themselves; for L MSS, where we are dealing with prose, no comparison of line numbers is possible.

Subtitles; capitals and paragraph marks for subdivisions. We have noted the presence of these items in the belief that they will be useful in helping to determine textual relationships.

4. Notes of ownership and provenances. We have recorded the names of all medieval owners which we know about from the manuscripts themselves or from other sources and have added provenances, certain or possible, where available. Where we were unable to determine medieval ownership or provenance (and in some cases even where we were able to do so), we have noted post-medieval owners and provenances up to about the year 1650. We have not, however, tried to give the complete sales histories of the MSS. Our aim has been to put the MSS in their medieval context or in the closest possible context (in time) to that one. If no owner or provenance before 1650 is known to us, category 4 has been silently omitted.

5. Dialect. The remarks made earlier in section ii will indicate that what can be said about dialect necessarily varies in precision from one MS to another. The notes are intended, by the way they are phrased, to bring out the fact that the texts fall roughly into three categories:

1. That large majority which can with some confidence be placed within an area which at most corresponds to the size of an average county. If the notes suggest a more precise location, then the text in question is entered on the appropriate map at that location, e.g., MV 5, 6; if they do not, then the place where it is entered has only the rather broader implications conveyed in the notes, e.g., MV 3, 4.
2. Those which, for one reason or another indicated in the notes, cannot be localized firmly enough to be worth entering on a map but about the linguistic composition and affinities of which something positive can nevertheless be, and has been, said, e.g., MV 1, 10.
3. Those about the dialectal make-up of which no more at best than very guarded suggestions can at present be made, e.g., MV 2, 13.

It should also be said that not all texts of the *Prick of Conscience* have been analysed in their entirety so that some changes of dialect where the hand itself does not change (as in MV 39) may have passed unnoticed; a fuller linguistic scrutiny of some texts from this point of view is desirable. Furthermore, much more could probably be said about a number of the texts which fall in classes 2 and 3 above if they were subjected to close analysis of a kind that was, in general, far beyond the scope of the present guide.

6. Bibliography, divided into three sections:

First line. First we give the *IMEV* number(s) where appropriate and available; we do not, however, give the corresponding numbers in Carleton Brown, *A Register of Middle English Religious & Didactic Verse*, II (Oxford: Bibliographical Society, 1920), for *IMEV* has superseded Brown, and moreover the Brown numbers can be found in Appendix I of *IMEV*. We follow this with any earlier owners or names by which the MS is known in the literature on *PC* (except when the name of an earlier owner is incorporated in the present shelfmark, as, e.g., with MV 16). As in category 4, we have not tried to give a complete sales history here, but it is important for anyone reading the literature to know that, e.g., SR 12 is number 2322 in the *Summary Catalogue* (*SC*), or that MV 56 was the Corser MS, or that SR 15 was a Yates MS.

Second line. Here we refer to the most recent authoritative

published description(s) of the MS. Usually we list only one item, but in cases where an unpublished description supersedes the published description or where other books or articles measurably supplement the published description, we give two, and occasionally more than two, items. We have not attempted to list all printed descriptions of a MS, though in nearly every case the item(s) we do list will contain a bibliography of earlier descriptions.

Third line. Here we list, in alphabetical order, all references to *PC* in the MS in question that we have found in the relevant scholarly literature. Our criterion for inclusion is that the reference must be to the text of *PC* in a specific MS, though we have occasionally added references that deal with other aspects of the MS if we thought they would be relevant to a study of *PC* (e.g., Doyle and Robbins in MV 83). We have tried to be as thorough as possible in this section of category 6, with the following exclusions and exceptions: we have not repeated the reference to the description of the MS from the preceding section of category 6, nor have we noted earlier printed descriptions of the MS; all references to specific MSS of *PC* in Wells's bibliographies will be found under the names of the authors who discuss them rather than under Wells; and for MV 27, which was Morris's base MS, we do not list brief mentions after 1863, the date of publication of his edition (see further MV 27, category 6). Allen ('Authorship', passim) summarizes and refers to earlier scholarship on *PC*, and we have relied heavily on and are greatly indebted to her for bibliographical information before the middle of the 19th c. We have used the phrase '(as above)' to refer to an item that is mentioned earlier in category 6 for the same MS but nowhere else in the guide (e.g., MV 43).

7. Notes on textual relationships and other matters. In category 7 we comment briefly and tentatively on the textual relationships of the MSS, based for MV MSS on our collations correlated with the findings of the various writers on the subject (see notes 16 and 17), for SR MSS primarily on the work of McIntosh *et alii* (see note 26) and Waters, and for E, S, and L MSS primarily on the work of Lewis. In no sense are these to be considered exhaustive comments, but rather reflections of what little work has already been done on the MSS and suggestions of relationships to be pursued by others. For MV MSS we have

given their group number (I, II, III, or IV) and the most closely related MSS; for SR MSS we have given the most closely related MSS as well as Waters's divisions (A and B) for Book V; and for all MSS we have made whatever additional textual comments seemed to us useful and appropriate. Occasionally we have commented on non-textual matters (e.g., MV 67), but in general category 7 is confined to the textual relationships of the MSS. When we have nothing to say on the subject, category 7 has been silently omitted.

GUIDE TO THE MANUSCRIPTS

I
The Main Version

MV 1 Aberystwyth, National Library of Wales, Porkington 20, ff. 1–94v, s. xv[1].

1. Parchment, ii + 106 + ii ff. (with end flyleaves foliated 107–08), 210×150 mm. Written in anglicana formata. Single columns, 40–46 ll. per page in first quire (ff. 1–8v), 47–52 thereafter. Catchwords and signatures.

2. Two items in addition to *PC*: *Trentalle Sancti Gregorii* (*IMEV* 3184) and Richard Maydestone's version of the Seven Penitential Psalms (*IMEV* 1961), ending imperfectly at l. 941.

3. No title; colophon (in margin): 'Explicit tractus stimulus conscience Here endeþ þe tretyce þat is callede þe prykke of conscience.' Inc: 'þe miȝt of þe fadyr alle myȝtty'; expl: 'þat for oure hele on rode gan hynge'. Slightly abbreviated text (*c.* 9077/9624 ll.). Latin titles in text to all books except IV, where it is in the margin; English titles in margin at beginnings of all books; running Latin titles. Many rubrics and a number of additions in the margins, presumably from a MS other than the exemplar; interlinear and marginal corrections throughout. Prol: 1; I: 5; II: 11; III: 18v; IV: 28v; V: 41; VI: 64; VII: 74v; Epil: 93v.

5. Monmouthshire, west Gloucestershire, or possibly South Wales.

6. *IMEV* 3428.80; formerly Ormsby-Gore.
   Alfred J. Horwood, 'The Manuscripts of J. R. Ormsby-Gore, Esq., M.P., of Brogyntyn, Co. Salop.', *Second Report of the Royal Commission on Historical Manuscripts* (London: Eyre and Spottiswoode, 1874), Appendix, No. 20, pp. 84–85; unpublished description by Daniel Huws at the National Library of Wales.
   Allen, *Writings*, p. 373, n. 1; Waters, p. 49.

7. Has characteristics of both Groups III and IV, perhaps a MS anterior to Group IV with additions supplied from a MS of Group III.

MV 2 Arundel Castle, Sussex, Library of His Grace the Duke of Norfolk, E.M., MS of the *Stimulus Conscientie*, ff. 1–141v, s. xiv ex.

1. Parchment, 141 ff. (plus one parchment leaf, glued to a paper backing, inserted loosely in the MS), 228 × 156 mm. Text written in anglicana formata, with titles, subtitles, and Latin quotations in textura. Single columns, 31 ll. per page. Catchwords. MS unfoliated.

2. *PC* the only item in the MS except for an English proverb in a late 15th-c. hand on f. 141v.

3. Title: 'Iste liber vocatur Stimulus consciencie'; no colophon. Inc: 'The myght of the fadir almyghty'; expl: 'þat for oure hele on þe roode gan hynge Amen'. Text slightly abbreviated (8994/ 9624 ll.), with more abbreviation in IV–VI than before or after. Latin titles in margin to Books I–V, in text to VI–VII; English title in text to III; running Latin titles throughout. Occasional English subtitles in text. Capitals for subdivisions. Prol: 1; I: 6v; II: 15; III: 26; IV: 41v; V: 59v; VI: 95; VII: 111; Epil: 140.

4. Note of medieval ownership at the top of the parchment side of the inserted leaf, in a different hand from that of the text: 'Istum librum legavit frater thomas de Geytington dummodo fuit secularis post vitam suam et fratris sui conmunitati fratrum minorum eboraci' (= York, Franciscan Convent); this note probably applies to the MS itself because an 18th-c. hand on the inserted leaf has also added English notes in the margins of the MS. The name 'Antony herst' is in the outside margin of f. 125, written in a 16th-c. hand, and there is a 'crude drawing of the Royal Arms of the style between 1420 and 1603' on f. 84 (Steer, as below).

5. North east Midlands with marked signs of a southeastern overlay.

6. Not in *IMEV*; formerly Monro/Munro.
  Francis W. Steer, *Bibliotheca Norfolciana* (privately printed, 1961), p. 25; for provenance see *MLGB*, pp. 218, 321.
  Allen, 'Authorship', p. 169; Allen, *Writings*, pp. 375-76; Britton, p. 333, n. 16; M.R., p. 386a; Ritson, p. 37; Warton-Price, p. 99, n. z (though not in original Warton); Waters, pp. 48-49.

7. Appears to be either a conflated or a contaminated MS. Group III to Book V, though Book II begins as in the MSS of Group II; probably Group II thereafter.

MV 3 Beeleigh Abbey, Maldon, Essex, Foyle MS of the *Prick of Conscience*, ff. 1-131v, 1465?

1. Parchment, iv + 146 + iii ff., 233 X 130 mm. *PC* written in anglicana formata. Single columns, 36 ll. per page. Catchwords. The date is from a note on f. ii by G(regory) L(ewis) Way, a former owner, who says that the MS originally contained a memorandum, later erased by the binder, on a blank parchment leaf at the beginning, to the effect that the MS was begun 'the xvii day of April in the iiii[th] yer of King Edwards Reinge'.

2. *PC* followed by Richard Rolle's *Form of Living* in English prose.

3. No title; colophon: 'Explicit tractatus stimulus consciencie nominatus.' Inc: 'þe myȝt of þe fadir al myȝty'; expl: 'þat for us fouchid save on rode to hynge Amen'. Text slightly reduced (9417/9624 ll.). Latin titles in text to all books. Capitals for subdivisions. Occasional source notes and numbers in margins; occasional interlinear additions to text. Prol: 1; I: 6; II: 13v; III: 23; IV: 36v; V: 54; VI: 87; VII: 102v; Epil: 130v.

4. On f. iv verso, in a 15th-c. hand (though not the same as that of the text), appears: 'Iste liber constat domine Alicie Burton nec non et Margarete consobrine eius.'

5. Probably Warwickshire.

6. *IMEV* 3428.74; formerly Amherst 29; then Harmsworth.
   Seymour de Ricci, *A Hand-list of a Collection of Books and Manuscripts Belonging to The Right Hon. Lord Amherst of Hackney at Didlington Hall, Norfolk* (Cambridge: Cambridge University Press, 1906), p. 135; Sotheby's Sale Catalogue, 17-19 Jan. 1921, Lot 629, No. 2088; see also Doyle, 'Survey', II, 57-58.
   Allen, *Writings*, p. 262.

7. Group I. Related to MV 9, 10, 87, and 90 and, in Books I and II, to MV 24.

MV 4   Brussels, Bibliothèque Royale Albert I, IV 998, ff. 1-105v, s. xv in.

1. Parchment, 105 ff., 164 × 112 mm. A mixed hand for text (basically anglicana, but with characteristics of both bastard anglicana and secretary). Single columns, 33-44 ll. per page. Catchwords visible through f. 89v; signatures (modern). Illustrated initial on f. 1 representing Christ displaying the wounds on his hands.

3. Title impossible to read (the first page of text is damaged); no colophon, text ending imperfectly at l. 9320. Inc: 'The m[. . .]'; expl: '[. . .] perre'. Prologue slightly expanded, but the whole text considerably reduced (*c.* 7988/9221 ll.), with one omission within remaining text: one leaf between ff. 31 and 32 containing ll. 2631-727. Latin titles in both text and margins to all books except I and IV (the latter imperfect at beginning). Both capitals and paragraph marks for subdivisions. Latin quotations in text to f. 15v, thereafter in margins, usually in a hand different from that of the text. In addition, the top, bottom, and outside margins are filled with Latin prose, apparently in same hand as the text, though in a slightly more formal variety; it appears to be primarily a combination of (a) further quotations from the Latin sources used by the author of *PC* as well as quotations from other relevant sources and (b) a Latin paraphrase of portions of the English text (though it is not the Latin translation described later in this guide). Also marginal

source and topical notes in Latin. Prol: 1; I: 6; II: 13; III: 21; IV (begins imperfectly at l. 2728): 32; V: 46; VI: 73; VII: 86.

4. On f. 20v is a 16th-c. note of ownership: 'John Syngle hys booke [. . .].'

5. Devonshire.

6. Not in *IMEV.*
   Cinq années d'acquisitions 1974-1978 (Brussels: Bibliothèque Royale Albert Ier, 1979), pp. 69-71, item 32 (description by Jan Deschamps).
   McIntosh, 'Two', passim.

7. Group IV. A member of a subgroup of four very closely related MSS (along with MV 24, 63, and 72) that is derived from the Vernon subgroup (see MV 70, Category 7) and is also related to the Lichfield subgroup (see MV 23, Category 7).

MV 5 Cambridge, Fitzwilliam Museum, McClean 131, ff. 1-113v, s. xiv ex.

1. Parchment, i + 113 + i ff., 222 × 133 mm. Four hands, all anglicana formata, with Latin quotations in textura (except for a few in bastard anglicana at the beginning of Hand 4): (1) ff. 1-1v; (2) ff. 2-43v, l. 12; (3) ff. 43v, l. 13, to 85v; (4) ff. 86-end. Collation: 1^{12} (lacks 1) 2^{12} 3^{10} 4^{10} (lacks 5-6) 5^{10} (lacks 1-2) 6-8^{12} 9-10^{10} 11^{10} (lacks 2-9) 12$^{?}$ (only 1 and 2 remain). Single columns, 35-37 ll. per page in Hands 1-3, 32-38 ll. per page in Hand 4. Catchwords.

3. No title, text beginning imperfectly at l. 73; no colophon, text ending imperfectly at l. 9606. Inc: 'Til his liknes in semely stature'; expl: 'Or over mekille hardende in wickidnes.' Slightly abbreviated text (*c.* 8082/8569 ll.), with five omissions: (1) ll. 1-72 (one leaf) at beginning; (2) ll. 2861-3007 (two leaves) between ff. 37 and 38; (3) ll. 3296-441 (two leaves) between ff. 41 and 42; (4) ll. 8393-9062 (eight leaves) between ff. 106 and 107; (5) ll. 9607-end (one leaf) at end. Latin titles in text to

Books I, VI, and VII, in margin to III; English titles in text to II, IV, and V. Occasional capitals for subdivisions. Some correction, both marginal and (primarily) interlinear, in Hands 2 and 3; occasional notes and a few fanciful decorations in Hand 4. Prol (begins imperfectly at l. 73): 1; I: 4v; II: 12; III: 22; IV: 35; V: 48v; VI: 80; VII: 94v; Epil: 112v.

5. Hands 2, 3, and 4 all suggest north west Yorkshire; Hands 2 and 3 are linguistically so similar as to suggest the same place of scribal origin for both.

6. *IMEV* 3428.38; formerly Ashburnham Appendix 135.
    M. R. James, *A Descriptive Catalogue of the McClean Collection of Manuscripts in the Fitzwilliam Museum* (Cambridge: Cambridge University Press, 1912), p. 278.
    Britton, passim.

7. Group I. Related to MV 20 and 60, though perhaps contaminated, for Book II begins as in the MSS of Group II.

MV 6   Cambridge, Gonville and Caius College, 386, ff. 1-96, s. xv¹.

1. Paper, i + 98 + i ff., 213 × 146 mm. Text of *PC* in anglicana, with Latin quotations in anglicana formata. Single columns, 24-30 ll. per page, with the length of lines increasing in the second half of the MS. Signatures.

2. *PC* the primary item, with a 15th-c. deed and a spurious papal document on ff. 96v-97.

3. Title: 'Hic incipit stimulus conciencie compilatus per Ricardum heremitam'; colophon: 'Amen Amen Amen Explicit stimulus conciencie.' Inc: 'The mygth of þe fader almythy'; expl: 'þat for hus was born of a mayden and ded hup on þe rode henge'. Text greatly abbreviated in total number of lines (c. 5292/9624 ll.) and heavily revised: as the scribe-editor progresses, he begins to combine two lines into one, and by the time he is into Book V this is his dominant pattern. Running Latin titles along tops

of many pages, but nothing in text or margins except 'Prima de miseria humane condicionis' in text at l. 234 on f. 5. Some interlinear correction in same hand as text; occasional source notes. Prol: 1; I: 7v; II: 17v; III: 29; IV: 44; V: 59; VI: 78v; VII: 86v.

4. On f. 96v there is a deed by Jon Brythwald of Mildenhall, Suffolk (15th c.); at Gonville and Caius College by 1600.

5. West Suffolk.

6. *IMEV* 3428.32.
   M. R. James, *A Descriptive Catalogue of the Manuscripts in the Library of Gonville and Caius College, Cambridge*, II (Cambridge: Cambridge University Press, 1908), 446–47.
   Allen, 'Authorship', p. 121; Allen, *Writings*, p. 375; Oudin, col. 928; Pits, p. 466; Ritson, p. 34; Walter W. Skeat, ' "The Pricke of Conscience" ', *Notes and Queries*, 4th Series, 1 (1868), 65; Tanner, p. 375, n. q.

7. Probably Group IV, though a very independent MS, especially from Book VI on; very closely related to MV 76 and occasionally to MV 81 to the beginning of Book V.

MV 7 Cambridge, Magdalene College, F.4.18 (18), ff. 1–110v, s. xiv ex.

1. Parchment, 110 ff., 238 × 152 mm. Written in anglicana formata. Single columns, 38 ll. per page. Catchwords, beginning with f. 1v (probably seven leaves omitted at beginning). MS paginated rather than foliated from f. 3 on, beginning with page 3.

3. No title, text beginning imperfectly at l. 542; colophon: 'Explicit liber qui dicitur stimulus consciencie.' Inc: 'he says a man is borne to travaylle ryht'; expl: 'þat vouched sauf for us on rode to hyng Amen'. Text reduced by c. 8 per cent (8360/9083 ll.). Latin titles in text to all remaining books; running Latin titles throughout. Capitals for subdivisions. Occasional marginalia, including chapter numbers for each book; there also appears an English couplet (repeated) on f. 108v (p. 214) in two late

15th- or early 16th-c. hands. Occasional corrections in text. I (begins imperfectly at l. 542): 1; II: 5v (p. 8); III: 13 (p. 23); IV: 25v (p. 48); V: 39 (p. 75); VI: 70v (p. 138); VII: 84v (p. 166); Epil: 109v (p. 216).

4. Some names in margins (William birch, Thomas, Thomas becke, Robert, Robert Beck, Ric*ardus* reshe), late 15th or early 16th c.

5. Hiberno-English: Dublin Pale, County Louth (?).

6. *IMEV* 3428.33.
   Magdalene Cat., p. 45.

7. Group II. Related to MV 19, 22, 53, and 85.

MV 8 Cambridge, St John's College, 80 (D.5), ff. 1–118, s. xiv/xv.

1. Parchment, 121 ff., 270 × 165 mm. Two hands: (1) ff. 1–26, l. 26, an idiosyncratic anglicana formata, often approaching bastard anglicana, especially in the Latin quotations; (2) ff. 26, l. 27 to end, anglicana. Single columns, 32–41 ll. per page for Hand 1; 35-44 ll. per page for Hand 2, gradually increasing as the text progresses. Catchwords irregularly. MS unfoliated.

2. *PC* followed by Articles Concerning London (ff. 118v-121).

3. No medieval title, but f. 1 is torn in the upper right hand corner and may have had a title originally; colophon: 'Explicit trattus [*sic*] qui dicitur consciencie stimulus Here endes þe tretice þat es cald þe key of knowyng' ('þe kay of knawyng' also at l. 9551). Inc: [þ]e myghte of [. . .]'; expl: 'þat for us vouched save on rode to hyng'. Text considerably reduced (*c.* 7881/9624 ll.). English titles in text to I, IV, and VI; Latin titles in margin to III and VII. Occasional corrections, both interlinear and marginal. Prol: 1; I: 2v; II: 9; III: 16; IV: 27; V: 48v; VI: 81v; VII: 96v; Epil: 117.

4. Below the colophon on f. 118 is a bond with the names 'Cetezein Coiffer of london' and 'R of Watford in the Counte of hertford husbandeman' in a hand of the 15th-16th c.

5. Both hands fully northern, though almost certainly from different places.

6. *IMEV* 3428.35.
St John's Cat., pp. 107–08.
Allen, *Writings*, pp. 386 and 386, n. 3; Britton, passim.

7. Group II. A member of the 'Key of Knowing' subgroup, along with MV 33, 41, 58, 64, 86, and perhaps 92; occasionally closer to MV 41 than to the other MSS. Has a conflated colophon.

MV 9 Cambridge, St John's College, 137 (E.34), ff. 1–113v, s. xv in.

1. Parchment, 113 ff., 210 X 152 mm. Text written in anglicana, with Latin quotations in anglicana formata. Collation: 1^8 (lacks 1) $2-5^8$ 6^8 (lacks 3–4) 7^8 (lacks 4–5) $8-12^8$ 13^8 (with 7 a fragment) 14^8 15^8 (lacks 5–6). Single columns, 35–44 ll. per page. MS unfoliated.

3. No title, text beginning imperfectly at l. 69; colophon: 'Explicit tractatus Stimulus consciencie nominatus Here endiþ þe tret[. . .] þat prik of conscience clepid ys', followed by 'Floure of maydens alle Tu gloria virginitatis / Whan we to þe calle Rege nos sociando beatis / He þat wrote þis tretis / God graunte hym hevene blis' and then 'Nomen scriptoris est Ricardus plenus amoris'. Inc: 'God to mannys kynde had grete love'; expl: 'þat for us vouched saufe on rode to hynge / þerfore þu us fecche to þy blisful wonynge / with outen endynge Amen Amen Amen'. Very little abbreviation in the text (*c.* 8909/9079 ll.), but with four omissions: (1) ll. 1–68 (one leaf) at beginning; (2) ll. 3437–596 (two leaves) between ff. 41 and 42; (3) ll. 4171–330 (two leaves) between 48 and 49; (4) ll. 9276–432 (two leaves) between ff. 110 and 111. Latin titles in text to all books. Capitals for subdivisions. An occasional source note. Prol (begins imperfectly at l. 69): 1; I: 5; II: 12; III: 21; IV: 33; V: 46; VI: 74v; VII: 88v; Epil: 112.

4. On f. 113v: 'Amen quod Robertus Lefdys cui constat iste libellus' in a later 15th-c. hand; probably given to St John's by Richard Spinke, of Driffield, Yorkshire (B.A. 1623-24, M.A. 1627; died 1634).

5. Berkshire.

6. *IMEV* 3428.36, 812.
St John's *Cat.*, pp. 173-74.
Allen, *Writings*, p. 376.

7. Group I. Related to MV 3, 10, 87, and 90 and, in Books I and II, to MV 24.

MV 10 Cambridge, University Library, Dd.11.89, ff. 9-162, s. xiv ex.

1. Parchment, i + 196 + i ff., 197 X 133 mm. Two MSS bound together, the second of which (ff. 9-196), containing *PC*, is in several anglicana hands of different degrees of formality; at least two hands in *PC*, with a change on f. 123. Single columns, 25-34 ll. per page, with a larger average per page before f. 123 than after. Catchwords.

2. The first MS contains prose and verse on the Ten Commandments (the verse is *IMEV* 1856) and the *Abbey of the Holy Ghost*; the second MS contains *PC*, the *Speculum Gy de Warewyke* (*IMEV* 1101), a remembrance of the Passion (*IMEV* 2613), and an Exposition of the *Pater Noster* (*IMEV* 958).

3. No title; colophon: 'Explicit tractatus qui dicitur stimulus consciencie / Here endeþe þe tretys þat ys cald þe prykke off conciense / Here endeþe [*sic*] þe sermon þat a clerk made þat was cleput / Alquyn To gwy of Warwyk.' Inc: 'þe myth of þe fadur almy3ty'; expl: 'þat for us vouched save on rode to hyng Amen Amen Amen'. Text only slightly reduced (*c.* 9382/9624 ll.). English titles in text to all books except II; English subtitles in text. Paragraph marks and occasional capitals for subdivisions. Ff. 70 and 74 each have at the bottom four lines of comment

on and paraphrase of the text written by a 15th-c. hand in an East Anglian dialect: f. 70—ll. 4065 (omitted in text), 4084 varied, 4101-02 varied, the last two marked for insertion at l. 4101 on f. 70v by a +; f. 74—ll. 4563-64 paraphrased, two lines similar in sense to 4405-10. Prol: 9; I: 14v; II: 23; III: 34; IV: 49; V: 68v; VI: 106; VII: 123v; Epil: 160v.

5. Both main hands have strong ingredients of a Gloucestershire or Worcestershire character but with marked traces of dialectal forms from elsewhere.

6. *IMEV* 3428.29.
   CUL Cat., I, 481-82; Pink.
   Robbins, p. 389.

7. Group I. Related to MV 3, 9, 87, and 90 and, in Books I and II, to MV 24. Though the text of MV 10 is different from that of MV 67, the two have the same configuration of colophons, with the error 'endeþe þe sermon'—an error because the *Speculum Gy de Warewyke* follows *PC* in MV 10.

MV 11   Cambridge, University Library, Dd.12.69, ff. 37-97v, s. xiv ex.

1. Parchment, ii + 95 + iv ff. (ff. 23 and 35 lost), 197 × 127 mm. Two hands in the MS, changing at f. 37. *PC* written in anglicana formata. Single columns. 30-34 ll. per page. Catchwords in *PC*.

2. *PC* preceded by *Dieta Salutis*, verses added on f. 24v on the Articles of Faith, and short explanations of various theological subjects, ending imperfectly on f. 34v.

3. Title: 'Hic incipit stimulus consciencie'; no colophon, text perhaps ending imperfectly (but cf. MV 14); Inc: 'þe myth of þe fader almyghy [*sic*]'; expl: 'to þe whiche joye he us brynge / þat of noȝth haþ made alle þynge' (cf. ll. 9532 and 9622-23). Text greatly reduced: only 38 per cent of the total number of lines remains (*c.* 3654/9624 ll.). Text very paraphrastic. Latin titles in text to all books. Capitals for subdivisions. Marginal

source notes in Latin; an occasional marginal note in English (ff. 72-72v, 76v). Occasional corrections, both in text and (primarily) in margins. Prol: 37; I: 41; II: 45; III: 49v; IV: 54v; V: 62; VI: 81; VII: 89.

4. On beginning flyleaf ii verso is an erased early 15th-c. inscription indicating that the MS was given to the Shermanbury, Sussex, Parish Church by a John Haynes, followed by 'Sussex/ Thomas'; on end flyleaf iv is a long note in Latin, dated 1460, relating to the accession of Edward IV.

5. A probably Sussex transcription of an exemplar in a rather standard form of language.

6. *IMEV* 3428.30.
   CUL Cat., I, 506; Pink; for provenance see *MLGB*, pp. 223, 324.

7. Highly condensed, paraphrastic text, but appears to be Group I; nearly identical to MV 14. The highly abbreviated and altered *Speculum Huius Vite* was probably made from the version contained in MV 11 and 14.

MV 12   Cambridge, University Library, Ll.2.17, ff. 2-145, s. xv².

1. Parchment, 143 ff. (ff. 3-6 lost; ff. 1 and 147 pastedowns), 311 X 222 mm. Text written in bastard anglicana, with Latin quotations in textura. Single columns, 30 ll. per page. Catchwords.

3. No title; colophon: 'ffinito libro reddatur gloria Christo'. Inc (at the top of f. 2): 'Off many thynges I knowe and se' (l. 179; text begins here by intention with an elaborate gold capital); expl (at bottom of f. 145): 'That has bene and is and yet shal be' (l. 9570; text ends here, probably by intention because the colophon follows and f. 145v is blank). Text reduced by nearly 9 per cent (8358/9145 ll.), with one omission: ff. 3-6, which would have contained ll. 239-495. English titles in text to Books II-IV, VI-VII (the beginning of I is omitted); Latin title

in margin to Book V. Capitals and paragraph marks for subdivisions. Topical marginal notes in Latin throughout. Prol (begins at l. 179): 2; I (begins imperfectly at l. 496): 7; II: 14; III: 26; IV: 42v; V: 62v; VI: 98; VII: 113v; Epil: 144v.

4. On f. 1v is 'Hub Freake me tenet' (16th c.).

5. South east Nottinghamshire.

6. *IMEV* 3428.31.
   CUL Cat., IV, 44; Pink.

7. Group II.

MV 13 Cambridge, University Library, Additional 6693, ff. 1-179, s. xiv ex.

1. Parchment, 179 ff., 179 X 118 mm. Two similar textura hands at work in *PC*: (1) ff. 1-175v; (2) ff. 176-79. Collation: 1-2⁸ 3⁸ (lacks 1) 4-22⁸ 23⁷⁶ (lacks 1, 6). Either the last quire of the original MS has been lost, and ff. 176-79 added from another copy of the poem, or the last quire is a six, with the outer bifolium lost. Single columns, 26 ll. per page. Catchwords.

2. *PC* the only item in the MS except for the beginning of an English poem (*IMEV* 1781) and a line of Latin on f. 179 in two different but still medieval hands.

3. No title, though the running title on the first few pages is 'Prologus stimuli consciencie'; no colophon. Inc: 'Th[. . .]th of þe fadir al my3thi'; expl: 'þat for us fouchid save on roode to hyng Amen'. Text slightly reduced (9196/9516 ll.), with two omissions: (1) one leaf containing ll. 833-84 between ff. 15 and 16; (2) probably one leaf containing ll. 9416-71 between ff. 175 and 176. Latin titles in text to all books; running Latin titles to f. 175v. Occasional marginal notes; a few corrections in text. Prol: 1; I: 8 (though the title is on f. 5v between ll. 234 and 235); II: 17v; III: 31v; IV: 50; V: 73v; VI: 119v; VII: 140v; Epil: 177.

4. Late 15th-c. scribbles on f. 179 include the names 'Anne drure' and 'baﾃtimas allyn'.

5. Berkshire, Oxfordshire, or Northamptonshire?

6. *IMEV* 3428.92; formerly Ashburnham Appendix 136 (not 236, as in Supplement to *IMEV*).
   Catalogue of the Manuscripts at Ashburnham Place Appendix (London: Charles Francis Hodgson, 1861), item 136 (repeated in Sotheby's Sale Catalogue, 1 May 1899, p. 49, lot 84); unpublished description by R. A. B. Mynors at Cambridge University Library.

7. Erratic MS, appearing to shift relationships: Group II in Books II and IV, Group I in book V, etc.

MV 14 Cambridge, Massachusetts, Harvard University Library, English 515, ff. 1-77, s. xiv².

1. Parchment, 77 ff., 180 × 120 mm. Written in anglicana formata. Three leaves omitted at the beginning of the text. Single columns, 23 ll. per page. Catchwords.

3. No title, text beginning imperfectly at l. 161; no colophon. Inc: 'But gret perel ys þat man ynne'; expl: 'To þe whuche joye he us brynge / þat of nouȝt haþ made alle þynge [cf. ll. 9532 and 9622-23] / Amen amen so mote hyt be / Seye we alle par charyte Amen.' Text greatly reduced: only 37 per cent of the total number of lines remains (3492/9464 ll.). Text very paraphrastic. Latin titles in text to all books except I. Capitals for subdivisions. Some interlinear corrections in same hand as text. Prol (begins imperfectly at l. 161): 1; I: 3v; II: 8v; III: 14; IV: 20v; V: 29v; VI: 55; VII: 65v.

4. Belonged to a 'John Kyng' in the 15th c. His name is on f. 77v following the words 'Iste liber constat', which are in the same hand as the text, but the name is in a later hand and may be over an erasure (of the former owner's name?).

5. Probably Worcestershire, but with suggestions of a Gloucestershire dialectal element.

6. *IMEV* 3428.82; formerly Halliwell.
   Census, I, 966.
   Allen, 'Authorship', pp. 124 and 126, n. 1.

7. Highly condensed, paraphrastic text, but appears to be Group I; nearly identical to MV 11. The highly abbreviated and altered *Speculum Huius Vite* was probably made from the version contained in MV 11 and 14.

MV 15   Canterbury, Cathedral, Lit. D. 13 (66), ff. 1-144v, s. xiv med.

1. Paper, iv + 144 ff., 222 X 140 mm. Written in anglicana. Some leaves out of order: the correct order between ff. 14 and 23 should be 14, 17, 15-16, 19-22, 18, 23. Eight leaves missing after f. 132. Single columns, 24-30 ll. per page. Frequent catchwords.

3. No title, and no space for one; no colophon, text ending imperfectly at the bottom of f. 144v with l. 8720, but in the bottom margin of the same page a later hand (15th c.) has added 'Explicit liber Stimulus consciencie.' Inc: 'þe miȝtte of þe fader al miȝtty'; expl: 'þat folwide none oþer lawe bote cristes'. Text slightly abbreviated (*c.* 7768/8282 ll.), especially in Book VI, where it jumps from l. 7296 to l. 7520, as do other MSS. Eight leaves missing between ff. 132 and 133 which would have contained ll. 7558-996. English titles in text to all books. Many rubrics throughout; some interlinear correction. Prol: 1; I: 7v; II: 16; III: 30; IV: 48v; V: 72v; VI: 116v; VII: 132.

4. Late 15th-c. notes on beginning flyleaves, one of which is 'Iste liber constat domino Rectori de Borton', suggesting ownership by Nicholas Moyn or Mayne, whose will begins on f. iv verso; the name 'Willelmus Mayne' appears on f. ii verso.

5. Wiltshire.

6. *IMEV* 3428.54.
  MMBL, II, 281 (superseding the description published in 1911 by C. Eveleigh Woodruff).
  Waters, p. 48.

7. Group III.

MV 16 Charlottesville, Virginia, University of Virginia Library, Hench 10, ff. 1–136v, *c.* 1370.

1. Parchment, 136 ff., 270 × 180 mm. Written in anglicana formata throughout. The original ff. 1–2 have been missing since at least 1610 and have been replaced by two parchment leaves copied from a MS in the British Library by H(enry) H(ucks) G(ibbs), first Lord Aldenham, in the 19th c., as he himself says on beginning flyleaf ii. Single columns, 33–41 ll. per page. Catchwords beginning on f. 8v.

3. No title on either f. 1 or f. 3; no colophon originally, but a very faint 'Explicit stimulus consciencie' added in a 15th-c. (?) hand. Inc (f. 1): 'þe myght of the fader almyghty'; inc (f. 3): 'To mekenesse and to love and drede'; expl: 'þat on þe rode for oure love gan hynge Amen'. A nearly complete text (*c.* 9565/9624 ll.). English titles in text to all books except VII; running Latin titles throughout. Occasional English subtitles in text. Many marginal source notes; occasional corrections in text and a few lines added in margins where omitted in text originally. Prol: 1 (original MS begins on f. 3); I: 5v; II: 12v; III: 23; IV: 37v; V: 55v; VI: 91; VII: 107; Epil: 135.

4. A Walter Loveden owned the MS in 1610 (his name appears twice on f. 3 with the dates 24 April 1610 and 15 June 1610).

5. Warwickshire.

6. *IMEV* 3428.87; formerly Aldenham.
  Faye and Bond, p. 515a; Henry Hucks Gibbs, *A Catalogue of Some Printed Books and Manuscripts at St. Dunstan's, Regents Park, and Aldenham House, Herts.* (London:

privately printed, 1888), p. 159; see also Sotheby's Sale Catalogue, 22-24 March 1937, p. 132, Aldenham lot 310. Waters, pp. 48-49.

7. Group III.

MV 17   Chicago, Illinois, Newberry Library, 32.9, ff. 1-99, s. xiv^2.

1. Parchment, i + 114 ff., 197 X 133 mm. *PC* written in anglicana formata. Single columns, 23-31 ll. per page. Catchwords. London binding of *c*. 1540. MS unfoliated. In four small roundels at the corners of f. 1 are the letters 'P', 'F', 'M', 'S' (clockwise, from upper left), which probably stand for 'Pater', 'Filius', 'Mater', 'Spiritus'.

2. *PC* followed by the *Lapidarye of Philippe Kynge of France*.

3. No title; colophon: 'Here than endes the tretice alle / which that men Prik of conscience kalle / Explicit expliceat sic benedictus eat / Amen.' Inc: 'The mighte of þe fader al my3ty'; expl: 'God bringe us thidre whan we hennes wende' (l. 9532), followed by 'And that it mote so be / With herte stedfaste Amen say we.' Text greatly reduced, by over 42 per cent (*c*. 5536/9624 ll.), mainly by omission rather than by paraphrase. English titles in text to all books except IV and VII; occasional English subtitles in text. Capitals for subdivisions. Prol: 1; I: 7v; II: 13; III: 19v; IV: 28v; V: 37; VI: 71v; VII: 84.

4. The *Lapidarye* ends with 'quod Hull' (f. 113v).

5. Possibly Northamptonshire but with evidence of a more northerly underlay.

6. *IMEV* 3428.76; formerly Helmingham Hall LJ.II.1; the Silver MS.
Sotheby's Sale Catalogue, 6 June 1961, lot 8; Saenger.
Allen, *Writings*, p. 373, n. 1; Waters, p. 49.

7. Group III. Related to MV 38.

MV 18 Chicago, Illinois, Newberry Library, 33 (C. 19169), pp. 1-198, s. xiv².

1. Parchment, 99 ff., 210 × 110 mm. Written in anglicana formata. Collation: 1⁸ (stubs only) 2⁸ (1-2 stubs only) 3-13⁸ 14⁸ (lacks 2-7) 15⁸ (4-8 stubs only) 16² (stubs only). Single columns, 39 ll. per page. MS paginated rather than foliated.

3. No title, text beginning imperfectly at l. 797; no colophon, text ending imperfectly at l. 9571. Inc: 'And lackeþ ȝong men þat now are seene'; expl: 'þus may þis tretis with þe sentence'. Text reduced by c. 7 per cent (7710/8298 ll.), with three omissions: (1) ten leaves at beginning containing ll. 1-796; (2) six leaves between pp. 190 and 191 containing ll. 8780-9256; (3) one leaf at end containing ll. 9572-624. Latin titles in text to all remaining books. I (begins imperfectly at l. 797): 1; II: 4; III: 22; IV: 46; V: 75; VI: 133; VII: 159; Epil: 198.

5. Probably south west Lincolnshire but with various more northerly forms especially at the beginning.

6. IMEV 3428.85; formerly Peterborough Central Library; Hope Emily Allen Additional MS I (Writings, p. 374).
Census, I, 541; Saenger.
Allen, Writings, p. 373, n. 1; Lewis, 'Relationship', pp. 257, 259, and n. 26; McIntosh, 'Two', pp. 69 and 69, n. 1.

7. Group IV. Closely related to the Vernon subgroup (see MV 70, Category 7) in Book V.

MV 19 Douai Abbey, Woolhampton, Berkshire, 7, ff. 2-150, s. xiv/xv.

1. Parchment, ii + 150 + ii ff., 175 × 113 mm. Written in anglicana. Single columns, 27-34 ll. per page.

3. Title: 'Hic incipit liber qui vocatur stimulus consciencie'; colophon: 'Explicit liber qui vocatur stimulus consciencie Deo gracias Amen.' Inc: 'The might of þe fader almighty'; expl: 'þat

for us vouchid save on rode to hyng'. Text slightly abbreviated
(c. 8883/9562 ll.), with one omission: ll. 7316-77 (one leaf)
between ff. 115 and 116. Book IV ends at bottom of f. 63; f.
63v is blank; Book V begins at the top of f. 64 (a new quire).
Latin titles in text to all books. Capitals for subdivisions. Occa-
sional interlinear additions to the text; occasional marginalia of
various kinds. Prol: 2; I: 8; II: 17; III: 28v; IV: 43v; V: 64; VI:
102; VII: 118v; Epil: 148v.

4. 'Dan harri of beyston' on verso of front pastedown in a hand
of the 15th/16th c.

5. South Lancashire.

6. *IMEV* 3428.94.
   MMBL, II, 416.

7. Group II. Related to MV 7, 22, 53, and 85.

MV 20 Dublin, Trinity College, 156 (D.4.8), ff. 2-136v, s. xv in.

1. Parchment, i + 140 ff. (with beginning flyleaf foliated 1),
c. 216 X 141 mm. Probably two hands at work in *PC*, both
anglicana (with textura for Latin quotations and titles): (1) ff.
2-66v, 75-136v; (2) ff. 67-74v. Collation: 1-7⁸ 8⁸ + 1 leaf 9-
10⁸ 11¹⁰ 12-14⁸ 15⁸ (lacks 1) 16¹⁰ 17⁸. Single columns, 32-33
ll. per page, except for an added leaf (f. 66), which has 17 on
the recto and 16 on the verso; f. 66 was probably added later by
the first scribe to fill out the text missing between his own f. 65v
and the beginning of f. 67, which had already been copied by
the second scribe. Catchwords.

2. *PC* followed by Richard Maydestone's version of the Seven
Penitential Psalms (*IMEV* 1961), ending imperfectly.

3. No title; no colophon, text ending imperfectly (though by in-
tention) at l. 9474. Inc: 'The might of the father on high' (on
f. 1v, written by a Johannes Fleming in the 17th c. because gall
has obliterated most of the first page of the medieval text on

f. 2); expl: 'Whar throw we may come to his blis amen.' Text re-
duced by over 9 per cent (*c.* 8647/9560 ll.), mainly from Book
VI to the end. One leaf, which would have contained ll. 7801-
64, omitted between ff. 116 and 117. Latin titles in text to all
books except I, with colophon to preceding book. Capitals for
subdivisions. Prol: 2 (with the first 22½ ll. also written by Flem-
ing on f. 1v); I: 7; II: 15v; III: 26v; IV: 41v; V: 61v; VI: 97v;
VII: 122v.

4. In the margin of f. 78 is a 16th-c. copy of a writ to the Sheriff
of Dublin during the reign of Henry VIII, and on ff. 1-1v is a
deed made in Dublin referring to the year 1618 and mentioning
the names James Ware and Matthew Tirrel, witnessed by men
whose names are White, Criffe (?), and William Blauer.

5. Hiberno-English: Dublin.

6. *IMEV* 3428.65.
  Abbott, p. 20.
  Allen, *Writings*, pp. 381-82; Andreae, p. 23; Benskin and
    Laing, pp. 99-100, n. 13; Bülbring, *ES*, passim; Bülbring,
    Trans., passim; Ritson, p. 34.

7. Group I. Related to MV 5 and 60.

MV 21 Dublin, Trinity College, 157 (D.4.11), ff. 1-89, s. xv in.

1. Parchment, 90 ff., 212 × 158 mm. Written in anglicana for-
mata. Probably one quire (of ten?) omitted at beginning. Single
columns, 39 ll. per page. Catchwords. MS unfoliated.

2. *PC* the only item in the MS, though there are six lines of
Latin and fifteen of English prose on f. 89v and a list of Latin-
English equivalents and twelve lines of English prose on f. 90.

3. No title, text beginning imperfectly at l. 446; no colophon,
text ending, perhaps by intention, at l. 9472 at the bottom of
f. 89. Inc: 'His moder consayved hym sinfully'; expl: 'thurgh þe
prayer of his moder mylde Amen', followed by a long line that

summarizes the next two lines (9473-74; possibly 9621-24?), 'ffolowes vertus and hates s[mutilated] ffor sua may ȝe to h[mutilated]'. Text considerably reduced, by *c.* 23 per cent (6972/9087 ll.), with many lines omitted, much condensation, and some paraphrase. English titles in text to all remaining books. Capitals for subdivisions. I (begins imperfectly at l. 446): 1; II: 6v; III: 13v; IV: 23v; V: 35v; VI: 62; VII: 73.

5. Fully northern.

6. *IMEV* 3428.66.
   Abbott, p. 20.
   Andreae, p. 23; Britton, passim; Bülbring, *ES*, passim; Bülbring, *Trans.*, passim; D'Evelyn, pp. 190-91 and 191, n. 21.

7. Group IV, though with a number of idiosyncratic readings. Related to MV 49 from l. 2850 on and to MV 95 in Books VI-VII. See also E 4, Category 7.

MV 22 Dublin, Trinity College, 158 (D.4.15), ff. 1-81v, s. xv[1].

1. Parchment (for *PC*) and paper, 93 ff., 195 X 131 mm. Text of *PC* in anglicana, with Latin quotations usually in anglicana formata. Collation: 1^{12} 2^{12} (lacks 3, 10) 3^{12} (lacks 3-4, 9-10) 4^{12} (lacks 2-3, 5-8, 10) $5-6^{12}$ 7^{10} 8^{12}. Single columns, 26-35 ll. per page. Catchwords.

2. *PC* followed by miscellaneous medicinal recipes, etc.

3. No title; no colophon, text ending imperfectly at l. 6428. Inc: 'the myght of þe ffader allemyghty'; expl: '[. . .] ay when he þere on thoght', plus catchwords 'ffor drede'. Text reduced by *c.* 4 per cent (*c.* 5290/*c.* 5528 ll.). A number of omissions in the remaining text: (1) one leaf with ll. 882-945 between ff. 14 and 15; (2) one leaf with ll. 1338-405 between ff. 20 and 21; (3) two leaves with ll. 1660-785 between ff. 24 and 25; (4) two leaves with ll. 2058-199 between ff. 28 and 29; (5) two leaves with ll. 2399-*c.* 2535 between ff. 31 and 32; (6) four leaves with ll. 2607-891 between ff. 32 and 33; (7) one leaf with

ll. 2974-3045 between ff. 33 and 34. Latin titles in text to Books I, V, VI; Latin titles in top margins to II (f. 15), III (f. 21), and V (f. 47). Running Latin titles irregularly. Occasional marginal notes. Prol: 1; I: 7; II (begins imperfectly at l. 946): 15; III (begins imperfectly at l. 1786): 25; IV (begins imperfectly at l. 2892): 33; V: 47; VI: 81v.

4. Later 15th-c. names on ff. 82-93 passim (Rogerus Jekyn, Rycardus Fykerot, Lady Preston, etc.) are associated with the area of Killeen, County Meath, Ireland.

5. North Lancashire.

6. *IMEV* 3428.67.
   Abbott, p. 21.
   Andreae, p. 23; Britton, passim; Bülbring, *ES*, pp. 28-30.

7. Group II. Related to MV 7, 19, 53, and 85.

MV 23 Holkham Hall, Wells, Norfolk, Library of the Earl of Leicester, 668, ff. 1-134v, s. xiv/xv.

1. Parchment, 134 ff., 230 × 145 mm. At least three hands at work: (1) anglicana formata, from the beginning to l. 1047, ll. 1076-2112, and 8086-9624, alternating with Hand 2 elsewhere; (2) anglicana formata, from ll. 4482-5480, 5498-767, and 5818-8085, alternating with Hand 1 elsewhere; (3) anglicana formata, ll. 1048-75 on f. 16v; (4) perhaps a fourth hand for a few lines on f. 104v. Hand 1 is the same as Hand 1 of MV 89. Single columns, 33 ll. per page. Catchwords. First and last leaves badly stained. MS unfoliated.

3. No medieval title; colophon: 'Explicit tractatus qui dicitur Stimulus consciencie Deo gracias', followed by 'Nomen scriptoris Johannes plenus amoris [. . .] benedicat rex orientis.' Inc: 'Here bygynnyþ [. . .]'; expl: '[. . .] for oure h[. . .] roode con [. . .] Amen.' Text reduced by over 8 per cent (8824/9624 ll.), with the greatest reduction in Books III-V and VII. No titles anywhere. Occasional capitals for subdivisions. Occasional marginal corrections; marginal notes in a 15th-c. anglicana hand.

Prol: 1; I: 6v; II: 14v; III: 25; IV: 39v; V: 56; VI: 89; VII: 105;
Epil: 133.

5. The two main hands, at least, belong to the Lichfield area.

6. *IME V* 1193.4.
*A Handlist of the Manuscripts in the Library of the Earl of
Leicester at Holkham Hall Abstracted from the Catalogues
of William Roscoe and Frederic Madden and Annotated by
Seymour de Ricci* (Oxford: Oxford University Press, for
the Bibliographical Society, 1932), p. 56, based on a fuller
unpublished description at Holkham Hall done by Roscoe
and Madden in 1816-28 (MS 770, VII, 609-10).
Allen, *Writings*, p. 373, n. 1; Dareau and McIntosh, pp. 20-22;
Lewis, 'Relationship', pp. 257-59 and n. 22; Yates, p. 335.

7. Group IV. A member of the Lichfield subgroup (along with
MV 45, 54, 57, 68, 88, and 89), whose ultimate exemplar may
have been MV 31.

MV 24   Leeds, University Library, Brotherton 500, ff. 1-147v,
s. xiv/xv.

1. Parchment, xii + 147 + ii ff., 205 X 125 mm. Written in
anglicana. Single columns, 27-35 ll. per page.

2. *PC* the only item in MS except for some Latin additions on
various theological topics on ff. 44-44v and 147v.

3. Title: 'Hic incipit quidam tractatus Roberti Grostehed epi-
scopi lincolliensis qui nominatur stimulus consciencie Prima
pars qualiter homo factus est et omnia propter eum'; no colo-
phon. Inc: 'þe myȝt of þe fader al myȝty'; expl: 'Jesus kyng
over uch kynge [*sic*] Amen.' Text considerably reduced (*c.*
8378/9624 ll.), with the greatest reduction in Books III-VII,
and it shows signs of having been put together in somewhat
careless fashion. Book III ends one quarter of the way down
f. 44; there are some Latin additions on the rest of f. 44 and on
f. 44v; Book IV begins at the top of f. 45 (the beginning of a

new quire), without title but with a two-line capital. Latin titles
in text to all books except IV and V; Latin title in margin to V.
Occasional capitals for subdivisions. Much correction, both
interlinear and marginal, in both the hand of the text and a later
hand. Prol: 1; I: 7v; II: 17; III: 29v; IV: 45; V: 62v; VI: 97v;
VII: 113v; Epil: 146.

5. North west Worcestershire.

6. *IMEV* 3428.75; formerly Neale; then Harmsworth; Hope
    Emily Allen Additional MS III (*Writings*, p. 374).
    Humphreys and Lightbown, pp. 29-30; Ker.
    Allen, *Writings*, p. 377; Humphreys and Lightbown, pp. 35-
    38; McIntosh, 'Two', passim.

7. Group I in Books I and II; Group IV thereafter, where it is
a member of a subgroup of four closely related MSS (along with
MV 4, 63, and 72) that is derived from the Vernon subgroup
(see MV 70, Category 7) and is also related to the Lichfield sub-
group (see MV 23, Category 7).

**MV 25   Leeds, University Library, Brotherton 501, ff. 1-58v,
s. xv[1].**

1. Paper, iii + 122 + iii ff., 222 × 200 mm. *PC* written in a neat
anglicana and (for Latin quotations) textura. Single columns,
31-38 ll. per page, with couplets written as single lines. Catch-
words.

2. Fifteen items in addition to *PC*: religious works, in English,
in prose and verse, including Richard Lavynham's *Litil Tretys
on the Seven Dedly Synnys*, Thomas Wimbledon's sermon *Redde
Racionem*, the *Spiritus Guidonis* (*IMEV* 2725), the prose *Gospel
of Nicodemus*, and the prose translation of Pseudo-Bonaventure's
Stimulus Amoris.

3. No title, text beginning imperfectly at ll. 1130-31; colophon:
'Explicit tractatus qui vocatus Stimulus consciencie.' Inc: 'Omne
quod est in mundo aut est concupiscencia carnis aut est'; expl:

'To whych place he us all bryng þat for oure hele on rode ded hyng Amen.' Text slightly abbreviated (c. 8048/8495 ll.), with Book VII the only one that deviates greatly from Morris's text. Latin titles in text to all remaining books. Occasional capitals for subdivisions. Source notes (in textura), occasional other notes (in anglicana). II (begins imperfectly at ll. 1130-31): 1; III: 4v; IV: 12v; V: 21; VI: 38; VII: 45; Epil: 58.

4. A number of untraceable names at various places in the MS; the earliest ones are 'Thomas Pell' (ff. 57, 73v) and 'Thomas fotucehithe' (f. 57), both early 16th c.

5. South Lincolnshire.

6. IMEV 3428.77, 3428.89; formerly Horton Old Hall.
Art, item 133; Humphreys and Lightbown, pp. 30-34; Ker. Humphreys and Lightbown, pp. 35-38.

7. Group IV.

MV 26   London, British Library, Arundel 140, ff. 41v-146v, s. xv[1].

1. Paper, 185 ff. (including two scraps before f. 144 foliated 144[1-2] and two scraps before f. 165 foliated 165[1-2]), c. 290 × c. 215 mm. PC written basically in secretary but with some anglicana features. Single columns, 35-44 ll. per page. Catchwords.

2. PC preceded by Ipotis (IMEV 220) and Mandeville's Travels in English prose and followed by the Speculum Gy de Warewyke (IMEV 1101), The Sevyn Sages of Rome (IMEV 3187), and Chaucer's Tale of Melibeus.

3. No title; colophon: 'Here endyth þat tretys þat is called þe pryke of conscience', followed by 'Deo gracias Amen quod R T.' Inc: 'In þe myght of þe fadyr alle myghty'; expl: 'þat for oure love made heven and erþe and alle þynge Amen'. Text slightly reduced (c. 8400/8730 ll.), with a number of omissions: (1) two

leaves between ff. 51 and 52 containing ll. 856-1011; (2) one leaf between ff. 76 and 77 containing ll. 2965-3034; (3) two leaves between ff. 88 and 89 containing ll. 3976-4140; (4) two leaves between ff. 106 and 107 containing ll. 5674-841; (5) two leaves between ff. 114 and 115 containing ll. 6475-636; (6) two leaves between ff. 144 and 145 containing ll. 9304-467, but they remain as scraps and are bound between ff. 143 and 144. English titles in text to all books except II, which is imperfect at the beginning; English subtitles in text. Capitals for subdivisons. Occasional corrections in text. Prol: 41v; I: 46; II (begins imperfectly at l. 1011): 52; III: 60; IV: 73; V: 88v; VI: 114; VII: 124; Epil: 145v.

5. South east Midlands with possibly a central Midlands underlay.

6. *IMEV* 3429.5.
> *Catalogue of Manuscripts in the British Museum*, New Series, I (London: Trustees of the British Museum, 1834), *Part I. The Arundel Manuscripts*, p. 38a; John M. Manly and Edith Rickert, *The Text of the Canterbury Tales* (Chicago: University of Chicago Press, 1940), I, 52-54.
> Andreae, passim; Bülbring, *Trans.*, passim; D'Evelyn, passim; Morris, p. 1; Waters, passim (esp. p. 48).

7. Group III, with some similarity to MV 32.

MV 27   London, British Library, Cotton Galba E. IX, ff. 76a-113a, s. xiv ex.

1. Parchment, iii + 111 ff. (with beginning flyleaves foliated 1-3 by the most recent foliator), 335 X 220 mm. Six hands in the MS, of which the hand that writes *PC* (only), in textura, is the fifth. Double columns, 48 ll. per column. Catchwords irregularly.

2. Fourteen items in all in the MS, including *Ywaine and Gawin* (*IMEV* 259), *The Sevyn Sages of Rome* (*IMEV* 3187), *The Gospel of Nicodemus* (*IMEV* 512), 'The Book of Penance' (*IMEV* 694), historical poems by Laurence Minot (*IMEV*, p. 767), and a prophecy of Merlin (*IMEV* 1112).

3. No original title; colophon: 'Explicit tractus qui dicitur stimulus consciencie / here endes þe tretice þat es called pryk of conscience.' Inc: 'þe myght of þe fader almyghty'; expl: 'þat for us vouched safe on rode to hyng Amen'. 7144/7144 ll., with two omissions: (1) one leaf between ff. 83 and 84 containing ll. 1538-729; (2) probably twelve leaves between ff. 110 and 111 containing ll. 6923-9210. English titles in text to I, II, IV, and V; no title to VI, and III and VII begin imperfectly. Capitals for subdivisions. Some correction, nearly all interlinear. Prol: 76a; I: 77vb; II: 80vb; III (begins imperfectly at l. 1730): 84a; IV: 89a; V: 95va; VI: 108b; VII (begins imperfectly at l. 9211): 111a; Epil: 112va.

5. Fully northern.

6. *IMEV* 3428.39.

> *Cotton Cat.*, pp. 363b-364a; Bogislav von Lindheim, *Studien zur Sprache des Manuskriptes Cotton Galba E IX*, Wiener Beiträge zur englischen Philologie, 59 (Vienna and Leipzig: Wilhelm Braumüller Universitäts-Verlagsbuchhandlung, 1937), pp. 4-6, 87-89.

> After the publication of Morris's edition (1863), this MS is frequently mentioned by name by writers whose main interest is in a variant text or a different MS. The following contain more than just a mention of or quotations from the MS: Allen, 'Authorship', passim; Andreae, passim; Britton, passim; Bülbring, *Trans.*, passim; Campbell, pp. 110-11; Dareau and McIntosh, passim; Lewis, 'Relationship', passim; Lightbown, passim; Morris, passim; Waters, pp. 7, 9, 17, 25. Before 1863 see Yates, p. 335. For dialect see Lindheim (as above), pp. 86-130.

7. Group I. Closely related to MV 34 and 83. The MS used by Morris as the base MS for his edition, except for ll. 1538-729 and 6923-9210, which he took from MV 34.

MV 28 London, British Library, Cotton Appendix VII, ff. 3-145v, s. xv in.

1. Parchment, ii + 145 + i ff., 240 × 145 mm. Two hands at work in *PC*: (1) ff. 3-4v, 7-20v, 22-145v, anglicana formata;

(2) ff. 5-6v, 21r-v, secretary. Collation: $1^?$ (2 remain) 2^8 (lacks 1) $3-10^8$ 11^8 (lacks 4) $12-15^8$ 16^8 (lacks 2, 6) $17-18^8$ 19^{10} $20^?$ (1 remains). Single columns, 26-34 ll. per page. Catchwords.

2. *PC* preceded by The Four Daughters of God (*IMEV* 1879), ending imperfectly on f. 2v.

3. No title, f. 3 mutilated; no colophon, text ending imperfectly at l. 9604, but 'Explicit stimulus consciencie' appears on f. 144 between ll. 9474 and 9475. Inc (first recognizable words, from l. 8): 'And graunte us heven'; expl: 'And mey nouȝt þerby stered be.' Text reduced by *c.* 9 per cent (*c.* 8492/9344 ll.), with four omissions: (1) one leaf between ff. 3 and 4 containing ll. 56-109; (2) one leaf between ff. 76 and 77 containing ll. 4794-865; (3) one leaf between ff. 113 and 114 containing ll. 7319-91; (4) one leaf between ff. 116 and 117 containing ll. 7570-630. No titles originally to any books; Latin titles in margin to II and III in a late 15th-c. hand. Prol: 3; I: 8v; II: 17v; III: 29v; IV: 45v; V: 64v; VI: 99v; VII: 116; Epil: 144v.

4. A 16th-c. (?) note at the bottom of f. 3 indicates that the poem was 'Script*us* a fratre Tho de Ascheburne ord*inis* fratris b*eate* M*a*rie genet*ricis* dei de mo*nte* Carm conventus Northampton Anno 1384', from which Allen, *Writings*, pp. 379-81, speculates that it is not impossible that Ashburn was the original author. Because of the date of the MS, Ashburn was probably not the owner of the MS, though the reference to Northampton-shire may provide a lead as to provenance. A note of ownership on the end flyleaf (f. 146) in a late 15th-c. hand, but nearly impossible to make out, even under ultraviolet light. 16th-c. notes of payment on f. 37v to 'gorge kyrby', 'thomas howerd', and 'wyllaym hudford'.

5. Hand 1 is probably east central Lincolnshire; Hand 2 is probably south west Lincolnshire.

6. *IMEV* 3428.40.
   Cotton Cat., p. 614b; see also Karl Brunner, 'Der Streit der vier Himmelstöchter', *Englische Studien*, 68 (1933-34), 188-89.
   Allen, *Writings*, pp. 379-81; Edwin Guest, *A History of*

English Rhythms (London: William Pickering, 1838), II, 418 (same reference in 1882 edition); Lewis, 'Relationship', p. 258; Ritson, p. 17; Robbins, p. 389; Waters, pp. 21-22.

7. Group IV. Related to at least MV 29, 35, 43, 62, 93, and 94 and, in Book V, to MV 40.

MV 29 London, British Library, Egerton 657, ff. 1-95v, s. xiv².

1. Parchment, i + 96 + i ff. (including an unfoliated parchment leaf inserted between ff. 39 and 40), 235 × 132 mm. Written in anglicana. Single columns, 38-45 ll. per page. Catchwords; signatures occasionally visible.

3. No title, text beginning imperfectly at l. 608; no colophon, text ending imperfectly at l. 9138. Inc: 'ffor þi alle þat have skylle and mynde'; expl: 'A poynte of swylk bryghtnes als þere salle be', plus catchwords 'Ilk lane in hevene.' Text reduced by *c.* 8 per cent (*c.* 7764/8430 ll.), with one omission in remaining text: one leaf between ff. 39 and 40 containing ll. 4003-104, replaced by a blank unfoliated parchment leaf. Latin titles in margins to all remaining books except II. Some Latin source notes in margins. I (begins imperfectly at l. 608): 1; II: 5; III: 14; IV: 25v; V: 39v; VI: 65v; VII: 77v.

5. North Lincolnshire.

6. *IMEV* 3428.41.
   List, 1838, p. 26.
   Andreae, passim; Bülbring, *ES*, pp. 28-30; Bülbring, *Trans.*, passim; Lewis, 'Relationship', p. 258.

7. Group IV. Related to at least MV 28, 35, 43, 62, and 94 and, in Book V, to MV 40.

MV 30 London, British Library, Egerton 3245, ff. 2-156, s. xiv ex.

1. Parchment, v + 202 ff. (including an unfoliated parchment leaf inserted between ff. 197 and 198), 215 × 145 mm. *PC* written in anglicana formata. f. 1 not part of original quiring. Single columns, 26-33 ll. per page. Catchwords. On f. 1v is an unfinished miniature with an architectural frame having windows and a canopy but with the central portion unfilled (perhaps designed for a Trinity?).

2. *PC* followed by the *Abbey of the Holy Ghost* (with the *Charter*) and miscellaneous English verse (primarily devotional lyrics, *IMEV* 271, 3882, 1368, 1951, 1761, 1781, 246, 3557, 1729, 1691, 196.5, 2035, and 615 respectively).

3. *PC* preceded on f. 1v by an eight-line invocation (below the miniature) beginning 'ffadir sone and holy gost', at the end of which are two lines, in a 15th-c. anglicana hand, introducing the poem: 'To þe blisful trinite be don al reverens / In whos name I begyn þe prikil of consciens.' Title (on f. 2), part of which is cut away: '[. . .]r of þe holy trinite / [. . .]niþ stimulus consciencie'; colophon: 'Here endiþ as ȝe may see / Stimulus consciencie / Aftir Richard þe holy ermyte / that soþly þus gan þis book endyte / Hampool'. Inc: '[þ]e myht of þe ffadir almyghtty'; expl: 'that for our hele on roode gan hyng'. Text reduced by *c.* 7 per cent (*c.* 8940/9624 ll.). Latin titles in text to all books; Latin colophons in text to Books II-VI. Latin running titles irregularly. Occasional Latin source notes in margins. Prol: 2; I: 8; II: 17; III: 29; IV: 45; V: 64; VI: 102v; VII: 120v; Epil: 154v.

4. 16th-c. owners' names: John Danyell (f. 26), Robert Holgate (ff. 93, 109v, 110).

5. Suffolk.

6. *IMEV* 3428.70, 790, 1197.1, 3769.8; formerly Macro; then Gurney.
   The British Museum Catalogue of Additions to the Manuscripts

1936-1945 (London: Trustees of the British Museum, 1970), Part I, 358-60; see also Robbins, pp. 372-87. Allen, *Writings*, pp. 375-76; Robbins, pp. 371, 389.

7. Group IV. Related to MV 50.

MV 31 London, British Library, Harley 1205, ff. 1-125, s. xiv ex.

1. Parchment, 125 ff., *c.* 185 X 115 mm. Written in anglicana formata; same scribe as MV 54. Single columns, 28-29 ll. per page. Catchwords; signatures usually visible.

2. *PC* the only item in the MS except for some Latin words and French and Latin scribbles written later on f. 125r-v.

3. No title, text beginning imperfectly at l. 1772; colophon: 'Explicit expliceat ludere scriptor eat.' Inc: '[. . .] ferþe for he is uncertayne'; expl: 'That for oure heele on roode gan hynge AMEN.' Text reduced by *c.* 10 per cent (6949/7739 ll.), with one omission in remaining text: probably two leaves between ff. 124 and 125 containing ll. 9508-621. Running English titles throughout, but no other titles. Paragraph marks for subdivisions. Latin source notes in margins throughout; occasional topical notes in margins in a different hand from that of the text. III (begins imperfectly at l. 1772): 1; IV: 14v; V: 35; VI: 75; VII: 93; Epil: 125.

4. The name of a possible 16th-c. owner appears on f. 125v: 'Thomas Chawmber'.

5. Lichfield.

6. *IMEV* 3428.42.
   Harley Cat., I, 597a.
   Andreae, passim; Bülbring, *ES*, pp. 28-30; Bülbring, *Trans.*, passim; Dareau and McIntosh, pp. 22 and 26, n. 5; Lewis, 'Relationship', pp. 255, 257, 259, and nn. 14, 17, 21, 22, 26; Angus McIntosh, 'A New Approach to Middle English

Dialectology', *English Studies*, 44 (1963), 7, n. 16; McIntosh, 'Two', pp. 69 and 69, n. 1.

7. Group IV. Closely related to MV 70 and 82 throughout, MV 40 from ll. 1–c. 3783 and 4621–end, to MV 36 to Book IV, to MV 59 and 77 to at least Book V, and to MV 18 in Book V; also related to the Lichfield subgroup (see MV 23, Category 7) throughout and may have been its ultimate exemplar.

MV 32   London, British Library, Harley 2377, ff. 1-106v, s. xiv/xv.

1. Parchment, 106 ff., 222 X *c.* 145 mm. Written in anglicana formata. MS bound incorrectly: the correct order of leaves should be: ff. 1-34v, 67-106v, 35-66v; text on ff. 64 and 65 is reversed, no doubt because of a faulty exemplar. Single columns, 34 ll. per page except for the quire of eight on ff. 75-82v, which has 32 ll. per page. Catchwords visible irregularly.

3. No title, text beginning imperfectly at l. 1152; no colophon, text ending imperfectly at l. 9153. Inc: 'God made þe world so seyþ holy wryt'; expl (on f. 66v): 'In hevene where þei schul ever more wonne', plus cut-off catchwords. Text slightly reduced (7432/7581 ll.), with one omission in remaining text: perhaps six leaves between ff. 1 and 2 containing ll. 1221-651. English titles in margin to Books III, V-VII; many English subtitles in margins. Paragraph marks for subdivisions. All Latin quotations are in margins; some Latin source and topical notes also in margins. Some correction in text. II (begins imperfectly at l. 1152): 1; III: 2; IV: 16; V: 34v: VI: 99v; VII: 43.

4. Probably owned by Lord William Howard (1563-1640).

5. Dialectally has two or more Midland ingredients, with Warwickshire and possibly Huntingdonshire components.

6. *IMEV* 3429.8.
   Harley Cat., II, 673b; Wright, pp. 198-99.
   Andreae, passim; Britton, p. 333, n. 16; Bülbring, *Trans.*,

passim; D'Evelyn, passim; Morris, pp. i–ii and ii, n. 2; Waters, passim (esp. pp. 48–49); Yates, p. 335.

7. Group III, with some similarity to MV 26, though perhaps contaminated, for Book II begins as in the MSS of Group II.

MV 33 London, British Library, Harley 2394, ff. 1–129, s. xv.

1. Primarily paper but with occasional parchment leaves near the beginning, 129 ff., *c.* 210 × *c.* 140 mm. Four (?) hands at work: (1) ff. 1–22v, anglicana; perhaps (2) ff. 23–34v, anglicana; (3) ff. 35–127v, mixed, showing characteristics of both anglicana and secretary; and (4) ff. 128–29, a 16th- or 17th-c. hand. Collation: 1^{22} 2–8^{12} 9–10^{10} 11 (only 1 remains, with two later leaves added to complete the poem). Single columns, 35–40 ll. per page for (1), 34–39 for (2), 29–32 for (3), and for (4) 29, 32, and 34 on ff. 128, 128v, 129 respectively. Catchwords beginning on f. 34v; signatures throughout. The first eight leaves are mutilated.

3. No title, f. 1 mutilated; no colophon (though 'the key of knowing' appears at l. 9551 in the later addition). Inc (first recognizable line is l. 18): 'with outen any be gynnyge [*sic*]'; expl (in the later hand): 'þat for oure Redemption on the Rood did hynge Amen', with the last line of the medieval text (l. 9509, on f. 127v) reading: 'for if we never suld hel se'. Text reduced by *c.* 12 per cent (*c.* 8460/9624 ll.), with much of the reduction in Books V–VII. Latin titles in margins to Books I–III, in text to Books V–VII; running titles in Latin on rectos to f. 30. Many corrections and marginal notations (especially of biblical references) in Hand 4. Prol: 1; I: 6; II: 12v; III: 22v (with first 24 ll. repeated on f. 23); IV: 36v; V: 56; VI: 90; VII: 105v; Epil: 128.

4. Hugo, the third scribe of the MS, wrote an inscription in code on f. 45, which, if solved, might provide some information on provenance.

5. The medieval hands are fully northern.

6. *IMEV* 3428.43.
   Harley Cat., II, 682b.
   Allen, *Writings*, pp. 386 and 386, n. 4; Andreae, passim; Britton, passim; Bülbring, *Archiv*, pp. 391–92; Bülbring, *Trans.*, passim; Morris, pp. i–ii, ii, n. 2, and 212 (variant reading); Yates, p. 335.

7. Group IV on ff. 1–22v, though with corrections probably from the exemplar of ff. 23–129; Group II on ff. 23–129, where it is a member of the 'Key of Knowing' subgroup, along with MV 8, 41, 58, 64, 86, and perhaps 92. Though ff. 128–29 are written in a later hand, they doubtless reflect the same exemplar as ff. 23–127v.

MV 34 London, British Library, Harley 4196, ff. 215va–258va, s. xiv ex.

1. Parchment, 258 ff., 380 × 275 mm. Five hands in the MS, the last of which, in textura, writes *PC*. Double columns, 48 ll. per column. Catchwords.

2. *PC* preceded by the expanded *Northern Homily Cycle*, saints' legends in verse (*IMEV* passim), and *The Gospel of Nicodemus* (*IMEV* 512).

3. No original title, but added in the margin of f. 215v in a 16th-c. hand is 'This booke here followyng is *Call*yd the prycke of conscience'; colophon: 'Explicit tractus qui dicitur stimulus consciencie.' Inc: 'þe myght of þe fader all myghty'; expl: 'þat for us vouchen safe on rode to hyng Amen'. 8276/8279 ll., with one omission: seven leaves between ff. 228 and 229 containing ll. 2593–3937. English titles in text to all books except IV, which is imperfect at the beginning, and VI; Latin title in margin to V. Capitals for subdivisions. Prol: 215va; I: 217b; II: 220b; III: 224a; IV (begins imperfectly at l. 3938): 229a; V: 229a; VI: 241vb; VII: 247vb; Epil: 258a.

4. Owned by William Browne in 1622.

5. Fully northern.

6. *IMEV* 3428.44.
Harley *Cat.*, III, 124b; Wright, p. 85; Saara Nevanlinna, ed.,
The Northern Homily Cycle, Mémoires de la Société Néo-
philologique de Helsinki, 38 (Helsinki: Société Néophilolo-
gique, 1972), pp. 5-8.
This MS is frequently mentioned by writers whose main in-
terest is in a variant text or a different MS: Allen, 'Author-
ship', p. 119, n. 4; Andreae, passim; Britton, passim; Bül-
bring, *Archiv*, p. 390; Bülbring, *ES*, p. 11; Bülbring, *Trans.*,
passim; Campbell, p. 211; Doyle, 'Survey', II, 47-49;
Horstman, II, xli; Humphreys and Lightbown, p. 35; Light-
bown, passim; Morris, passim (including variants and glos-
sary); Waters, pp. 7, 9, 17.

7. Group I. Closely related to MV 27 and 83. The base MS for
ll. 1538-729 and 6923-9210 of Morris's edition of *PC*. See also
E 1, Category 7.

MV 35 London, British Library, Harley 6923, ff. 2-117v, s. xiv
ex.

1. Paper and parchment, i + 116 ff. (with post-medieval begin-
ning flyleaf foliated 1; ff. 105, 106 mutilated and others torn),
175 × 130 mm. Text written in anglicana formata, with Latin
quotations in bastard anglicana. Single columns, 28-38 ll. per
page, the number increasing as the text progresses. Catchwords
occasionally visible.

3. No original title ('Stimulus Conscienciae or The Prick of
Conscience' on beginning flyleaf in an early 18th-c. hand); no
colophon, text ending imperfectly at l. 8798. Inc: 'þe myght of
þe fader alle myghty'; expl: 'Of god almyghty richly dyȝt.' Text
reduced by nearly 7 per cent (*c.* 7825/8388 ll.), with five omis-
sions in remaining text: (1) one leaf between ff. 2 and 3 contain-
ing ll. 59-118; (2) one leaf between ff. 10 and 11 containing ll.
612-79; (3) one leaf between ff. 49 and 50 containing ll. 3328-
405; (4) one leaf between ff. 69 and 70 containing ll. 4901-68;
(5) probably two leaves between ff. 81 and 82 containing ll.
5878-6023. Latin titles in margin to Books I, IV, V, VII; English

title in margin to Book VI; Books II and III introduced by a rhyming couplet. Paragraph marks for subdivisions. Prol: 2; I: 7; II: 15; III: 25v; IV: 41; V: 58v; VI: 87; VII: 102v.

4. Many names of possible owners in 16th-17th-c. hands, including John Sanford 'of Combeflorye in the Countye Somerset' (f. 29), John Holmens (f. 69), John Luydall (f. 69v), George Murray (f. 79v), and Johan Wilton (?) dated 1 September, 15 Henry VIII (f. 101v).

5. Fully northern.

6. *IMEV* 3428.45.
Harley Cat., III, 449a; Wright, pp. 195, 296.
Andreae, passim; Britton, passim; Bülbring, *ES*, pp. 23–28 passim; Bülbring, *Trans.*, passim; Lewis, 'Relationship', p. 258; Morris, pp. i–ii, ii, n. 2, and variants passim; Ritson, p. 34; Yates, p. 335.

7. Appears to be a conflated MS. Group II to Book III, where it has similarities with the so-called Lollard subgroup (MV 51, 56, 61, 73) and MV 42 and 92; Group IV thereafter, where it is related to at least MV 28, 29, 40, 43, 62, 93, and 94 in Book V.

MV 36   London, British Library, Lansdowne 348, ff. 2–127v, s. xv in.

1. Parchment, i + 126 ff. (with beginning flyleaf foliated 1), 170–75 × 110–15 mm. Written in anglicana formata. Single columns, 27–34 ll. per page. Catchwords; signatures occasionally visible.

3. No original title; colophon: 'Explicit expliceat ludere Scriptor eat þis Boke is Calde Prik of Conciense.' Inc: 'þe myght of þe fader alle mighti'; expl: 'þat for oure love on Rode can hynge'. Text reduced by nearly 8 per cent (*c.* 7883/8510 ll.), with two omissions: (1) one quire of eight leaves between ff. 57 and 58 containing ll. 3842–4394; (2) one quire of eight leaves between ff. 65 and 66 containing ll. 4960–5520. Part of text

out of order in Books I and II: ll. 950–1181 are inserted after
l. 585 on f. 12 and extend to f. 15v, where the text returns to
l. 586; these lines are then omitted from their proper place on
f. 21v. Latin titles in text to Books I–IV and VI, in margin to
VII. Latin source notes in the margins throughout; occasional
corrections, both in text and in margins. Prol: 2; I: 8v (though
the title is on f. 4 between ll. 114 and 115); II: 21v; III: 29;
IV: 43v; V (begins imperfectly at l. 4395): 58; VI: 78; VII:
94v; Epil: 126.

4. On the verso of the beginning flyleaf, which was probably
not part of the original MS, appear 'Heare begynneth ye [. . .]
booke of cresyse' and then the name 'Jhon boyce' in a 16th-c.
hand; there is also a 'Johan b' on f. 21.

5. Central Staffordshire.

6. *IMEV* 3429.9.
   *A Catalogue of the Lansdowne Manuscripts in the British
   Museum* (London: R. and A. Taylor, 1819), Part II, 107a.
   Andreae, passim; Bülbring, *ES*, pp. 28–30; Bülbring, *Trans.*,
   passim; D'Evelyn, passim; Lewis, 'Relationship', pp. 255,
   257, 259, and nn. 14, 16, 17, 19, 21, 26; Morris, pp. i–iii,
   ii, n. 2, and variants passim; Warton-Price, p. 91, n. w (not
   in 1871 edition); in a new edition of Warton-Price, with
   notes by Frederic Madden and others (London: Thomas
   Tegg, 1840), extracts from MV 36 are given (II, 36–42);
   Waters, passim.

7. Group IV. Closely related to MV 31, 40, 59, 70, 77, and 82
to Book IV; also related to the Lichfield subgroup (see MV 23,
Category 7) to Book IV.

MV 37 London, British Library, Sloane 1044, item 235, s. xv[1].

1. Sloane 1044 is a collection of leaves from various MSS, pri-
marily medieval. For item 235: parchment, 170 × 95–98 mm.;
written in anglicana; single columns, 34 ll. per page.

3. Item 235 is a leaf from a MS of the *PC* containing 68 ll. corresponding to ll. 2755–829, with ll. 2792–829 on the recto and ll. 2755–89 on the verso. Inc: '*Within*ne fourty ȝere here as þe bok says'; expl: 'but fro þe lowest helle whyt owtyn doute'.

5. Norfolk.

6. *IMEV* 3428.46.

    Ayscough, I, 384, 399 (but inadequate); *Catalogus Librorum Manuscriptorum Bibliothecae Sloanianae* (printed but unpublished, 1837–40), pp. 210b-211a.

7. Too little evidence on which to place this MS in one of the four groups.

MV 38   London, British Library, Sloane 2275, ff. 150a-183b, s. xiv².

1. Parchment, ii + 244 + ii ff. (with first end flyleaf foliated 245), 240–50 × 176–85 mm. An irregular, idiosyncratic hand in *PC*, perhaps by a single scribe who attempted to write basically anglicana formata but in the process experimented with both his duct and his letter forms. Double columns, 36–51 ll. per column, with the whole *PC* written as if it were prose. Catchwords at the beginnings of quires irregularly; signatures.

2. Seventeen items, all of which are religious and (except for *PC*) in Latin, including works by Rolle (*Melum Contemplativorum, Contra Amatores Mundi, Incendium Amoris, Super Lectiones Job*, and *Emendatio Vite*), meditations attributed to Anselm, Augustine, Bernard, and Bonaventure, Pope Innocent III's *De Miseria Humane Conditionis*, and the *Elucidarium* of Honorius of Autun, ending imperfectly, plus two English poems (*IMEV* 1709.5 and 2602.4) and some Latin lines on f. 245.

3. Title: 'Incipit stimulus consciencie'; colophon: 'Explicit Stimulus consciencie.' Inc: 'þe miȝt of þe fadre almiȝty'; expl: 'God bring us quen we hethen wende' (l. 9532), followed by 'And þat it miȝt riȝt so be Amen Amen pur charite.' Text

greatly reduced, by over 41 per cent (*c.* 5639/9624 ll., though because the whole *PC* is written in prose, it is difficult to take an actual count), with much condensation and some rearrangement of text. Latin titles in text to all books. Marginal corrections. Prol: 150a; I: 152va; II: 154b; III: 156b; IV: 159a; V: 161vb; VI: 173vb; VII: 178b.

5. Cheshire.

6. *IMEV* 3428.47.
Ayscough, I, passim (list of contents can be put together only from Index I at the end of Vol. II); unpublished handwritten catalogue of the Sloane MSS at the British Library, pp. 436–38.
Waters, p. 48.

7. Group III. Related to MV 17.

MV 39 London, British Library, Additional 11304, ff. 71v–194, s. xiv².

1. Parchment, i + 195 + ii ff. (f. 195 is a pastedown, with the two end flyleaves between ff. 194 and 195), *c.* 220 X *c.* 150 mm. Three hands at work in *PC*: (1) ff. 71v–175v, anglicana formata, with Latin quotations in textura; (2) ff. 176–87, anglicana; (3) ff. 187v–94, anglicana formata. Single columns, 35 ll. per page. Catchwords and signatures visible for Hand 1, occasionally for Hands 2 and 3. On f. 71v the scribe appears to be experimenting with styles before going on to do the rest of the text.

2. *PC* preceded by Rolle's *Super Lectiones Job*, the 'Passio Domini Nostri' according to John on f. 70r-v, and some miscellaneous Latin lines passim on ff. 69v–71.

3. Title: 'Hic incipit liber qui vocatur stimulus conciencie et continet in se septem libros', followed by a brief table of contents to the seven books in Latin; no colophon, text ending imperfectly at l. 9472, presumably by design. Inc: 'þe myht of þe fadyr alle myhty'; expl: 'þoro prayer of is moder mylde

Amen'. Text reduced by over 11 per cent (8538/9624 ll.), with the greatest reduction in Book VII. Latin titles in text to Prologue and all books, with colophons to Books I–IV; running book numbers along tops of the rectos. Paragraph marks for subdivisions. Much Latin marginalia and a few omitted lines added in the margins. Prol: 72; I: 77; II: 85; III: 95; IV: 108; V: 124v; VI: 158v; VII: 173v.

5. Hands 2 and 3 suggest south west Norfolk or north west Suffolk; Hand 1 is linguistically very mixed, with a strong northerly element especially to the top part of f. 74v.

6. *IMEV* 3428.48.
   List, 1838, p. 2.
   Andreae, passim; Bülbring, *ES*, pp. 23-28 passim; Bülbring, *Trans.*, passim; D'Evelyn, p. 191, n. 21.

7. Group II, though with a number of idiosyncratic readings.

MV 40   London, British Library, Additional 22283, ff. 243a–259va, s. xiv ex.

1. Parchment, 172 ff. (of more than 379 originally; foliated 178–377, with omissions), *c.* 590 X *c.* 390 mm. At least four hands in the MS, the second of which, in anglicana formata, writes *PC* (the same hand as MV 70). *PC* is on leaves originally foliated 243a–59va and is in triple columns, 90 ll. per column. Catchwords.

2. Forty-four items in the extant MS, almost exclusively English, some of the most important of which are the *Northern Homily Cycle*, the *Speculum Vite* (*IMEV* 245), Robert Grosseteste's *Castle of Love* (*IMEV* 3270), *Ipotis* (*IMEV* 220), the *Book of Vices and Virtues*, the English translation of Pseudo-Bonaventure's *Stimulus Amoris*, Richard Rolle's *Form of Perfect Living* and *Ego Dormio*, the *Scale of Perfection*, the *Abbey of the Holy Ghost*, and *A Talkyng of the Love of God*.

3. Title (on f. 242va, at the end of the *Speculum Vite*, with a two-line space left for it on f. 243a; cf. MV 70): 'Prikke of

Conciens hette þis book / Whoso wol may rede and look'; no colophon, and no space for one. Inc: 'þe miȝt of þe ffader al-michti'; expl: 'þat for ure hele on Rode gan hinge Amen'. Text reduced by over 7 per cent (8919/9624 ll.), with nearly all of the reduction in Books III-VII. Part of text out of order in Books I and II: ll. 950-1181 are inserted after l. 585 on f. 244a and extend to f. 244c, where the text returns to l. 586; these lines are then omitted from their proper place on f. 245b. Latin titles in text to Books I and VI; English title in text to Book VII; space left in text for titles to Books II-V. Capitals and occasional paragraph marks for subdivisions. Prol: 243a; I: 243vb (with titles both here and on f. 243b between ll. 114 and 115); II: 245a; III: 246a; IV: 247vb; V: 249vc; VI: 254a; VII: 255vc; Epil: 259c.

4. Because of dialectal and textual similarities with British Library MS Additional 37787, this MS may be from a Cistercian house in northern Worcestershire or Warwickshire, perhaps Bordesley Abbey in northeastern Worcestershire, for which see Sajavaara, pp. 437-39 and note 3 on pp. 439-40, who develops an earlier suggestion by Baugh, p. 39. On the possibility that the MS was owned by Joan Bohun (d. 1419), see Doyle, 'Survey', II, 162-64, following up a discovery by Hope Emily Allen that the name 'Joan boun' appears once in the MS in a tiny hand perhaps of the early 15th c.

5. North Worcestershire; essentially the same as MV 70.

6. *IMEV* 3428.49; the Simeon MS.
   Catalogue of Additions to the Manuscripts in the British Museum, in the Years MDCCCLIV-MDCCCLX (London: Trustees of the British Museum, 1875), pp. 623-26; for general discussions see Doyle, 'Shaping', and Sajavaara; for provenance see Doyle, 'Survey', II, 162-66, and Lewis, 'Relationship', p. 252 and n. 4 (the latter based partly on notes and correspondence by Hope Emily Allen now housed at Bryn Mawr College).
   Allen, 'Authorship', pp. 128, n. 5, and 168-69; Allen, '*SV*', p. 162, n. 67; Allen, *Writings*, p. 385; Andreae, passim; Bülbring, *ES*, pp. 28-30; Bülbring, *Trans.*, passim; Doyle, 'Shaping', pp. 337 and 340, n. 36; Lewis, 'Relationship',

passim; McIntosh, 'Two', p. 69, n. 1; Morris, pp. i–iii, ii, n. 2, and variants on 14, 15, 83, 105.

7. Group IV. Nearly identical to MV 70 from ll. 1–*c*. 3783 and 4621–end; closely related to MV 31 and 82 at the same lines and to MV 36, 59, and 77 to l. 3783; also related to the Lichfield subgroup (see MV 23, Category 7) from ll. 1–*c*. 3783 and 4621–end. Changes textual affiliations from ll. 3784–4620, where it is related to at least MV 28, 29, 35, 43, 62, 93, and 94.

MV 41 London, British Library, Additional 24203, ff. 1–150v, s. xiv ex.

1. Parchment, 150 ff., *c*. 185 X *c*. 110 mm. Written in anglicana formata. Single columns, 26 ll. per page. Catchwords; signatures visible in quire f (ff. 97–102). MS damaged on ff. 1–62 'by the application of an extract of galls to bring out the writing' (*Additional Cat. 1877*, p. 22).

3. f. 1 probably had a title and a table of contents (continuing to l. 12 on f. 1v) in red, but it is now impossible to read any of it; colophon: 'Explicit liber qui dicitur clavis sciencie' ('kay of knawyng' at l. 9551). Inc (on f. 1v): '[. . .] might of þe fadir alle mighty'; expl: 'þat for us vochede save to hynge / AMEN Quod Bagby'. Text reduced by *c*. 19 per cent (7720/9562 ll.), with one omission: one leaf between ff. 107 and 108 containing ll. 6726–87. English titles in text to Books I–III and V; Latin titles in text to Books VI–VII. Capitals for subdivisions. Some correction in text. Prol: 1v; I: 4; II: 13v; III: 23v; IV: 38v; V: 62v; VI: 102v; VII: 120v; Epil: 149.

4. Fountains Abbey: text written 'Per fratrem Johannem de Bageby commonachum Monasterii beate Marie de fontibus' (f. 150v).

5. Fully northern.

6. *IMEV* 3428.50.
   Additional Cat. 1877, pp. 22–23; for provenance see *MLGB*, pp. 88, 263.

Allen, 'Authorship', pp. 126 and 126-28, n. 5; Allen, *Writings*, pp. 386 and 386, n. 4; Andreae, passim; Britton, passim; Bülbring, *Trans.*, passim; W. J. Walter, *An Account of a Manuscript of Ancient English Poetry, Entitled Clavis Scientiae, or, Bretayne's Skyll-Kay of Knawing, by John de Wageby, Monk of Fountains Abbey* (London: Keating, Brown, and Keating, 1816); Waters, p. 5.

7. Group II. A member of the 'Key of Knowing' subgroup, along with MV 8, 33, 58, 64, 86, and perhaps 92; occasionally closer to MV 8 than to the other MSS.

MV 42 London, British Library, Additional 25013, ff. 1-136, s. xv[1].

1. Paper, 136 ff., 215 × c. 145 mm. Written in anglicana formata. Single columns, 23-38 ll. per page, with the number decreasing (and the hand getting larger) as the text progresses. Catchwords; signatures occasionally visible.

2. *PC* the only item in the MS except for the poem 'Of þo Flode of þo World' (*IMEV* 1014) based on it, which is inserted without comment on ff. 15v-18v between ll. 1224 and 1225.

3. No title, text beginning imperfectly at l. 79; colophon: 'Explicit liber qui vocatur stimulus concientie.' Inc: 'For to chese and f[...]'; expl: 'þat of noght made alle thynge'. Text reduced by over 4 per cent (c. 8973/9321 ll.), with three omissions: (1) one leaf at the beginning containing ll. 1-78; (2) two leaves between ff. 50 and 51 containing ll. 3702-853; (3) one leaf between ff. 62 and 63 containing ll. 4727-99. Latin titles in margin to Books I-IV and VI; Latin title in text and English title in margin to Book V. Running Latin titles on rectos; Latin subtitles in margin in Book I. Paragraph marks for subdivisions throughout. Corrections in text throughout and in margins occasionally. Prol (begins imperfectly at l. 79): 1; I: 4v (with titles both here and on f. 2v at l. 235); II: 11v; III: 24; IV: 37; V: 52v; VI: 84v; VII: 100; Epil: 134v.

5. South west Yorkshire.

6. *IMEV* 3428.51.
Additional Cat. 1877, p. 140.
Andreae, passim; Britton, passim; Bülbring, *ES*, pp. 23-28
passim; Bülbring, *Trans.*, passim; for the poem 'Of þo
Flode of þo World' inserted on ff. 15v-18v see Horstman,
II, 67-70 (text taken from British Library, MS Royal 17
B.xvii).

7. Group II, with similarities with the so-called Lollard sub-
group (MV 51, 56, 61, 73) and the 'Key of Knowing' subgroup
(MV 8, 33, 41, 58, 64, 86) and, in Books II and III, with MV
35 and 92. See also E 1, Category 7.

**MV 43 London, British Library, Additional 32578, ff. 1-103,
1405.**

1. Paper, 140 ff., *c.* 210 X *c.* 135 mm. *PC* written in one angli-
cana hand, with Latin quotations in anglicana formata. Single
columns, 35-56 ll. per page. Catchwords irregularly.

2. *PC* followed by a poem on the Apostles' Creed (*IMEV* 2700),
the verse *Templum Domini* (*IMEV* 967), *The Gospel of Nico-
demus* (*IMEV* 512), and a short religious poem (*IMEV* 1456).

3. No title, text beginning imperfectly at l. 183; colophon:
'Laus tibi rex Christe quoniam liber explicit iste Explicit tracta-
tus qui Dicitur stimulus consciencie.' Inc: 'Many man has likynge
truflus to here'; expl: 'þat for oure hele on rode gan hynge
Amen'. Text reduced by over 8 per cent (*c.* 8640/9442 ll.).
Latin title in margin to Book II only. Capitals for subdivisions.
Occasional corrections, primarily in the margins. Prol (begins
imperfectly at l. 183): 1; I: 3v; II: 10v; III: 18v; IV: 30; V:
44v; VI: 72; VII: 83; Epil: 102.

4. Colophon is followed by 'Anno Domini millesimo cccc^{mo}
quinto secundum manum Johannes ffarnelay capellani manen-
tis in bolton ffini ffinito libro sit laus et gloria Christo Amen',

with 'Johannes' written over another name, perhaps 'Roberti', and 'manentis in bolton' added at the end of the line in another hand. At the end of the poem on the Apostles' Creed (f. 105v) also appears 'amen quod ffamelay'. A number of other names of owners and possible owners, all of which are 16th or 17th c., are on ff. 33v, 76v, 102v, 103v, and 140.

5. North east Lancashire, or possibly extreme west Yorkshire.

6. *IMEV* 3428.52.
   Catalogue of Additions to the Manuscripts in the British Museum in the Years MDCCCLXXXII–MDCCCLXXXVII (London: Trustees of the British Museum, 1889), p. 157; facsimile of f. 76 in C. E. Wright, *English Vernacular Hands from the Twelfth to the Fifteenth Centuries* (Oxford: Clarendon Press, 1960), item 16, with some description in the headnote.
   Andreae, passim; Britton, passim; Bülbring, *Archiv*, pp. 391–92; Bülbring, *Trans.*, passim; Lewis, 'Relationship', p. 258; Robbins, p. 389; Wright (as above), item 16 (facsimile of f. 76).

7. Group IV. Related to at least MV 28, 29, 35, 62, and 94 and, in Book V, to MV 40.

MV 44 London, British Library, Additional 33995, ff. 102a–155a, s. xiv ex.

1. Parchment, 156 + i ff., *c.* 305 X *c.* 200 mm. Two anglicana hands in MS, the second slightly more formal than the first: (1) ff. 1-101v; (2) ff. 102-56v, with Latin quotations in anglicana formata. Collation: $1-8^{12}$ 9^9 (1 is a single leaf, with its stub showing between ff. 105 and 106) $10-11^{12}$ 13^{16} (lacks 16). Double columns, 42-50 ll. per column. Catchwords. Signatures visible from f to i, occasionally before and after.

2. *PC* preceded by the *Speculum Vite* (*IMEV* 245) and the *Stimulus Consciencie Minor* (*IMEV* 244) and followed by the 'Bande of Lovyng' (*IMEV* 11), ending imperfectly.

3. No title; colophon: 'Explicit tractatus qui dicitur stimulus consciencie Here endes þe tretice þat es called Pryk of conscience.' Inc: 'þe might of þe fadir allemighty'; expl: 'þat for us vouched save on rode to hyng AMEN'. Text only slightly reduced (c. 9481/9624 ll.). English titles in text to all books; running English titles throughout. Capitals and paragraph marks for subdivisions. Topical notes in English in the margins throughout; occasional source notes in the margins; an occasional correction in the text. Prol: 102a; I: 103vb; II: 107a; III: 111b; IV: 117a; V: 124b; VI: 138a; VII: 144b; Epil: 154va.

5. Fully northern.

6. *IMEV* 3428.53.
   Catalogue of Additions to the Manuscripts in the British Museum in the Years MDCCCLXXXVIII-MDCCCXCIII (London: Trustees of the British Museum, 1894), pp. 156-57.
   Allen, 'Authorship', pp. 169-70; Britton, passim; Doyle, 'Survey', II, 46.

7. Group I. Closely related to MV 96.

MV 45 London, College of Arms, LVII, ff. 133a-175vb, s. xiv ex.

1. Parchment, i + 175 ff., c. 318 × 216 mm. *PC* written in anglicana formata. Double columns, 40 ll. per column. Catchwords.

2. *PC* preceded by the *Cursor Mundi*, with its first leaf cut out (*IMEV* 2153); the 14th-c. flyleaf contains nine lines of text and music.

3. No title, text beginning imperfectly at l. 802; no colophon, text ending imperfectly at bottom of f. 175vb with l. 8278. Inc: 'ʒit ben þer moo þen I have tolde'; expl: 'As here doþ any his sister or broþere' (plus catchwords 'And knowe'). Text reduced by nearly 8 per cent (6900/7477 ll.). Omissions: (1) ll. 1-801

(five leaves) at beginning; (2) ll. 8279-9624 (probably one quire of eight leaves) at end. No titles anywhere. Source notes in margins for the great majority of Latin quotations. I (begins imperfectly at l. 802): 133a; II: 133vb; III: 138b; IV: 144a; V: 151a; VI: 165a; VII: 171va.

5. Lichfield.

6. *IMEV* 3428.56.
   W. H. Black, *Catalogue of the Arundel Manuscripts in the Library of the College of Arms* (London: unpublished, but printed by S. and R. Bentley, 1829), pp. 101-03; see also Sarah M. Horrall, ed., *The Southern Version of Cursor Mundi*, I (Ottawa: University of Ottawa Press, 1978), 13-14. Allen, *Writings*, p. 373, n. 1; Dareau and McIntosh, pp. 20-22; Lewis, 'Relationship', pp. 257-59, 263, and nn. 22, 26.

7. Group IV. A member of the Lichfield subgroup (along with MV 23, 54, 57, 68, 88, and 89), whose ultimate exemplar may have been MV 31. Because MV 45 omits the beginning of the text, it is impossible to know whether it originally contained twenty-two prefatory lines (as in MV 88) or ten prefatory lines (as in the other MSS of the subgroup), though because of its textual affiliations it probably contained only ten.

MV 46 London, Lambeth Palace, 260, ff. 101a–139vb, s. xv in.

1. Paper, i + 139 + i ff., 275 X 205 mm. *PC* written in anglicana, with titles and Latin quotations in bastard anglicana. f. 137 is a blank leaf added later. Double columns, 57-68 ll. per column. A few faint signatures.

2. Five items in addition to *PC*, including the *Northern Homily Cycle*, the *Convertimini* perhaps by Robert Holkot, a collection of tales in Latin (with passages in English), some Latin sermons, and Sacrobosco's *De Sphera*.

3. No substantive title, but across the top margin of f. 101 is 'Jesus Maria [*sic*] filius'; colophon (f. 136vb); 'Explicit tractus

qui vocatur stimulus consciencie interioris per sanctum Ricardum heremitam de hampole.' Inc: 'The myght of þe fadyr almyghty'; expl: 'at for owre hele on þe rode wald hyng Amen'. Very little abbreviation in the text (c. 9196/9372 ll.). One leaf omitted between ff. 102 and 103, which would have contained ll. 474-725. Latin title in text to Book I, English titles in text to all other books; running Latin titles and book numbers throughout. Capitals for subdivisions. Much Latin marginalia, mainly source notes, but also notes on topics in the poem especially in Books VI and VII. Prol: 101a; I: 102va; II: 103vb; III: 106va; IV: 110va; V: 115b; VI: 124va; VII: 128vb; Epil: 136b.

ff. 138-39v contain a table of contents to PC, beginning 'Incipit tabula stimulus consciencie secundum alphabetum', in three columns per page and perhaps in the same hand as that of the text. The table contains both topics (avis, arbores, venacio, ve, etc.) and grammatical forms (qua, qui, quia, quanto, e.g.), and most items seem to be correlated by number to medieval folio numbers that are still visible at the bottoms of the rectos.

4. At bottom of f. 1 is 'Robert Bukstede' (or 'Bulstede') in a late 15th-c. hand.

5. Fully northern.

6. IMEV 3428.57; formerly Savile 42.
   Lambeth Cat., Part III, 406-9.
   Allen, 'Authorship', p. 125, n. 3 from p. 124; Allen, Writings,
   pp. 372-73, 375, 376-77, 385; Britton, passim; Bülbring,
   ES, pp. 11-18; Ritson, p. 34; Tanner, p. 375, n. q.

7. Group I.

MV 47 **London, Lambeth Palace, 491, ff. 296-323, s. xv¹.**

1. Paper and parchment, 329 ff., 220 × 145 mm. PC written in anglicana, with Latin quotations in anglicana formata (with occasional textura features). Two MSS of the 15th c. bound toggether and foliated as one, separated by four leaves (ff. 291-94) of blank, modern paper; PC appears in the second, paper

MS (ff. 295-329) and is written in single columns, 33-43 ll. per page.

2. In the second MS the *PC* is preceded by poems on the creed, the five bodily wits, the seven works of bodily and ghostly mercy (*IMEV* *30/*851.6, 1815, 3040, 3262), and a short Latin prose work entitled 'þies condiciones agh a preste to have if he be mad a preste of god' and followed by memorial lines and verses and sermons or notices of certain feasts and church days in both Latin and English.

3. Title: 'In dei nomine Amen' (though preceded by 'Ric Hampole Stimulus Conscientiae' in a later hand, perhaps of the 18th c.); no colophon, text ending imperfectly and abruptly at l. 2485 one third of the way down f. 323. Inc: 'The myght of the fader that is almyghty'; expl: 'A thowsende synnes to one gode dede.' Text reduced by over 8 per cent (*c.* 2130/2327 ll.), mainly by the scribe's skipping from l. 8 to l. 179 in the Prologue. One omission: ll. 2227-384 (two leaves?) between ff. 321 and 322. English titles in text to all remaining books. Capitals for subdivisions. Prol: 296; I: 298v; II: 305v; III: 315.

5. North east Nottinghamshire.

6. *IMEV* 3428.58.
   Bülbring, *Archiv*, pp. 383-92; *Lambeth Cat.*, Part V, 681-84.
   Bülbring, *Archiv*, pp. 390-92; Waters, p. 11.

7. Group IV.

MV 48 London, Lambeth Palace, 492, ff. 1-56v, s. xiv ex.

1. Parchment, ii + 56 ff., *c.* 250 X *c.* 130 mm. Written in anglicana formata, with titles and Latin quotations in bastard anglicana. Single columns, 43 ll. per page. Catchwords.

3. Title: 'Hic incipit liber qui vocatur stimulus consciencie et ex dictis doctorum colligitur atque tractatur et dividitur in septem partes videlicet prima pars de natura humana secunda de mundo

tercia de morte quarta de purgatorio quinta de die Judicii sexta
de penis inferni septima pars de gaudiis celi'; no colophon, text
ending imperfectly at l. 5868. Inc: 'þe myhte of þe fadire alle
myhty'; expl: 'Off sonnes and douthers þat þei fforth brouth',
plus catchwords 'þe whiche þei here'. Text considerably reduced
(4805/5868 ll.), with a great deal of paraphrase. Latin titles in
text to all books (and, in addition, in margin to Book I); run-
ning Latin titles to f. 48. Occasional capitals for subdivisions.
Some marginalia (primarily source notes) to Book IV; virtually
none in V. Prol: 1; I: 5; II: 11; III: 17v; IV: 26; V: 37.

4. The beginning flyleaves contain a 15th-c. document that has
connections with the Dioceses of Lincoln and Norwich.

5. South east Norfolk.

6. *IMEV* 3428.59.
   Lambeth Cat., Part V, 684.
   Waters, p. 3; Henry Wharton, Appendix to William Cave's
   *Scriptorum Ecclesiasticorum Historia Literaria a Christo
   Nato usque ad Saeculum XIV* (London: Richard Chiswell,
   1689), p. 35.

7. Group IV, though with a number of idiosyncratic readings.

**MV 49 London, Sion College, Arc. L. 40. 2/E. 25, ff. 48-133v,
s. xiv/xv.**

1. Paper, ii + 133 + ii ff. (end flyleaf i is a parchment binding
leaf, formerly used as a pastedown, and is foliated 134), c. 215
X 142 mm. Three hands in *PC*: (1) ff. 48-70v, anglicana, with
Latin quotations usually in bastard anglicana; (2) ff. 71-101v,
anglicana, but with moments of greater formality than Hands 1
or 3; (3) ff. 102-33v, anglicana. Single columns, 28-35 ll. per
page for Hand 1, 44-53 ll. per page for Hand 2, 34-44 ll. per
page for Hand 3.

2. Four items in addition to *PC*: a 'treatise on shrift' in verse
(*IMEV* 557.3), *The Gospel of Nicodemus* in verse (*IMEV* 512),

a Dialogue between St Bernard and the Blessed Virgin (*IMEV* 771), and part of the office for Friday of the third week of Advent.

3. No title, but has a very large incipit; no colophon, text ending imperfectly at l. 9220. Inc: 'þe myght of þe fader almyghty'; expl: 'Als wele þai þat sall be far*er*.' Text considerably reduced (*c.* 7002/8191 ll.), with much condensation from Book IV on. Omissions in MS: (1) one leaf between ff. 59 and 60 containing ll. 748-821; (2) one leaf between ff. 94 and 95 containing ll. 4107-220; (3) one leaf between ff. 96 and 97 containing ll. 4429-537; (4) two leaves between ff. 97 and 98 containing ll. 4641-848; (5) one leaf between ff. 101 and 102 containing ll. 5321-447; (6) three leaves between ff. 113 and 114 containing ll. 6720-7034; (7) perhaps one leaf between ff. 127 and 128 containing ll. 8421-502. English titles in text to all books except IV. Capitals for subdivisions. Source notes in margins nearly always (except on ff. 93-101v); some correction, primarily interlinear, with occasional addition of originally omitted lines. Prol: 48; I: 53v; II: 61v; III: 71v; IV: 83; V: 93v: VI: 111; VII: 119.

4. On f. 134: 'Iste liber pertinet ffratri Johanni holonde Monacho Westm*onasterii*'—a John Holonde, monk of Westminster, whose first mass was in 1472 and who was sub-prior in 1500.

5. All hands fully northern.

6. *IMEV* 3428.64.
   MMBL, I, 289.
   Allen, 'Authorship', p. 126; Britton, passim; Bülbring, *ES*, pp. 1-6; Doyle, 'Survey', II, 47-49.

7. A conflated MS: Group I to the beginning of Book IV (l. 2850); Group IV thereafter, related to MV 21 and, in Books VI-VII, to MV 95.

MV 50 London, Society of Antiquaries, 288, ff. 1-120v, s. xv[1].

1. Paper, i + 120 + i ff., 210 × 140 mm. Written in anglicana. ff. 13-120v are in single columns, 28-32 ll. per page. ff. 1-12v

are a 16th-c. modernization of ll. 1384-2320, in single columns,
36 ll. per page; because the last line of this modernization dupli-
cates the first line of the medieval text and because every page
but one (f. 9v) has catchwords, including f. 12v, this moderniza-
tion may originally have gone beyond l. 2320. Medieval catch-
words from f. 24v on.

3. No title on either f. 1 or f. 13, text beginning imperfectly in
both cases; no colphon, text ending imperfectly at l. 9604,
though 'Prekyl of conscience' appears in l. 9551. Inc to modern-
ized version: 'Benot farre from me lord sayeth hee' (l. 1384);
inc to medieval text on f. 13: 'þat sey a devyl in his figure
Ryth' (l. 2320). Expl to modernized version on f. 12v: 'That see
a devell in his shape Right' (l. 2320), plus catchword 'That';
expl to medieval text: 'and may nout þerby steryd be'. Medieval
text reduced by 10 per cent (c. 6591/7283 ll.). Latin titles in
medieval text to all remaining books; smaller Latin titles in mar-
gins to Books IV, V, and VII probably in same hand; running
Latin titles with just book and number throughout. Various
marginalia: source notes, English rubrics, some Latin notes,
occasional addition of lines omitted originally. II in modernized
version (begins imperfectly at l. 1384): 1; III: 4. III in medieval
text (begins imperfectly at l. 2320): 13; IV: 18; V: 36v; VI:
72v; VII: 88v; Epil: 119v.

5. West Norfolk.

6. Not in *IMEV*; formerly Umfreville.
   MMBL, I, 310.

7. Group IV. Related to MV 30.

MV 51 London, Society of Antiquaries, 687, pp. 5-358, s. xv[1].

1. Paper, ii + 279 + ii ff. (with beginning flyleaves paginated
1-4 and end flyleaves paginated 559-62), c. 215 × 145 mm. *PC*
written in anglicana. Single columns, 27-36 ll. per page in *PC*

section of MS. Signatures; frequent catchwords. MS paginated rather than foliated.

2. Seven items in English, including, in addition to *PC*, the Pater Noster, Ave, and Creed; a form of confession found also in Bodleian Library, MS Douce 60; Richard Lavynham's *Litil Tretys* on the Seven Deadly Sins; *Tractatus de Decem Preceptis Diversis*; an A-text of *Piers Plowman* (*IMEV* 1459); and a treatise on excommunication; and one item in Latin, the *Speculum Sacerdotis Secundum Visionem Sancti Edwardi Regis et Confessoris*.

3. No title, and no space for one; no medieval colophon, text ending imperfectly on p. 358 with l. 9554. But on p. 1, in an 18th-c. (?) hand, appears 'Prick of Conscience—The title of this booke as appeareth in ye ende of it' and then at the bottom of p. 358, in the same hand, appears: 'A leafe wanting where in conclusion of all are these 3 verses / God save the king and speeden ye plough / And senden the prelatti care inough / inough inough inough inough.' Inc: 'þe mythe of þe ffadyr alle mythy'; expl: 'It may hys concyence tendyr make.' Text expanded by 13 per cent (*c*. 10791/9554 ll.), mainly by the addition, in Book VI, of Latin prose (pp. 231-39), Latin and English interspersed (pp. 240-63), and more Latin prose (pp. 263-76). English titles in text to Books IV, VI, and VII only; no indication, by the use of a capital, of where Book I is intended to begin. Prol: 5; I: 17; II: 35; III: 59; IV: 91; V: 135; VI: 216; VII: 297; Epil: 358.

5. Probably north Norfolk, but just possibly east Lincolnshire; other hands in same MS East Anglian rather than Lincolnshire.

6. *IMEV* 3428.69; formerly Bright; Hope Emily Allen Additional MS VI (*Writings*, p. 374).
   MMBL, I, 314.
   Allen, *Writings*, p. 394; Britton, p. 333, n. 16.

7. Group II. A member of the so-called Lollard subgroup, along with MV 56, 61, and 73, though it has only the second interpolation.

MV 52　Longleat, Wiltshire, Library of the Marquis of Bath, 31, ff. 1-146v, s. xv in.

1. Parchment, ii + 146 + ii ff., 220 × 170 mm. Text written in anglicana, with Latin quotations in textura. One leaf omitted at beginning, perhaps one quire of eight leaves at end. Single columns, 28-32 ll. per page. Catchwords.

3. No title, text beginning imperfectly at l. 57; no colophon, text ending imperfectly at l. 9115. Inc: 'Syn the creaturys that skyl has nan'; expl: 'and the wonyng stedys that are ther Inne' (plus the catchwords 'I lykene here'). Text slightly abbreviated (c. 8740/9119 ll.). Some peculiarities in the text, no doubt due to some leaves being out of place in the scribe's exemplar: (1) the text on f. 8v and the text on f. 9 should be reversed; (2) ff. 27 and 28 should be reversed; (3) the text is out of order between ll. 6138-509 (on ff. 99v-106, all within one quire), appearing as follows: 6138, 6448 (f. 99v)-6507, 6202 (f. 101v)-6447, 6139 (f. 104v)-6201, 6509 (f. 106). The scribe notes the first two peculiarities in his MS and, for the third, indicates that Book V resumes on f. 101v. f. 91 is an extra leaf from the last (now missing) quire inserted between f. 90v, which ends with l. 5625, and f. 92, which begins with l. 5626; it contains ll. 9241-300. English titles in text to all books. Source notes for Latin quotations nearly always in first three books, occasionally thereafter; occasional other notes. Prol (begins imperfectly at l. 57): 1; I: 6; II: 15; III: 28; IV: 44; V: 64v; VI: 104v; VII: 121.

5. Probably a somewhat artificial mixture of two not very different kinds of central Midlands English.

6. *IMEV* 1193.4.
   Alfred J. Horwood, 'The Manuscripts of the Most Honourable the Marquis of Bath, at Longleat, Co. Wilts.', *Third Report of the Royal Commission on Historical Manuscripts* (London: Eyre and Spottiswoode, 1872), Appendix, p. 181b.

7. Group I.

MV 53 Manchester, Chetham's Library, Mun. A.4.103 (8008), ff. 1–115v, s. xiv ex.

1. Parchment, iii + 115 + ii ff., 204 × 137 mm. Written in anglicana. Collation: 3–7⁸ 8⁸ (lacks 3–6) 9–16⁸ 17⁸ (lacks 8); quires 1–2 and 18 missing. Single columns, 32 ll. per page. Signatures at ends of quires.

3. No title, text beginning imperfectly at l. 1048; no colophon, text ending imperfectly at l. 9082. Inc: 'Of þe las worlde [. . .]'; expl: 'þat gode men in hevyn schal fele and se'. Text slightly abbreviated (7419/7794 ll.). An omission of four leaves between ff. 42 and 43 that would have contained ll. 3930–4202. Latin titles in text to all remaining books. Capitals for subdivisions. II (begins imperfectly at l. 1048): 1; III: 10; IV: 24v; V (begins imperfectly at l. 4203): 43; VI: 76; VII: 92v.

4. On f. 19, in a 16th-c. hand, is 'hyt is master *Ha*rt is boke'.

5. Hiberno-English: Dublin Pale, County Louth (?).

6. *IMEV* 3428.55.
   J. O. Halliwell, *An Account of the European Manuscripts in the Chetham Library, Manchester* (Manchester: Sims and Dinham, 1842), p. 16; Ker.

7. Group II. Related to MV 7, 19, 22, and 85.

MV 54 Manchester, John Rylands University Library, English 50, pp. 1–204, s. xiv ex.

1. Parchment, vi + 112 + v ff., 250 × 150 mm. Written in anglicana formata; same scribe as MV 31. Single columns, 33 ll. per page. Catchwords. MS paginated rather than foliated.

2. *PC* followed by the first 659 ll. of the *Speculum Gy de Warewyke* (*IMEV* 1101).

3. No medieval title ('Stimulus conscientiae' in a 16th-c. hand), but 'The Prologe' appears just before the text begins; colophon:

'Explicit hic quidem tractatus vocatus Stimulus consciencie ffinito libro sit laus et gloria Christo.' Inc (difficult to read because this part of the page is badly stained, but probably): 'Her beginneþ þe soþ to say'; expl: 'That for oure heele on roode con hinge Amen.' Text reduced by nearly 7 per cent (6643/7176 ll.), with the reduction mainly in Books III–VII. Omissions: (1) ll. 395–527 (two leaves) between pp. 12 and 13; (2) ll. 2552–625 (one leaf, an unnumbered scrap of which remains) between pp. 70 and 71; (3) ll. 2705–3956 (one leaf plus probably two quires of eight leaves) between pp. 72 and 73; (4) ll. 4595–5016 (six leaves) between pp. 90 and 91; (5) ll. 6825–7392 (one quire of eight) between pp. 140 and 141. English titles in text to all books except IV. Capitals for subdivisions. Occasional marginal notes in a medieval hand but not the same as that of the text. Prol: 1; I: 12; II: 25; III: 46; IV: 72; V: 73; VI: 129; VII: 145; Epil: 201.

5. South east Staffordshire.

6. *IMEV* 3428.62, 1193.3.
   Ker; Tyson, p. 163.
   Dareau and McIntosh, pp. 20–22 and 26, n. 5; Lewis, 'Relationship', pp. 257–59 and n. 22.

7. Group IV. A member of the Lichfield subgroup (along with MV 23, 45, 57, 68, 88, and 89), whose ultimate exemplar may have been MV 31.

MV 55 Manchester, John Rylands University Library, English 51, ff. 5–116v, s. xv in.

1. Parchment, vii + 130 + iv ff. (with the 130 ff. of the text foliated 4–134), 175 × 120 mm. *PC* written in a rather careless anglicana formata. Single columns, 38–40 ll. per page. Catchwords.

2. *PC* followed by Richard Maydestone's version of the Seven Penitential Psalms (a defective text: see *IMEV* 3755.7). MS originally bound with other works that are now missing (a list appears on f. 2).

3. No title, text beginning imperfectly at l. 76; colophon: 'Here endeþ þe pricke of conscience ffinito libro reddatur gloria Christo Qui scripcit carmen sit benedictus Amen.' Inc: 'and ȝaf hym skille witt and mynde'; expl: 'þat for us made heven erþe and al þinge'. Text reduced by 7 per cent (c. 8714/9356 ll.), some of which is due to either an intended omission or an eye-skip from l. 7295 to l. 7520 on f. 90v. Omissions: (1) ll. 1–75 (one leaf) before f. 5; (2) ll. 154-229 (one leaf) between ff. 5 and 6; (3) ll. 1688-838 (two leaves) between ff. 23 and 24. English titles in text to all books, with indication of the book in top margin in Latin. Capitals for subdivisions. Occasional marginal notes. Prol (begins imperfectly at l. 76): 5; I: 7v; II: 14v; III: 23v; IV: 34; V: 50; VI: 80; VII: 91; Epil: 115v.

4. 'Thomas Day of Brystow' is written by a late 15th-c. hand on f. 125.

5. Southern or south west Midlands but with few marked dialectal characteristics.

6. *IMEV* 3428.61.
   Ker; Tyson, p. 163.
   Allen, *Writings*, p. 373, n. 1; Waters, p. 48.

7. Group III.

MV 56 Manchester, John Rylands University Library, English 90, ff. 2a-62vb, s. xiv/xv.

1. Parchment, v + 64 + v ff. (with the 64 ff. of the text foliated 2-65), 343 × 245 mm. *PC* written basically in anglicana. Double columns, 47-52 ll. per column. Catchwords.

2. *PC* followed by Wyclif on the Pater Noster (no title; colophon: 'Explicit pater noster') on ff. 63a-65va.

3. No title and no colophon. Inc: 'The myȝt off þe fadur al-myȝti'; expl (on f. 62va): 'þat for ous fouched saff to henge', followed immediately by fifty-two lines of Latin prose on

conscientia on ff. 62va–62vb. Text expanded by 24 per cent (*c.* 11938/9624 ll.), mainly by the addition of much Latin prose and English verse on ff. 2vb–7b and on ff. 39b–48b; contains a Book VIII on ff. 61b–61vb made from material normally in Book V. f. 11vb is blank, but no text is missing between ff. 11va and 12a; some blank spots in Book VI (three quarters of a column on f. 40vb, a whole column on f. 41a, etc.). Latin titles in text to all books. An occasional marginal note. Prol: 2a; I: 8a; II: 11a; III: 14vb; IV: 19va; V: 25vb; VI: 37a; VII: 51va; VIII: 61b; Epil: 62b.

4. In St Albans in 15th/16th c., for on f. 1v is the following note of that date: 'Iste sunt testes hugone Chattok Taylor of Sint Albons Wyllyham scheddebolt Bayly araunt dwelling in the same Toune.'

5. South east Shropshire.

6. *IMEV* 3428.60, 3428.68; formerly Mainwaring; then Corser; then Ashburnham Appendix 243 (not 136, as in *IMEV*).
  Ker; Tyson, p. 169.
  Allen, *Writings*, pp. 388–89, 393, 404; Britton, p. 333, n. 16; Bülbring, *ES*, passim; Bülbring, *Trans.*, passim.

7. Group II. A member of the so-called Lollard subgroup, along with MV 51, 61, and 73; contains both interpolations and the rearrangement that produces a Book VIII and thus represents the fullest state of the subgroup.

MV 57 New Haven, Yale University Library, Osborn a 13, ff. 2–139, s. xv[1].

1. Parchment, vii + 138 + iii ff. (with the 138 ff. of the text foliated 2–139; f. 55 blank and modern), 240 × 155 mm. Written in anglicana formata. Single columns, 32–33 ll. per page. Catchwords and signatures.

3. No title, text beginning imperfectly at l. 38; no colophon. Inc: 'And no quyk creature bot þay'; expl: 'þat for oure hele

on rode con hyng Amen'. Text reduced by 7 per cent (*c.* 8729/ 9379 ll.), with the reduction increasing slightly as the text progresses. Omissions in MS: (1) one leaf (ll. 1–37 plus probably twenty-two prefatory lines) at beginning; (2) one leaf (ll. 3672– 742) between ff. 54 and 56 whose place is now filled by a blank modern f. 55; (3) probably two leaves (ll. 9479–614) between ff. 138 and 139. English titles in text to all books; running titles throughout. Capitals for subdivisions. Prol (begins imperfectly at l. 38): 2; I: 7; II: 15v; III: 26v; IV: 41v; V: 59; VI: 94v; VII: 111; Epil (begins imperfectly at l. 9615): 139.

5. Lichfield area.

6. *IMEV* 3428.71; formerly Phillipps 8343; then Greg.
   Faye and Bond, p. 100a; unpublished description by Cora E. Lutz at Yale University Library.
   Allen, *Writings*, p. 382; Dareau and McIntosh, pp. 20–22; Lewis, 'Relationship', pp. 257–59 and n. 22.

7. Group IV. A member of the Lichfield subgroup (along with MV 23, 45, 54, 68, 88, and 89), whose ultimate exemplar may have been MV 31. Because MV 57 omits the beginning of the text, it is impossible to know for certain whether it originally contained twenty-two prefatory lines (as in MV 88) or ten prefatory lines (as in the other MSS of the subgroup), though because of the probable number of lines on the missing first leaf and because of textual similarities with MV 88, it probably contained twenty-two.

MV 58 New York, Pierpont Morgan Library, Bühler 13, ff. 1– 107, s. xiv/xv.

1. Parchment, 107 ff., 230 × 150 mm. Written in anglicana formata. Collation: 1$^{?8}$ (lacks 1–3) 2^8 3^7 4–5^8 6 (lacks) 7–9^8 10^8 (lacks 1–6) 11–13^8 14 (lacks) 15–16^8 17 (1–5 remain). Single columns, 29 ll. per page. Catchwords. MS unfoliated.

3. No title, text beginning imperfectly at l. 414; colophon: 'Here endith þe tretis þat is clepid the keye of knowyng.' Inc: 'Memento

queso quod sicut lutum feceris me'; expl: 'That for us vowchid saf on rode to henge / Amen amen seith 3e / 3ong and olde pur charite.' Text considerably reduced (6129/7482 ll.), with three omissions (in addition to the 413 lines at the beginning): (1) ll. 2848-3343 (probably one quire of eight leaves) between ff. 36 and 37; (2) ll. 4805-5335 (probably six leaves) between ff. 60 and 61; (3) ll. 7373-8074 (probably one quire of eight leaves) between ff. 86 and 87. Latin titles in text to Books II-VI and Epilogue (and, in addition, in top margin at beginning of Book VI). Capitals for subdivisions. Source notes in margins throughout; topical notes in margins from Book V on. I (begins imperfectly at l. 414): 1; II: 9v; III: 17v; IV: 34; V: 47v; VI: 71v; VII (begins imperfectly at l. 8075): 87; Epil: 105v.

5. Dialectally mixed, with south east Midlands ingredients.

6. *IMEV* 3428.73; formerly Leighton; then Harmsworth; Hope Emily Allen Additional MS II (*Writings*, p. 374).
Faye and Bond, p. 389b.
Allen, *Writings*, pp. 386 and 386-87, n. 4; Britton, p. 333, n. 16.

7. Group II. A member of the 'Key of Knowing' subgroup, along with MV 8, 33, 41, 64, 86, and perhaps 92.

MV 59   Oxford, Bodleian Library, Ashmole 41, ff. 1-130, s. xiv ex.

1. Parchment, vii + 160 + v ff. (with the leaf between ff. 2 and 3 unfoliated), 265 X *c.* 175 mm. *PC* written in anglicana formata throughout. Two MSS bound together and foliated consecutively; *PC* appears in the first MS (ff. 1-133) and is written in single columns, 34 ll. per page. Catchwords.

2. *PC* the only item in the first MS; the second contains the prose *Chastisyng of Goddes Children* (ending imperfectly) and, on ff. 134-36, scraps of religious prose and verse (*IMEV* *69/ *3719.5, 1781).

3. No title, text beginning imperfectly at l. 63 (though a 16th-c. hand has added 'Stimulus consientie [*sic*] thys boke ys namyd I tel the' in the top margin of f. 1); no colophon (though the same 16th-c. hand has added 'Stimulus consientie Thys boke ys I telle the' below the 'Amen' on f. 130). Inc: 'Monkynde is to godus wille'; expl: 'þat for oure love on rode gan hynge Amen'. Text reduced by *c.* 7 per cent (8860/9491 ll.), with two omissions: (1) one leaf at beginning containing ll. 1–62; (2) one leaf between ff. 9 and 10 containing ll. 880–949. Latin titles in text to Books I and IV–VI and in margin to III. Paragraph marks for subdivisions. Source notes throughout. Prol (begins imperfectly at l. 63): 1; I: 4v (though the title is on f. 1v at l. 115); II (begins imperfectly at l. 950): 10; III: 20; IV: 33v; V: 50v; VI: 84; VII: 99v; Epil: 128v.

4. An 'Anthony Alderle' was the owner of the first MS in 1567 (see ff. 130 and 131).

5. Central Staffordshire.

6. *IMEV* 3428.10; *SC* 6921.
   Ashmole Cat., cols. 62–63.
   Lewis, 'Relationship', pp. 255, 257, 259, and nn. 14, 16, 17, 19; McIntosh, 'Two', pp. 69 and 69, n. 1; Warton-Price, pp. 91–96 (not in 1871 edition) and 91, n. w; Waters, pp. 3–4, 22.

7. Group IV. Closely related to MV 40 to Book IV, to MV 31, 36, 70, 77, and 82 to at least Book V, and to MV 18 in Book V; also related to the Lichfield subgroup (see MV 23, Category 7) to at least Book V.

MV 60   Oxford, Bodleian Library, Ashmole 52, ff. 1a–65a, s. xiv².

1. Parchment, i + 65 + i ff., 173 × 115 mm. Written in textura throughout. Double columns, 36 ll. per column. Signatures.

2. *PC* the only item in the MS except for four lines of English verse (*IMEV* 3196) written on f. 65v in a 15th-c. anglicana hand.

3. No title and no colophon. Inc: 'þe myth of þe fader al-
mythty'; expl: 'þat for us vouched save on rode to henge
Amen'. Text slightly reduced (9173/9624 ll.). No titles any-
where. Capitals for subdivisions. Some marginalia, primarily
source notes. Prol: 1a; I: 3va; II: 7b; III: 12b; IV: 18vb; V:
27va; VI: 43va; VII: 50 vb; Epil: 64b.

5. South Lincolnshire, with traces of features from further
west, perhaps Nottinghamshire.

6. *IMEV* 3428.12; *SC* 6936.
   Ashmole Cat., col. 91.
   Warton-Hazlitt, p. 240, n. 1; Warton-Price, p. 96, n. x.

7. Group I. Related to MV 5 and 20.

**MV 61   Oxford, Bodleian Library, Ashmole 60, ff. 1–138v,
s. xiv ex.**

1. Parchment, i + 138 + vii ff., *c.* 290 X *c.* 190 mm. Written
in anglicana formata. One leaf missing at beginning and one at
end. Single columns, 40 ll. per page. Catchwords.

2. Title (on f. 8): 'Incipit stimulus consciencie a Ricardo here-
mite de hampole compositus gracie dei subdito terminatur'; no
medieval colophon, text ending imperfectly with l. 9603 at
bottom of f. 138v (though a 16th- or early 17th-c. hand has
written 'Ricardus Rollo Eremita de Hampoll prope Dancaster').
Inc: 'The myȝt of þe fadir almyȝtty'; expl: 'And he þat shal it
here oþer see.' Text expanded by nearly 16 per cent (11020/
9526 ll.), mainly by the addition of Latin prose and English
verse in the Prologue and in Book VI (ff. 1–7v, 88–104 respec-
tively); contains a Book VIII made from material normally in
Book V. ff. 1–7v (with a preceding leaf missing) are marked for
insertion on f. 10 between ll. 192 and 193. Two omissions in
text: (1) one or more leaves between ff. 3 and 4; (2) one leaf
between ff. 23 and 24 containing ll. 1328–404. Latin titles
in text to all books; running Latin titles from Book I on. Para-
graph marks for subdivisions. Some Latin notes in margins in

same hand as that of the text. Prol: 8 (plus 1-7v); I: 12; II: 19; III: 27; IV: 39; V: 54v; VI: 82v; VII: 112; VIII: 136; Epil: 138.

4. The name 'Wyllyam Harrys' (16th c.) appears twice on f. 30.

5. Isle of Ely.

6. *IMEV* 3428.11; *SC* 6922.
   Ashmole Cat., cols. 104-05.
   Allen, 'Authorship', pp. 123 and 123, n. 4; Allen, *Writings*,
   pp. 374-75, 388, 389-94, 395, 397; Britton, p. 333, n.
   16; Bülbring, *ES*, pp. 23-30; Furnivall, pp. 62-64; Halli-
   well, pp. 259-61; Warton-Hazlitt, p. 240, n. 1.

7. Group II. A member of the so-called Lollard subgroup, along with MV 51, 56, and 73; contains the second interpolation and the rearrangement that produces a Book VIII within the text, with the first interpolation written on preceding leaves (ff. 1-7v) but marked for insertion at the appropriate place in the text (f. 10).

MV 62   Oxford, Bodleian Library, Bodley 99, ff. 1-120v, s. xiv ex.

1. Parchment, i + 120 ff., 200 X 130-38 mm. Text written in anglicana, with Latin quotations in anglicana formata. Single columns, 32-36 ll. per page. Catchwords. Medieval binding.

3. No title (though a 16th-c. hand has written 'Richard Rolle hermit of hampole' at the top of f. 1); no colophon, text ending imperfectly at l. 8837 at the bottom of f. 120v. Inc: 'þe myght of þe fadur allmyghty'; expl: 'Undur holy kirk þat here fightand es', with catchwords 'Er alle'. Text reduced by over 8 per cent (*c.* 8082/8837 ll.). English titles in text to all books. Prol: 1; I: 6; II: 14v; III: 24v; IV: 38v; V: 55; VI: 88v; VII: 103.

5. South Yorkshire.

6. *IMEV* 3428.5; *SC* 1944; formerly NE B. 1. 2.
   SC, II, Part I, 126.

Britton, passim; Lewis, 'Relationship', p. 258; Tanner, p. 375, n. q.

7. Group IV. Related to at least MV 28, 29, 35, 43, 93, and 94 and, in Book V, to MV 40.

MV 63 Oxford, Bodleian Library, Digby 14, ff. 2-158v, s. xv[1].

1. Parchment, iii + 166 + ii ff. (with third flyleaf at beginning foliated 1 and followed by six blank, lined, unnumbered leaves before *PC* begins on f. 2), 161 X 105-15 mm. Text of *PC* in anglicana, with Latin quotations in textura. Single columns, 28 ll. per page except for ff. 2 (20) and 3 (21). Foliation here follows that in MS.

2. *PC* followed, on ff. 159-60, by passages from Isidore and the names of the kings of England up to Henry VI.

3. Title: 'Hic incipit quidam tractatus Magistri Roberti Grosthed episcopi quondam lincolinensis [*sic*] doctoris que egregii in theologia et vocatur Stimulus consciencie'; no colophon. Inc: 'Prologus The my3t of the fader almy3ty'; expl: 'That for oure hele in rode gan honge Amen.' Text reduced by *c.* 8 per cent (8811/9624 ll.). Latin titles in text to all books except I. Occasional notes, primarily on sources, throughout. Prol: 2; I: 9; II: 18v; III: 31; IV: 47v; V: 67v; VI: 107; VII: 124v; Epil: 157.

5. Devonshire.

6. *IMEV* 3428.2; *SC* 1615.
   Digby Cat., col. 10.
   Allen, *Writings*, p. 377; McIntosh, 'Two', passim; Warton-Price, p. 96, n. y; Waters, p. 4.

7. Group IV. A member of a subgroup of four closely related MSS (along with MV 4, 24, and 72) that is derived from the Vernon subgroup (see MV 70, Category 7) and is also related to the Lichfield subgroup (see MV 23, Category 7).

MV 64 Oxford, Bodleian Library, Digby 87, ff. 1-133v, s. xiv ex.

1. Parchment, i + 134 + ii ff., 210 X 148 mm. Text written in anglicana, with Latin quotations in a slightly more formal variety of the same, sometimes approaching formata. Single columns, 28-32 ll. per page. Catchwords.

2. *PC* only item in MS except for ten lines of Latin on f. 134.

3. Title (at top of f. 1): 'De miseria humani generis' (probably borrowed from the second part of Book I); colophon: 'Here endit þe tretis þat is þe kye of knowyng.' Inc: 'þe my[. . .] of þe fader almythti'; expl: 'þat for us wousaved on rode to heynge / Amen Amen seyth ʒe / yinge and elde pur charite'. Text considerably reduced, by nearly 17 per cent (c. 7961/ 9557 ll.). One leaf missing between ff. 22 and 23 which would have contained ll. 1799-865. Latin titles in top margins to all books and often to subdivisions within books; Latin titles in text to Books II, VI, and VII; running titles irregularly. Capitals for subdivisions. Occasional marginal notes. Prol: 1; I: 3; II: 12; III: 20v; IV: 35; V: 56; VI: 91; VII: 107v; Epil: 132v.

4. At top of f. 134v: 'Iste liber pertinet W Worthyngtoun anno Domini millesimo cccclxxxviii v die mensis ffebruarii Joh ho mutuatus.' A 16th-c. hand has written 'Liber iste attinet Oswoldo Rydlye' on f. 134.

5. Cambridgeshire.

6. *IMEV* 3428.3; *SC* 1688.
   Digby Cat., col. 97.
   Allen, 'Authorship', p. 126; Allen, *Writings*, pp. 386 and 386, n. 4; Britton, p. 333, n. 16; Ritson, p. 36, n.; Tanner, p. 375, n. q; Warton-Price, pp. 91, n. w, 99, and 99, n. z.

7. Group II. A member of the 'Key of Knowing' subgroup, along with MV 8, 33, 41, 58, 86, and perhaps 92.

MV 65   Oxford, Bodleian Library, Digby 99, ff. 8v-156v, s. xiv ex.

1. Paper, ii + 158 + ii ff. (with the 158 ff. of text including a mutilated unfoliated leaf between ff. 12 and 13 and an additional smaller leaf between ff. 138 and 139 foliated 139a), 222 X 146 mm. *PC* written in an idiosyncratic anglicana formata. Single columns, 26 ll. per page. Catchwords and signatures.

2. *PC* preceded by synodal statutes of William Raleigh, Bishop of Norwich (1240-43), with some later additions; f. 139a contains the Pater Noster and Creed in English on the recto (probably in same hand as that of *PC*) and three medical exorcisms in Latin on the verso (in a different hand).

3. Title: 'Incipit liber qui vocatur stimulus conciencie'; colophon: 'Explicit liber qui vocatur stimulus conciencie.' Inc: 'þe myht of þe fadyr almyhty'; expl: 'þat for us on rode hyng Amen.' Text considerably reduced (7746/9557 ll.), with the greatest reduction in Book VI (over 70 per cent). One leaf missing between ff. 148 and 149 which would have contained ll. 9076-142. Latin titles in text to Books I-V; occasional Latin subtitles in text. Paragraph marks for subdivisions. Some marginalia of various kinds; a few corrections. Prol: 8v; I: 14v; II: 25; III: 38v; IV: 56v; V: 77; VI: 119; VII: 125; Epil: 155.

4. On f. 156v, in same hand as that of *PC*: 'ffrater Johannes stanys canonicus Thetfordie constat *i*stum librum' (= Thetford Cluniac Priory, Norfolk). Other names of owners on f. 1, the earliest of which (15th c.) appears at the top: Margarete Salis 'de Meȝthewoldde' (presumably Methwold in Norfolk); the others are Robertus Joley (16th-c.) and Johannes Fearneley (1598).

5. Though there is only one hand in the MS, at least three kinds of language can be distinguished: (a) ff. 8v-17v, probably 27v-78v, and 117-25: south Norfolk; (b) ff. 18-27: south east Lincolnshire; (c) ff. 79-116v and perhaps 126-56: central Norfolk.

6. *IMEV* 3428.4; *SC* 1700.
   Digby Cat., col. 113; for provenance see *MLGB*, pp. 189, 311.

Ritson, p. 34; Tanner, p. 375, n. q.

7. Group IV. The presence of at least three kinds of language in a single hand suggests either that the MS was copied from at least three separate exemplars or that it was copied from a single exemplar written by three different scribes.

MV 66   Oxford, Bodleian Library, Douce 126, ff. 1a–68vb, s. xv[1].

1. Parchment, iii + 96 + iii ff. (with three leaves foliated 20), c. 230 × 167 mm. PC written in anglicana formata throughout (though with occasional textura features in the Latin quotations). MS bound incorrectly: ff. 50–64 should follow f. 68. Double columns, 27–33 ll. per column. Catchwords.

2. PC followed by 'Titus and Vespasian' (IMEV 1881) beginning imperfectly with l. 2532 at the top of f. 69, a Dialogue between St Bernard and the Virgin (IMEV 1869), a Latin verse Ave Regina, and a Hymn to the Virgin (IMEV 1060).

3. Title: 'Hic incipit stimulus consciencie'; no colophon, text ending imperfectly at l. 8466. Inc: 'þe myȝth of fadyr almyȝthy'; expl (on f. 64v): 'But evere laste in reste and pes.' Text slightly reduced (c. 7866/8027 ll.). Two omissions within the text: (1) ll. 6127–353 (two leaves) between ff. 66 and 67; (2) ll. 7914–8126 (two leaves) between ff. 61 and 62. English titles in text to all books. Occasional capitals for subdivisions. Interlinear and marginal corrections throughout, though more frequent in the first half of the text than in the second. Marginal notes by Francis Douce referring to the texts of two other MSS of the PC owned by him, MV 68 (f. 50v) and MV 69 (f. 68v). Prol: 1a; I: 3vb; II: 8va; III: 15a; IV: 23b; V: 32vb; VI: 67va; VII: 58va.

4. On f. 93 is a note with the date 18 August 1499 in it; some names of possible 16th-c. owners, including 'hary Chamly grocer' (f. 3) and 'Wylliam hogson' (ff. 15, 22).

5. Essex.

6. *IMEV* 3428.21; *SC* 21700.
   SC, IV, 529.
   Lewis, 'Relationship', n. 20; Ritson, p. 34 (either this MS or
   Douce 156); Robbins, p. 389; Waters, pp. 48-49.

7. Group III.

**MV 67   Oxford, Bodleian Library, Douce 141, ff. 1-129v,
s. xv^1.**

1. Parchment, v + 151 + iii ff. (with the 151 ff. of text includ-
ing an additional modern leaf between ff. 102 and 103, foliated
103a, containing a handwritten excerpt from Yates, p. 330; first
end flyleaf foliated 151), 246 X 160 mm. *PC* in two hands: (1)
ff. 1-96v, basically textura but with some anglicana features off
and on; (2) ff. 97-129v, textura. Single columns, 36-37 ll. per
page. Catchwords. Whole MS is interleaved with blank modern
leaves; MS is foliated with Roman numerals but Arabic are used
here for consistency among descriptions.

2. *PC* followed by an Exposition of the *Pater Noster* (*IMEV*
958), the *Abbey of the Holy Ghost*, Richard Maydestone's para-
phrase of Psalm 51 (*IMEV* 2157), and a *cantus amoris*.

3. No medieval title; colophon: 'Explicit tractatus qui dicitur
stimulus conscientie / Here endeþ þe tretys þat ys called þe /
prykke of consciense / Here endeþ [*sic*] þe sermon þat a clerk
made þat was / clepyd alquim to Gy of warwyk.' Inc: 'þe my3t
of þe fader almy3ti'; expl: 'þat for us voched save on rode to
hynge Amen'. Text only very slightly abbreviated (9434/9624
ll.). English titles in text to all books. Occasional capitals for
subdivisions. Occasional corrections, usually in the margins.
Prol: 1; I: 5v; II: 13; III: 23; IV: 36v; V: 54; VI: 86v; VII:
101v; Epil: 128v.

5. South Warwickshire.

6. *IMEV* 3428.22; *SC* 21715; formerly Hood (= Haslewood).
   SC, IV, 535-6.

Allen, 'Authorship', pp. 124-25, n. 3, and 125, n. 1; Hood, passim; Robbins, p. 389; Waters, pp. 6, 48-49.

7. Group III. Though the text of MV 67 is different from that of MV 10, the two have the same configuration of colophons, with the same error, though in MV 67 the *Speculum Gy de Warewyke* does not follow *PC*—indeed, does not appear anywhere in the MS. The Hood article is pasted onto beginning flyleaves ff. ii–iii verso and has, in its margins, folio numbers from MV 67 for the various excerpts.

MV 68   Oxford, Bodleian Library, Douce 156, pp. 1–172, s. xiv ex.

1. Parchment, i + 87 + i ff., 252 × 150 mm. Written in anglicana formata. MS bound incorrectly: pp. 15-30 (one quire of eight leaves) inserted between pp. 72 and 73. Single columns, 35 ll. per page. Catchwords. MS paginated rather than foliated.

3. Title: 'Jesus assit principo [*sic*] sancta Maria meo'; no colophon, text ending imperfectly at l. 6682. Inc: 'Here bigynneþ þe soþ to say'; expl: 'þat hit may never slakid bee'. Text reduced by over 9 per cent (5992/6612 ll.), with the reduction increasing as the text progresses. One leaf missing between ff. 6 and 7 which would have contained ll. 207-76. English title in text only to Book II, but an English colophon appears at the end of V; English running titles throughout. Some marginal notes, mostly English but a few in Latin; an occasional correction. Marginal notes by Francis Douce referring to the texts of two other MSS of the *PC* owned by him, MV 69 (pp. 5 and 7) and MV 66 (pp. 9, 170, and 172). Prol: 1; I: 10; II: 25; III: 45; IV: 71; V: 104; VI: 166.

5. Central Midlands.

6. *IMEV* 1193.1; *SC* 21730.
   SC, IV, 540.
   Dareau and McIntosh, pp. 20-22; Lewis, 'Relationship', pp. 257-59 and nn. 22, 26; Ritson, p. 34 (either this MS or Douce 126).

7. Group IV. A member of the Lichfield subgroup (along with
MV 45, 54, 57, 88, and 89), whose ultimate exemplar may have
been MV 31.

**MV 69   Oxford, Bodleian Library, Douce 157, ff. 1-114v, s.
xiv ex.**

1. Parchment, xiii + 119 + iv ff. (with the 119 ff. of text con-
taining two leaves foliated 15, three leaves foliated 45, an un-
foliated leaf between ff. 72 and 73, an unfoliated leaf between
ff. 73 and 74, and the leaf after f. 78 foliated 79-80), 239-52
X 180 mm. Written in anglicana formata. Single columns, 36-
38 ll. per page. Catchwords and signatures.

3. Title: 'Incipit stimulus consciencie De trinitate'; colophon:
'Explicit stimulus conscience', followed on the same page by
a four-line exhortation in a 16th-c. hand (*IMEV* 1166). Inc:
'The myghte of þe ffader almyghtty', preceded by 'Prima pars
qualiter factus est mundus et omnia per ipsum'; expl: 'þat of
nouȝt made alle þynge Amen'. Slightly expanded Prologue and
Book I, but the rest of the text is reduced by over 10 per cent
(*c*. 8696/9624 ll.). Latin titles in text to all books. Capitals for
subdivisions. Some source notes. Marginal notes by Francis
Douce referring to the texts of two other MSS of the *PC* owned
by him, MV 66 (ff. 73[1] and 74) and MV 68 (ff. 3v and 75v).
Prol: 1; I: 6 (though the title is on f. 4v at l. 245); II: 14; III:
22v; IV: 34; V: 45[c]; VI: 73; VII: 87; Epil: 113v.

5. Two kinds of language in what seems to be the same hand:
(a) ff. 1-23v: suggests south west Lincolnshire with a slight
Essex overlay; (b) ff. 24-113v: probably south west Essex.

6. *IMEV* 3428.23, 1166; *SC* 21731; formerly Umfreville.
   SC, IV, 540.
   Allen, *Writings*, p. 382; Britton, p. 333, n. 16; Ritson, pp. 34,
   36-37, and 37, n.

7. Group II. See also E 1, Category 7.

MV 70 Oxford, Bodleian Library, English poetry a. 1, ff. 265c–284a, s. xiv ex. (after 1382).

1. Parchment, viii + 341 ff. (of more than 420 originally; foliated 1–413, with omissions), 572 × 394 mm. One anglicana formata hand (except for the table of contents and an English translation of Ailred of Rievaulx's *Informacio ad Sororem Suam*), the same hand as MV 40. For *PC*, triple columns, 80 ll. per column. Catchwords. ff. 273 and 276, which constitute the third bifolium of a quire of eight, are incorrectly foliated 276 and 273 respectively but are in their proper places textually. On f. 265c, at the beginning of the text of the *PC*, is a large miniature with Christ on the cross, God above, and a monk holding a scroll that begins 'Memento me deus secundum magnam misericordiam.'

2. 137 items (before losses), almost exclusively English, in verse to f. 318, mainly in prose from f. 319 on, some of the most important of which are the *South English Legendary*, Richard Maydestone's paraphrase of Psalm 51 (*IMEV* 2157), the *Northern Homily Cycle*, the *Speculum Vite* (*IMEV* 245), Robert Grosseteste's *Castle of Love* (*IMEV* 3270), *Ipotis* (*IMEV* 220), an English translation of Pseudo-Bonaventure's *Stimulus Amoris*, Richard Rolle's *Form of Perfect Living* and *Ego Dormio*, the *Scale of Perfection*, an English translation of Edmund of Abingdon's *Speculum Ecclesie*, the *Abbey of the Holy Ghost*, *A Talkyng of the Love of God*, the *Ancrene Riwle*, and an A-version of *Piers Plowman* (*IMEV* 1459).

3. Title: 'Prikke of conciens hette þis book / Hose wole mai rede and look'; no colophon. Inc: 'þe miht of þe ffadur almihti'; expl: 'þat for ure hele on roode can hinge Amen'. Text reduced by nearly 7 per cent (8892/9540 ll.), with nearly all of the reduction in Books III–VII. Part of text out of order in Books I and II: ll. 950–1181 are inserted after l. 585 on f. 266vb and extend to f. 267a, where the text returns to l. 586; these lines are then omitted from their proper place on f. 267vb. ll. 810–89 omitted on f. 267va (probably the scribe turned two leaves instead of one in his exemplar at this point). Latin titles in text to Books I, V, and VI; English title in text to Book VII; space left in text for title to Book IV. In the middle of f. 269b a small

piece of parchment containing ll. 1917–47 written in a late
15th- or early 16th-c. hand has been pasted in along its left-hand
side over the same lines in the MS, which are stained and partly
illegible (in both cases ll. 1938–43 have been omitted). Capitals
for subdivisions. Prol: 265c; I: 266b (with titles both here and
on f. 265vb just before l. 115); II: 267vb; III: 268vb; IV:
270vb; V: 273a; VI: 277vb; VII: 279vc; Epil: 283vb.

4. Because of dialectal and textual similarities with British
Library MS Additional 37787, this MS may be from a Cister-
cian house in northern Worcestershire or Warwickshire, perhaps
Bordesley Abbey in north-eastern Worcestershire, for which see
Sajavaara, pp. 437–39 and note 3 on pp. 439–40, who develops
an earlier suggestion by Baugh, p. 39. On f. 413v are Vernon
family names, the earliest of which is 1583.

5. North Worcestershire; essentially the same as MV 40.

6. *IMEV* 3428.8; *SC* 3938–42; the Vernon MS.
   SC, II, Part II, 789–92; for general discussions see Doyle,
   'Shaping', and Sajavaara; for the index see Mary S. Ser-
   jeantson, 'The Index of the Vernon Manuscript', *Modern
   Language Review*, 32 (1937), 222–61; for provenance see
   Doyle, 'Survey', II, 164–66, and J. Quinn, S.J., 'Earlier
   Owners of the Vernon Manuscript', *The Bodleian Library
   Record*, 4 (1952–53), 133–37.
   Allen, 'Authorship', p. 128, n. 5; Allen, '*SV*', p. 162, n. 67;
   Allen, *Writings*, p. 385; Doyle, 'Shaping', pp. 337 and
   340, n. 36; Lewis, 'Relationship', passim; McIntosh, 'Two',
   pp. 69 and 69, n. 1.

7. Group IV. Nearly identical to MV 40 from ll. 1–c. 3783 and
4621–end; closely related to MV 31 and 82 throughout, to MV
59 and 77 from the beginning to at least l. 4620, to MV 36 to
Book IV, and to MV 18 in Book V; also related to the Lichfield
subgroup (see MV 23, Category 7) throughout.

MV 71 Oxford, Bodleian Library, Junius 56, ff. 1–120v, s. xv[1].

1. Parchment, 120 ff., 206 × 134 mm. Written in textura. Single
columns, 30 ll. per page. Catchwords.

3. No medieval title, text beginning imperfectly at l. 182 (though Junius has added 'De notitia sui ipsius / What man is and was and schal be'); no colophon, text ending imperfectly at l. 8426. Inc: 'and to love and drede and leten al ylle'; expl: 'of þe douȝter þat was her dere', plus catchwords 'ne þe syster'. Text reduced by 9 per cent (7194/7899 ll.). Two omissions, in addition to three leaves at the beginning and an undetermined number after f. 120: (1) one leaf, which would have contained ll. 2214-75, has been torn out between ff. 32 and 33 (though bits of it remain); (2) four leaves, which would have contained ll. 2690-973, are missing between ff. 38 and 39. Latin titles in text to all books except IV, which begins imperfectly. Paragraph marks for subdivisions. Source notes throughout; occasional marginal notes in same hand as that of text. Junius has added his own Latin titles to books and some comments in the margins. A few corrections, both interlinear and marginal. Prol (begins imperfectly at l. 182): 1; I: 4; II: 13; III: 24v; IV (begins imperfectly at l. 2974): 39; V: 53v; VI: 90v; VII: 107.

5. East Worcestershire.

6. *IMEV* 3428.9; *SC* 5167*.
   SC, II, Part II, 977.

7. Group IV.

MV 72   Oxford, Bodleian Library, Laud Miscellaneous 486, ff. 1-122, s. xv in.

1. Parchment, i + 174 + ii ff. (with endleaves foliated 175-76), 207 X 137 mm. Written in anglicana formata. Single columns, 35-38 ll. per page. Catchwords. 15th-c. binding.

2. *PC* followed (on f. 123) by Gregory's *Pastoral Care*, ending imperfectly at the bottom of f. 174v.

3. Title: 'Stimulus consciencie et hec prima pars qualiter factus est homo et omnia propter ipsum et cetera'; colophon: 'Explicit tractatus venerabilis lincolniensis qui dicitur stimulus consciencie.' Inc: 'The myȝt of þe fader almyȝty'; expl: 'That for oure

hele on roude gan hyng.' Text reduced by nearly 7 per cent (c. 8974/9624 ll.). Latin titles in text to Books II, III, and VI (with space left for one in VII); Book I, which has no title and no capital at the normal place in the text, was thought to have begun at l. 1, as the main title indicates. Running Latin titles throughout at tops of rectos. Occasional marginal notes and corrections. *PC* preceded on f. i by fourteen lines of verse, probably based on ll. 9535–44, summarizing the seven parts of the poem (written in a late 15th-c. hand, which also adds the title 'þe prycke off concyens' inside the front cover). Prol: 1; I: 5v; II: 13; III: 23; IV: 35v; V: 50v; VI: 79v; VII: 93v; Epil: 121.

4. Probably belonged to an Eston family, for on f. 175v is this note in a late 15th- or early 16th-c. hand: 'Margareta de eston nata erat in die sancti mathie apostoli inter horam x^{am} et xi^{am} anno regis Edwardi iii^{a} post conquestum viii' (i.e., 1334).

5. South Gloucestershire.

6. *IMEV* 3428.1; *SC* 1186; formerly Laud G. 21.
   Laud Cat., fasc. 1, col. 350.
   Allen, *Writings*, p. 377; McIntosh, 'Two', passim; Tanner, p. 375, n. q; Warton-Price, p. 96, n. y; Waters, p. 4.

7. Group IV. A member of a subgroup of four closely-related MSS (along with MV 4, 24, and 63) that is derived from the Vernon subgroup (see MV 70, Category 7) and is also related to the Lichfield subgroup (see MV 23, Category 7).

MV 73 Oxford, Bodleian Library, e Musaeo 76, ff. 1–127, s. xv^{1}.

1. Parchment, i + 127 + ii ff., 283 × 190 mm. Written in anglicana formata, with influence from secretary. Single columns, 40 ll. per page. Catchwords.

3. No title; colophon: 'Here endith the pryk of conscience.' Inc: 'The my3th of the Fader almy3ty'; expl: 'That on rode for us wold hyng Amen Amen.' Text slightly expanded (9980/9624 ll.):

Book VI has been greatly expanded (1791/1111 ll.) by the addition of English verse and some Latin prose (ff. 83-92), but the rest of the text has been slightly reduced; contains a Book VIII made from material normally in Book V. English titles in text to Books I, II, and IV (and space left for one in III); Latin titles in text to Books VI-VIII; Latin titles in top margin at beginning of Books I-III. Prol: 1; I: 5; II: 12; III: 21; IV: 34; V: 49v; VI: 77v; VII: 100v; VIII: 124; Epil: 126.

4. On the originally blank f. 127v has been added a bond between William Ayer and Jefferye Skold regarding lands in Broomfield in Essex (16th c.); on f. 43, in a slightly later but still 16th-c. hand, is the name of a possible owner: 'Walter *H*oblinge'.

5. Essex.

6. *IMEV* 3428.7; *SC* 3679.
   SC, II, Part II, 728.
   Allen, *Writings*, pp. 388, 389, 393; Britton, p. 333, n. 16; Ritson, p. 34.

7. Group II. A member of the so-called Lollard subgroup, along with MV 51, 56, and 61; contains the second interpolation and the rearrangement that produces a Book VIII, but the first interpolation is represented only by one line of Latin (the same line that begins the interpolation in MV 61) and 'et cet' between ll. 192 and 193 on f. 3.

MV 74 Oxford, Bodleian Library, e Musaeo 88, ff. 1-92, s. xv¹.

1. Paper, ii + 94 + ii ff. (with the two end flyleaves foliated 95 and 96), 270 X 190 mm. Written in anglicana formata. MS bound incorrectly: the proper order of ff. should be 6v, 6r, 1-5, 8, 7, 16-22, 9-15, 23-70, 72-84, 86, 85, 87-90, 71, 91-94. Single columns, 39-46 ll. per page.

3. No title, text beginning imperfectly at l. 233; colophon: 'Here endeth the tretys that ys called the prykke of concience.'

Inc (on f. 6v): 'And whan he schal out of þys world wende'; expl: 'þat for oure love made heven and erthe and alle þynge'. Text reduced by over 15 per cent (7573/8986 ll.), primarily by the omission of ll. 5750-7008 on f. 62v (because of an imperfect exemplar?). Three omissions, in addition to the 232 ll. (probably three leaves) at the beginning: (1) ll. 728-896 (probably two leaves) after f. 5; (2) ll. 1421-502 (one leaf, a scrap of which remains) between ff. 19 and 20; (3) ll. 7465-817 (probably two leaves) between ff. 67 and 68. English titles in text to all remaining books. Frequent English subtitles in text. Occasional corrections, both interlinear and marginal. Prol (begins imperfectly at l. 233): 6v; I: 1v; II: 8; III: 21v; IV: 26v; V: 41v; VI (begins imperfectly at l. 7009): 62v; VII (begins imperfectly at l. 7618): 68; Epil: 91.

4. An owner's name on f. 87 in a late 15th- or early 16th-c. hand: John Hydley; other names (of possible owners?) in 16th-c. hands include John Alycoke (ff. 24, 82v), William Alycoke (f. 82v), Thomas Cowley (f. 93v), and Adam Benet, Davyt Edmoond, and Roberte Lowe (f. 94v).

5. Dialectally mixed, with suggestions of Gloucestershire and Wiltshire ingredients.

6. *IMEV* 3428.6; *SC* 3509.
   SC, II, Part II, 665.
   Ritson, p. 34; Waters, p. 48.

7. Group III.

MV 75 Oxford, Bodleian Library, Rawlinson A.366, pp. 1-250, s. xv in.

1. Parchment, ii + 125 + vi ff., 245 × 170 mm. Written in anglicana formata. Single columns, 32-34 ll. per page. MS is incorrectly bound: ff. 111-14 should go between ff. 122 and 123. Catchwords regularly to p. 96, irregularly thereafter. MS paginated rather than foliated. pp. 3-12, 109-10 are mutilated, with only bits of each remaining.

3. No title; no colophon, text ending imperfectly at l. 8998. Inc: 'The myght of the fader al myghty'; expl: 'Ben as nought to regard to the blisses of hevene', plus catchwords 'for as moche difference'. Text reduced by nearly 7 per cent (*c.* 8247/8849 ll.), with much of the reduction in Book VI. Two omissions within the existing text: (1) ll. 3377–446 (one leaf) between ff. 98 and 99; (2) ll. 3883-982 (two leaves) after f. 110. Latin title in text to Book II; English titles in text to Books III, IV, VI, and VII. Frequent English subtitles in text. Capitals for subdivisions. A textura hand has written marginal notes in Latin on pp. 33, 55, 79, 111, 117, 122, and 227. Prol: 1; I (begins imperfectly at l. 374): 12; II: 28; III: 49; IV: 78; V (begins imperfectly at l. 3983): 115; VI: 182; VII: 208.

5. East Cambridgeshire.

6. *IMEV* 3428.20; *SC* 15460; formerly Hearne.
   Rawlinson Cat., fasc. 1, col. 374.
   Thomas Hearne, ed., *Peter Langtoft's Chronicle* (Oxford: at the Theater, 1725), II, 527-28, 581-84; McIntosh, 'Scribal', pp. 231-32 and 231, nn. 1, 3; Waters, pp. 3, 48.

7. Group III.

MV 76 Oxford, Bodleian Library, Rawlinson C.35, ff. 1-117v, s. xv[1].

1. Parchment, ii + 117 + iii ff., 212 X 144 mm. Written in anglicana. Single columns, 33-35 ll. per page. Catchwords; signatures sometimes visible.

3. No title and no colophon. Inc: 'The myght of þe fader al my[. . .]'; expl: 'þat þey mowe to hevene cyte / Were evere more Joy and blysse ys plente Amen' (a paraphrase of ll. 9613-24). Text reduced by nearly 13 per cent (*c.* 7922/9062 ll.), with the greatest reduction in Book IV; text quite paraphrastic at least into Book VI. One omission: ll. 7989-8550 (probably one quire of eight leaves) between ff. 102 and 103. Latin titles to Books I (side margin), II (top margin), and III (text) only.

Paragraph marks for subdivisions. Latin source notes and rubrics in the margins in Books I-III; occasional corrections, both interlinear and marginal. Prol: I; I: 6 (though the title is on f. 4 at l. 235); II: 13v; III: 23; IV: 35v; V: 47v; VI: 80v; VII: 96v; Epil: 116.

4. On f. 57 are the names of seven Barkus brothers and the date 16 August, 20 Henry VIII.

5. South east Surrey.

6. *IMEV* 3428.13; *SC* 11901.
   Rawlinson Cat., fasc. 2, col. 11.
   Allen, *Writings*, pp. 382-83; Waters, pp. 48-49.

7. A conflated MS: probably Group IV to the beginning of Book V, where it is very closely related to MV 6 and occasionally to MV 81; Group III in Books V-VII; in Epilogue appears to become a SR text, along with MV 90. A note by Edward Umfreville on beginning flyleaf i.

MV 77 Oxford, Bodleian Library, Rawlinson C.319, ff. 1-140, s. xv[1].

1. Parchment, 140 + ii ff., *c.* 240 X *c.* 130 mm. Text written in anglicana formata, with titles and Latin quotations basically in textura (though with anglicana features off and on). Single columns, 30-38 ll. per page to f. 59, 26-31 thereafter. Catchwords regularly to f. 68v, irregularly thereafter. Medieval binding. A number of leaves mutilated, including the end flyleaves and a leaf preceding f. 1.

3. No title, text beginning imperfectly at l. 130, though there is a scrap preceding f. 1 on which the first word of l. 96 is visible at the bottom of the recto and part of the last word of l. 129 is visible at the bottom of the verso; colophon: only the first three letters of the first word are visible ('Sic') because both ff. 139 and 140 are scraps. Inc (l. 130): 'Hou strong god is and mitthi'; expl (f. 140): 'To wiche [. . .] / þat for [. . .]', though

the last full line visible is l. 9510, at the bottom of f. 138v: 'Ne summe schuld nevere punched be.' Text reduced by over 5 per cent (c. 8680/9190 ll., counting from 130–9510). Omissions in MS: (1) probably two leaves before f. 1 which would have contained ll. 1–129; (2) probably two leaves between ff. 8 and 9 which would have contained, in this order, ll. 1065–181, 586–615 (ll. 950–1064 having been added after l. 585 beginning on f. 7 and ll. 950–1181 having been omitted from their proper place on f. 13v); (3) one leaf between ff. 71 and 72 which would have contained ll. 5279–324; (4) one leaf between ff. 138 and 139 which would have contained ll. 9511–approximately 9560. Latin titles in text to Books I–VI and in margin to VII. Many marginal source notes; occasional interlinear corrections. Prol (begins imperfectly at l. 130): 1; I: 4 (though title appears on f. 4v between ll. 373 and 374); II: 13; III: 20; IV: 34; V: 51v; VI: 88v; VII: 105.

5. North west Suffolk but with strong south central Midlands underlay.

6. *IMEV* 3428.14; *SC* 12175.
   Rawlinson Cat., fasc. 2, col. 140.
   Lewis, 'Relationship', pp. 255, 257, 259, and nn. 17, 19, 26; McIntosh, 'Two', pp. 69 and 69, n. 1.

7. Group IV. Closely related to MV 40 to Book IV, to MV 31, 36, 59, 70, and 82 to at least Book V, and to MV 18 in Book V; also related to the Lichfield subgroup (see MV 23, Category 7) to at least Book V.

MV 78   Oxford, Bodleian Library, Rawlinson C.891, ff. 1–127, s. xv[1].

1. Parchment, i + 129 + i ff., 270 × 172 mm. Four different hands in *PC*: (1) ff. 1–3v, anglicana, with Latin quotations in anglicana formata; (2) ff. 4–34 (with f. 34v blank), anglicana; (3) ff. 35–111v, textura; (4) ff. 111v–27, anglicana, with Latin quotations in anglicana formata. Single columns throughout, 36 ll. per page for Hand 1, 32–40 for Hand 2, 35 for Hand 3,

and 28-33 for Hand 4. Catchwords to f. 105v. Medieval binding.

2. *PC* followed by Richard Maydestone's paraphrase of Psalm 51 (*IMEV* 2157) and brief annals of England from the Creation to 1377.

3. No title, text beginning imperfectly at l. 427; no colophon. Inc: 'Of such filþe man maked es'; expl (f. 111v): 'þat of nouȝt made alle þing Amen'. *c.* 8747/9124 ll., with the text in Hand 3 reduced by 5 per cent and the text in Hand 4 reduced by *c.* 14 per cent. Probably five leaves missing at beginning and one leaf between ff. 102 and 103 which would have contained ll. 8933-9006. Hand 2 ends abruptly on f. 34 with l. 2833 (Book IV), but this note follows, in Hand 4: 'partem purgatorii deficientem hic quere post gaudia celi ad hoc signum⸱⊞⸱'; Hand 3 begins at the top of f. 35 with a title to and the first line of Book V (3966) and continues to the end of the poem on f. 111v; the sign ⊞ follows immediately, l. 2833 is repeated, and the text continues from there to the last line of Book IV (3965) on f. 127, at which point Hand 4 writes 'quere in vᵃ partus [*sic*] hic ad hoc signum⸱⊹ ', which also appears on f. 35. English titles in text to Books II-IV and VI; Latin title in top margin to V; Latin title in text to VII. Latin running titles, in Hand 3 to f. 111 and in Hand 4 from ff. 111v-27. Occasional source notes (in Hand 2?) on ff. 1-34; occasional notes and corrections on ff. 35-111v in a hand other than Hand 3; occasional corrections and Latin marginal notes on ff. 111v-27. I (begins imperfectly at l. 427): 1; II: 8; III: 18; IV: 32 (and then continued on ff. 111v-27); V: 35; VI: 68v; VII: 83; Epil: 110.

5. Hand 1 probably north east Midlands; Hand 2 central Midlands; Hand 3 fully northern; Hand 4 dialectally very mixed but with a strong Fenland ingredient.

6. *IMEV* 3428.15; *SC* 12725.
   Rawlinson Cat., fasc. 2, col. 464.
   Britton, passim.

7. At least two different exemplars involved in the copying of MV 78: Group III for Hands 1 and 2; Group II for Hand 3. No data for the exemplar of the text written by Hand 4.

MV 79   Oxford, Bodleian Library, Rawlinson D.913, f. 9r–v, s. xiv².

1. Rawlinson D.913 is a collection of fragments primarily in French and English in both verse and prose bound together about 1861; 129 ff., thirty-four items in all. For f. 9: parchment, 207 X 159 mm.; written in anglicana formata; single columns, 31 ll. per page.

3. f. 9 is a leaf from a MS of the *PC* containing 62 ll. corresponding to ll. 9327–90 and thus has no title and no colophon. Inc: 'So fair a coroune [. . .]vere Noon sene'; expl: 'Evere sorowe and endeles paine.'

5. Passage too short for adequate assessment, but forms suggest Peterborough area.

6. *IMEV* 3428.16a; *SC* 13679.
   Rawlinson Cat., fasc. 4, cols. 136–43 (esp. 138).
   Allen, *Writings*, p. 373, n. 1.

7. Too little evidence on which to place this MS in one of the four groups.

MV 80   Oxford, Bodleian Library, Rawlinson D.913, f. 62r–v, s. xiv².

1. See MV 79. For f. 62: parchment, 150 X 130 mm. for each of two remaining leaves. One bifolium of the original MS folded open so as to make one leaf in Rawlinson D.913; the bifolium is bound along its top. Written in anglicana formata. Single columns, probably 28 ll. per page originally, but some lines have been cut off at the bottoms of the leaves (probably 2 ll. of the first and 5 ll. of the second).

3. f. 62 is a bifolium (the innermost one of a quire) from a MS of the *PC* containing *c.* 112 ll. corresponding to ll. 6492–604 and thus has no title and no colophon. f. 62 (top half) contains ll. 6553–75 and (bottom half) ll. 6523–48; f. 62v (top half)

contains ll. 6583-604 and (bottom half) ll. 6492-518. Inc (f. 62v): 'May nouȝt liȝtely turne agayne'; expl (f. 62v): '[. . .]elle schal be'. One English subtitle in text; one marginal source note; numbers next to the pains of Hell.

5. Passage too short for adequate assessment, but forms suggest south east Midlands.

6. *IMEV* 3428.16b; *SC* 13679.
   Rawlinson Cat., fasc. 4, cols. 136-43 (esp. 139-40).
   Allen, *Writings*, p. 373, n. 1.

7. Too little evidence on which to place this MS definitely in one of the four groups, though it may be Group III.

MV 81   Oxford, Bodleian Library, Rawlinson poetry 138, ff. 1-112v, s. xv[1].

1. Paper, i + 112 + i ff. (end flyleaf foliated 113), 222 X 148 mm. Text written in anglicana, Latin quotations in scripts ranging from textura to bastard anglicana to anglicana formata. Single columns, 32-39 ll. per page. Catchwords; quire numbers in top margins (once for each quire except the sixth).

2. End flyleaf contains an English couplet on pride, some English words, and a Latin riddle on *muscatum*.

3. Title: 'Assit principio sancta maria meo'; colophon: 'Explicit liber voca*tus* stimulus conciencie / [N]omen scriptoris salvet deus omnibus horis.' Inc: 'The myth of þe fadyr al myghty'; expl: 'þat wyt hys blod bowte us on þe rode tre Amen'. Text reduced by over 20 per cent (*c.* 7619/9624 ll.), with the greatest reduction in Book VII (over 53 per cent); most of Epilogue omitted, text skipping from l. 9522 to a two-line paraphrase of the last four lines of the poem. f. 103 contains lines that have already appeared on f. 100 (7680-735), with 'Vacat huc [*sic*]' at the bottom of the page, in the same hand as that of the text. Latin title in text to Book I only; occasional corrections, both interlinear and marginal. Prol: 1; I: 6 (though title is on f. 4r-v

between ll. 234 and 235); II: 14v; III: 24; IV: 37; V: 53; VI: 84; VII: 98.

4. May have a connection with the Augustinian Priory at Ulvers-croft (Leicestershire) because it contains a mid-15th-c. book-marker (now attached to f. i verso) referring to Ulverscroft; the name 'Phillip' appears in a late 15th-c. hand on f. 113v.

5. Norfolk.

6. *IMEV* 3428.17; *SC* 14632.
   SC, III, 311-12.

7. Group IV. Occasionally related to MV 6 and 76 to the begin-ning of Book V.

MV 82 Oxford, Bodleian Library, Rawlinson poetry 139, ff. 1-119, s. xiv².

1. Parchment, vi + 120 + ii ff., *c.* 260 × 138 mm. Written in textura throughout. Single columns, 37 ll. per page. Catchwords.

3. Title: 'Her bygynneþ in presence / The book cald pricke of conscience'; colophon: 'Jesus Jesus Jesus', though the MS may have had a substantive colophon originally: the bottom one third of f. 119 has been cut off, but there is a suggestion of at least one letter just below the extant colophon. Inc: 'þe my3t of þe fader almy3ti'; expl: 'þat for oure hele on rode can hynge Amen.' Text reduced by *c.* 9 per cent (8735/9624 ll.), with the reduction increasing as the text progresses. Latin titles in text to all books. Occasional interlinear corrections. Prol: 1; I: 6 (with titles both here and on f. 2v just before l. 115); II: 13v; III: 23; IV: 35v; V: 51; VI: 81; VII: 94; Epil: 118.

5. North east Shropshire.

6. *IMEV* 3428.18; *SC* 14633.
   SC, III, 312.
   Lewis, 'Relationship', pp. 255, 257, 259, and nn. 14, 16, 17.

7. Group IV. Closely related to MV 31 and 70 throughout, to MV 40 from ll. 1-c. 3783 and 4621-end, to MV 36 to Book IV, to MV 59 and 77 to at least Book V, and to MV 18 in Book V; also related to the Lichfield subgroup (see MV 23, Category 7) throughout.

MV 83   Oxford, Bodleian Library, Rawlinson poetry 175, ff. 1a-55b, s. xiv².

1. Parchment, i + 134 + ii ff. (with two leaves foliated 105), 268 X 190 mm. *PC* written in textura throughout. Double columns, 44 ll. per column. Catchwords irregularly.

2. Eleven items in English and Latin, both verse and prose, including (besides *PC*) 'Passiones Jesu Christi', 'The Book of Penance' (*IMEV* 694), 'The Gast of Gy' (*IMEV* 3028), *The Sevyn Sages of Rome* (*IMEV* 3187), and other, shorter religious pieces.

3. No title; colophon: 'Explicit tractatus qui dicitur stimulus consciencie Here endes þe tretyce þat es called þe pryk of conscience.' Inc: 'þe myght of þe fader all myghty'; expl: 'þat for us vouched safe on rode to hyng Amen'. A nearly complete text (9584/9624 ll.). English titles in text to all books. Occasional capitals for subdivisions. Prol: 1a; I: 3a; II: 6b; III: 10b; IV: 16a; V: 23b; VI: 37b; VII: 43va; Epil: 54vb.

4. At the top of f. 1 is the name 'Thomas Gyll', who may have been a chantry priest somewhere in Yorkshire in the early 15th c.

5. Fully northern.

6. *IMEV* 3428.19; *SC* 14667.
   SC, III, 321-22.
   Allen, 'Authorship', p. 124, n. 2; Allen, *Writings*, pp. 380-81, n. 4; Britton, passim; Campbell, passim; Doyle, 'Survey', II, 47-49; Robbins, p. 389; Waters, p. 11.

7. Group I. Closely related to MV 27 and 34.

MV 84 Oxford, Bodleian Library, Selden Supra 102*, ff. 15–16v, s. xv².

1. Selden Supra 102* is a series of pastedowns from Selden printed books: four items in all, of which the last (ff. 15–16v) is parchment, 188 × 116 mm.; in a mixed hand (with characteristics of both anglicana and secretary); in single columns, 26 ll. per page except for f. 16, which has 25.

3. ff. 15–16v are two leaves from a MS of the *PC* containing 103 ll. corresponding to ll. 7542–644 and thus have no title and no colophon. Inc: 'Bot gyfe he go bye þe way of wesdom'; expl: 'And þat heven is most nex our sy3t.'

5. Passage too short for adequate assessment: predominantly north east Midlands with evidence of some dialectal intermixture.

6. *IMEV* 3428.93.
   Neil R. Ker, *Fragments of Medieval Manuscripts Used as Pastedowns in Oxford Bindings*, Oxford Bibliographical Society Publications, New Series 5 (1951-52) (Oxford: A. T. Broome & Son, 1954), p. 157, item 1744.

7. Too little evidence on which to place this MS in one of the four groups.

MV 85 Oxford, St John's College, 57, ff. 1–137, s. xv (after 1432).

1. Paper, iii + 242 + ii ff., *c.* 304 × 215 mm. *PC* written in anglicana. Single columns, 29–35 ll. per page. Catchwords. The part of MS containing *PC* unfoliated.

2. In addition to *PC*, a list of mayors and sheriffs of London from 1 Richard I to 10 Henry VI, Chaucer's *Parlement of Foules* (*IMEV* 3412), and regulations for the army by Henry V.

3. No substantive title, but does have 'Prology' just before text and 'Prologus' in the margin by l. 1; colophon (on f. 135):

'Explicit stimulus consciencie.' Inc: 'The my3te of the ffadir almy3ty'; expl (on f. 135): 'That vouche saff for us on rode to hyng Amen.' Text reduced by 6 per cent (*c.* 8618/9216 ll.). Omissions in MS: (1) two leaves (ll. 67-198) between ff. 1 and 2; (2) one leaf (ll. 7536-66, 7592-627) between ff. 109 and 110; (3) two leaves (ll. 8246-381) between ff. 118 and 119; (4) one leaf (ll. 8517-680) between ff. 120 and 121. ff. 135v-37 contain lines, arranged by book (III-VII), that are for the most part omitted in the text, preceded by 'Hic suplemur defectus libri precedentis'. Latin titles in text to all books; running titles throughout. Occasional capitals for subdivisions. Prol: 1; I: 4v; II: 13; III: 24; IV: 38v; V: 57; VI: 93; VII: 109v; Epil: 134; added lines: 135v.

4. A number of 16th-c. names of owners and possible owners on the verso of f. i and on both the recto and verso of the first end flyleaf, including 'Thomas', 'Bodlay', 'mathew quytarod', 'John Spaeke', 'Thomas m[. . .]k', and 'Nicolass holdaornss'. Given to the College by John Davenant, a wine seller of Oxford, in 1576; his name is on f. 186.

5. Essex.

6. *IMEV* 3428.24.
   Coxe, II, Part 6, 16.

7. Group II. Related to MV 7, 19, 22, and 53.

MV 86 Oxford, St John's College, 138, ff. 1-126v, s. xv[1].

1. Parchment, i + 126 ff., 225 × 145 mm. Written in anglicana. Single columns, 30 ll. per page. Catchwords. MS unfoliated.

2. No title, text beginning imperfectly at l. 721, though at top of f. 1 is 'De medio [rest of running title torn away]'; no colophon, text ending imperfectly at l. 9482, though stubs of two additional leaves are visible. Inc: 'tranciat vespere decidat ind [rest of line torn off]'; expl: 'That arn evene contrarie ther to.' Text reduced by 13 per cent (7532/8649 ll.), with the greatest

reduction in Books II and VII. Probably one leaf missing between ff. 122 and 123, which would have contained ll. 9080–192. Latin titles and colophons in text to all remaining books; running titles (in Latin and occasionally in English) throughout. Capitals for subdivisions. Source notes, subtitles in Latin, and other notes throughout in same hand as that of the text; some interlinear corrections and a few marginal Latin comments in a later hand (late 15th or 16th c.). I (begins imperfectly at l. 721): 1; II: 4v; III: 13; IV: 29; V: 49v; VI: 86v; VII: 103v.

4. Given to the College in 1613 by Richard Butler, archdeacon of Northampton, through John Buckeridge, Bishop of Rochester (see margin of f. 2).

5. East Cambridgeshire.

6. *IMEV* 3428.25.
   Coxe, II, Part 6, 42; see also Richard Hunt, 'St. John's College Donors: Donors of Manuscripts to St. John's College Oxford during the Presidency of William Laud 1611-1621', in *Studies in the Book Trade in Honour of Graham Pollard*, Oxford Bibliographical Society Publications, New Series 18 (Oxford: The Oxford Bibliographical Society, 1975), pp. 63-64, 66.
   Britton, p. 333, n. 16.

7. Group II. Though MV 86 has no title and no colophon, it is textually a member of the 'Key of Knowing' subgroup, along with MV 8, 33, 41, 58, 64, and perhaps 92.

MV 87 Oxford, Trinity College, 15 (E. 15), ff. 1-203v, s. xv¹.

1. Parchment, i + 203 + i ff. (with end flyleaf foliated 104), 197 X 140 mm. Written in textura throughout. Single columns, 22-24 ll. per page. Catchwords. Parts of ff. 40, 41, 48, 203 mutilated.

3. No title; no colophon, the lower part of f. 203 torn away. Inc: 'The my3t of þe fader And allmi3ty'; expl: the last line of

the text is missing because the lower part of f. 203 is torn away, the last complete line (9606) reading 'Or ofer moche hardet in wickednes.' A nearly complete text (*c.* 9441/9624 ll.). Latin titles in text to all books. Occasional English subtitles in text. Occasional capitals for subdivisions. Marginal source and occasional other notes. Some correction, primarily interlinear, in same hand as that of the text; also some modern corrections, both marginal and interlinear, probably from another MS. Prol: 1; I: 8v; II: 20; III: 35; IV: 56; V: 82v; VI: 135; VII: 159; Epil: 202v.

5. Linguistically mixed but with characteristics suggesting it was copied in Worcester.

6. *IMEV* 3428.25.
   Coxe, II, Part 5, 7.

7. Group I. Related to MV 3, 9, 10, and 90 and, in Books I and II, to MV 24.

MV 88   Oxford, Trinity College, 16A (D. 16^A), ff. 1-116v, s. xv^1.

1. Parchment, i + 116 + i ff., 224 × 148 mm. Text written in anglicana formata, with Latin quotations mainly in textura (though with anglicana features off and on). Single columns, 32 ll. per page to f. 12v, 34 ll. per page from ff. 13-24v, 39-45 ll. per page thereafter.

3. No title, but in l. 3 of the twenty-two prefatory lines that precede the usual text appears 'of conciens pricke'; the only colophon is 'AMEN'. Inc: '[P] Rofitabule book ys þys to [erasure] lerune'; expl: 'þat for oure hele on rode con hyng'. Text reduced by *c.* 8 per cent (*c.* 8865/9624 ll.). English titles in text to all books. Occasional English subtitles in text. Capitals and paragraph marks for subdivisions. Occasional notes and primarily marginal corrections. Prol: 1; I: 7; II: 15v; III: 25v; IV: 37v; V: 51v; VI: 80; VII: 93; Epil: 115v.

4. On f. 116v, after the colophon, appears 'Liber Johannis leche' in a late 15th- or early 16th-c. hand.

5. South Shropshire.

6. *IMEV* 3428.27.
   Coxe, II, Part 5, 7.
   Dareau and McIntosh, pp. 20–22; Kaiser, pp. 234–42; Lewis, 'Relationship', pp. 257–59 and n. 22.

7. Group IV. A member of the Lichfield subgroup (along with MV 23, 45, 54, 57, 68, and 89), whose ultimate exemplar may have been MV 31. See also MV 57, Category 7.

MV 89 Oxford, Trinity College, 16B (D. 16^B), ff. 3–114, s. xiv/xv.

1. Parchment, i + 114 + i ff., 242 × 158 mm. Two anglicana formata hands in *PC*: (1) ff. 3–8v, l. 6, 30v, l. 19–31, 53, l. 28–78v, 84–84v, l. 24, 111v–14; (2) ff. 8v, l. 7–30v, l. 18, 31v–53, l. 27, 79–83v, 84v, l. 25–111. Hand 1 is the same as Hand 1 of MV 23. Single columns, 34–35 ll. per page. Catchwords.

2. *PC* preceded on ff. 1–2v by a fragment of a Latin missal in double columns.

3. No title; colophon: 'Explicit tractatus qui vocatur Stimulus consciencie Deo gracias.' Inc: 'Here bygynneþ þe soþe to say'; expl: 'þat for oure hele on rode gon hynge Amen.' Text reduced by *c.* 9 per cent (7756/8520 ll.), with three omissions: (1) three leaves containing ll. 3684–909 between ff. 51 and 52; (2) one leaf containing ll. 4658–743 between ff. 60 and 61; (3) probably eleven leaves (three plus one quire of eight) containing ll. 6141–7008 between ff. 78 and 79. An English title in text to Book II and an English colophon in text to Book VI, but no other titles anywhere in text. Occasional capitals (or spaces for capitals) for subdivisions. Prol: 3; I: 8v; II: 16; III: 26; IV: 39; V: 52v; VI (begins imperfectly at l. 7009): 79; VII: 86v; Epil: 112v.

4. On f. 114v are (1) a note of payment for bread to 'Upsenes wyfe' dated 1566 and (2) the name 'Robert cresswell grocer at the harrowe in bucklersburye' (Bucklebury in Berkshire, near Newbury?).

5. Lichfield for both hands.

6. *IME V* 1193.2.
    Coxe, II, Part 5, 7.
    Dareau and McIntosh, pp. 20-22; Lewis, 'Relationship', pp. 257-59 and n. 22.

7. Group IV. A member of the Lichfield subgroup (along with MV 23, 45, 54, 57, 68, and 88), whose ultimate exemplar may have been MV 31.

MV 90   Oxford, University College, 142 (D. 142), ff. 4-125v, s. xv in.

1. Parchment, iii + 127 ff. (with the whole MS foliated 1-130), *c.* 265 X *c.* 168 mm. *PC* probably all in one hand in spite of an apparent change at f. 16, l. 10: basically an attempt at textura, with some anglicana features. Single columns, 30-37 ll. per page. Catchwords. Medieval boards. MS paginated irregularly as well as foliated.

2. *PC* was the only item originally in the MS, but is now followed by 'A litel tretes' in prose (ff. 126v-27v; the first part of the *XII Profits of Tribulation* attributed to Adam the Carthusian), a prose work beginning 'Seven maysters of art fonden and noumbred þe evell houres and perilous days in the yer' (ff. 128v-29), two fragmentary pieces of verse (ff. 126, 128; *IME V* 3401 and 1184 respectively), and other bits of prose (ff. 126, 127v, 129v-30v).

3. No original title, but a later hand has added 'Stimulus consiencie'; colophon: 'Explicit stimulus consciencie', followed by 'Nomen scriptoris thomas plenus amoris' in same hand as that of the text. Inc: 'The myȝthe of the fader al myȝthy'; expl:

'þat for oure love made al þing Amen'. Text reduced by *c.* 13 per cent (*c.* 8264/9568 ll.), with one omission: one leaf containing ll. 596-751 between ff. 11 and 12. Latin titles in text to all books. Capitals for subdivisions. Occasional corrections, both in margin and in text. A list of topics in the poem on f. 1v in a different but contemporary hand. Prol: 4; I: 8v; II: 14; III: 23; IV: 37; V: 54; VI: 87; VII: 102; Epil: 124.

4. On f. 125v, in same hand as that of the text, appears the name of a possible contemporary owner: 'Ricardus Rauf P L'. Two 16th-c. owners' names appear on f. 130v: John and William Weston de Ocham. Other 16th-c. names on ff. 2v, 125v, 126, 129v, and 130v include Thomas Frelond, Johannes Ramsey, Henry and Wyllyam Russell, and William Sawyer.

5. South west Sussex.

6. *IMEV* 3428.28.
  Coxe, I, Part 1, 39; see also Gisela Guddat-Figge, *Catalogue of Manuscripts Containing Middle English Romances* (Munich: Wilhelm Fink Verlag, 1976), pp. 297-99.
  Allen, 'Authorship', p. 125, n. 3; Ritson, p. 34; Tanner, p. 375, n. q.

7. Group I until near the end of the text, where it is related to MV 3, 9, 10, and 87 and, in Books I and II, to MV 24; in Epilogue appears to become a SR text, along with MV 76, and ends with a SR explicit.

MV 91 Philadelphia, Pennsylvania, University of Pennsylvania Library, English 1, ff. 13-118, *c.* 1400.

1. Parchment, i + 120 + i ff., 250 × 170 mm. Text of *PC* in anglicana formata, with titles and Latin quotations in textura. Single columns, 40 ll. per page. Catchwords.

2. *PC* preceded by Richard Maydestone's version of the Seven Penitential Psalms (*IMEV* 3755) on ff. 1-12v, beginning imperfectly and with some text missing between ff. 5 and 6, and

followed by the English *Lamentacio Sancti Anselmi* (*IMEV* 3938) on ff. 118v-20v, ending imperfectly.

3. No title, text beginning imperfectly at l. 76; colophon: 'Explicit Tractatus qui dicitur Stimulus consciencie.' Inc: 'And þer to ʒaf him wit and skille'; expl: 'þat for oure love on rode gan hynge Amen'. A nearly complete text as far as the remaining lines indicate (8384/8487 ll.), but with a number of omissions: (1) one leaf at beginning with ll. 1-75; (2) two leaves with ll. 238-403 between ff. 14 and 15; (3) one quire of eight leaves with ll. 1960-2628 between ff. 33 and 34; (4) one leaf with ll. 3916-95 between ff. 49 and 50; (5) one leaf with ll. 6354-436 between ff. 78 and 79; (6) one leaf with ll. 7495-559 between ff. 91 and 92. English titles in text to all remaining books (II-IV); running Latin titles throughout. Capitals for subdivisions. Prol (begins imperfectly at l. 76): 13; I (begins imperfectly at l. 404): 15; II: 21; III: 30; IV: 34v; V (begins imperfectly at l. 3996): 50; VI (begins imperfectly at l. 6437): 79; VII (begins imperfectly at l. 7560): 92; Epil: 117.

4. The names of two former owners (?), 'Rycharde Hatter' and 'Franciscus Quawden', appear on f. 77 in a late 15th- or early 16th-c. hand.

5. Norfolk.

6. *IMEV* 3428.78; formerly Ireland Blackburne.
   Bruce Dickins, 'The Ireland Blackburne Manuscript of the Seven Penitential Psalms, the Pricke of Conscience and Lamentacio Sancti Anselmi', *Leeds Studies in English and Kindred Languages*, 3 (1934), 30-36; Faye and Bond, p. 479a; Zacour and Hirsch, p. 49.
   Waters, pp. 48-49.

7. Group III.

MV 92 Philadelphia, Pennsylvania, University of Pennsylvania Library, English 8, ff. 147a-159vb, s. xv in.

1. Parchment, 159 + i ff., 390 × 253 mm. Two hands in the MS: (1) ff. 1-146v and (2) ff. 147-59v, both of which are

anglicana, with Latin quotations in bastard anglicana. Double
columns, 42 ll. per column on ff. 147–51v, 45 ll. per column on
ff. 152–59v. Late 15th-c. binding by the 'Virgin and Child'
binder from the Winchester area.

2. *PC* preceded by Walter Hilton's *Scale of Perfection* (beginning
imperfectly), the English translation of Pseudo-Bonaventure's
Stimulus Amoris, and *Contemplations of the Dread and Love
of God.*

3. No original title, though a 20th-c. hand has put 'The Key of
Knowing' at the top of f. 147; no colophon, text ending imper-
fectly with new material that appears to be an expansion of ll.
2570–600 and especially 2643–73. Inc: '[þ]e miȝt of þe fader
almiȝty'; expl: 'þat wold nouȝt himself do'. Text expanded by
24 per cent (2277/c. 1830 ll.) by the addition of both Latin
prose and English verse, especially in Book III. One omission in
remaining text: probably two leaves containing ll. 240–410
between ff. 148 and 149. Latin titles in text to the two remain-
ing books (II and III). No capitals anywhere, but space is left
for them both at beginnings of books and at subdivisions. Prol:
147a; I (begins imperfectly at l. 411): 149a; II: 152b; III: 157b.

5. South east Lincolnshire. The language of the *Scale of Perfec-
tion* (in same hand) is more southerly, perhaps south Isle of Ely.

6. *IMEV* 3428.81; formerly Stonor Park.
 Faye and Bond, pp. 479b–80a; Jeanne Elizabeth Krochalis,
 'Contemplations of the Dread and Love of God: Two
 Newly Identified Pennsylvania Manuscripts', *The Library
 Chronicle*, 42 (1977), 11–13; Zacour and Hirsch, p. 50.
 Allen, *Writings*, p. 373, n. 1.

7. Group II. MV 92 has the title 'The Key of Knowing' but in a
20th-c. hand, though it may have been taken from part of the
text that is now missing, for the MS has some textual similarity
to the 'Key of Knowing' subgroup (MV 8, 33, 41, 58, 64, 86);
it also has some similarities with the so-called Lollard subgroup
(MV 51, 56, 61, 73) and, in Books II and III, with MV 35
and 42.

MV 93 Princeton, New Jersey, Princeton University Library, Taylor MS of the *Prick of Conscience*, ff. 1-126v, s. xiv^2.

1. Parchment, iii + 126 + iii ff., 184 × 121 mm. Text in anglicana formata, with Latin quotations in textura. Collation: 1^{12} (lacks 12) 2-4^{12} 5^{12} (lacks 7-8) 6^{12} 7^{10} + 2 leaves (lacks 4; the 2 leaves added between 8 and 9) 8^{10} 9-11^{12}. Single columns, 33-35 ll. per page. Catchwords. MS unfoliated.

3. No title; colophon: 'Explicit tractatus qui dicitur / Stimulus Consciencie / Here endes þe tretice þat es calde / Prikke of Conscience', followed by 'Si male quid feci veniam peto si bene gratis.' Inc: 'þe myght of þe fadir alle myghty'; expl: 'þat for oure hele one rode cane hynge'. Text reduced by *c*. 8 per cent (*c*. 8560/9326 ll.), with three omissions: (1) one leaf with ll. 757-826 between ff. 11 and 12; (2) two leaves with ll. 3948-4095 between ff. 53 and 54; (3) one leaf with ll. 5589-669 between ff. 72 and 73. English titles in text to all books except V, which is imperfect at the beginning. Capitals for subdivisions. Some correction in text. Prol: 1; I: 6; II: 13v; III: 23v; IV: 37v; V (begins imperfectly at l. 4096): 54; VI: 82v; VII: 97v; Epil: 125.

4. A note of ownership at the end, on f. 126v: 'Iste Liber Constat Johanni Aston De Croppil Botler' (Cropwell Butler, Nottinghamshire), in a different but contemporary hand.

5. Probably extreme south Yorkshire or north west Nottinghamshire.

6. *IMEV* 3428.88; formerly Horton Old Hall.
   Art, item 76; Maggs Bros. Sale Catalogue, No. 580 (1933), item 449.
   John V. Fleming, 'Medieval Manuscripts in the Taylor Library', *Princeton University Library Chronicle*, 38 (1977), 116-17.

7. Group IV. Related to at least MV 28, 35, 62, and 94 and, in Book V, to MV 40.

MV 94   San Marino, California, Huntington Library, HM 139, ff. 144a-187a, s. xv med.

1. Paper, 44 ff., 288 X 205 mm. Two hands: (1) ff. 144-55v, text in anglicana, and (2) ff. 156-87, text in anglicana formata, with Latin quotations in bastard anglicana in both hands. *PC* is on leaves foliated 144-87, indicating that it was originally part of another, longer MS. Double columns, 42-52 ll. per column on ff. 144-55v, 44-59 ll. per column on ff. 156-87.

2. *PC* the only item in the MS, though on f. 155v *PC* ends abruptly nine lines down column b with l. 2265 and is followed by 'In may quem [*sic*] ever þi hert is liȝt' (the first line of either *IMEV* 1505 or *IMEV* 1506?) in same hand; *PC* resumes with l. 2266 at the top of f. 156a.

3. Title (at the very top of f. 144): 'Assit principio sancta maria meo'; no colophon. Inc: 'þe myȝte of þe fadere almyȝtty'; expl: 'þat for oure hele on rode did hynge'. Text reduced by *c.* 8 per cent (*c.* 8830/9624 ll.). Latin title in text to Book I; no other titles, but space is left for them at the beginnings of Books VI and VII. Marginal Latin rubrics on ff. 180-82v passim. Prol: 144a; I: 146a (though title appears on f. 144v between ll. 114 and 115); II: 149a; III: 153a; IV: 158a; V: 163b; VI: 173vb; VII: 178va; Epil: 186vb.

4. Three appearances on ff. 155vb and 187v of the name of a former owner, John Wyldon, in two different 16th-c. hands; the name 'Jhon pendand' (15th-16th c.) is on f. 164va.

5. Yorkshire/Nottinghamshire border for Hand 1, with a slight change of language at f. 152v, l. 5; north Nottinghamshire for Hand 2.

6. *IMEV* 3428.84; formerly Phillipps 9412.
   Census, I, 56.
   Allen, *Writings*, pp. 373, n. 1, and 539-40; Lewis, 'Relationship', pp. 255, 258, and nn. 16, 23; McIntosh, 'Two', pp. 69 and 69, n. 1.

7. Group IV. Related to at least MV 28, 29, 35, 43, 62, and 93 and, in Book V, to MV 40.

MV 95   Shrewsbury, School, III (Mus. III. 39), ff. 1-27v, s. xv ex.

1. Paper, ii + 108 + iii ff. (with end flyleaves foliated 109-11), 216 × 152 mm. *PC* written basically in anglicana but with some secretary features. Single columns, 21-31 ll. per page. The MS is very frayed and torn, especially to f. 7.

2. *PC* followed by sermons and other theological tracts and notes, all in English (for which see Calvert's and Herbert's descriptions).

3. No title, text beginning imperfectly at l. 4892; no colophon, text ending imperfectly at l. 7542. Inc: The s[. . .] / As [. . .] / A [. . .]'; expl: 'butt he goo by the wey of wysdom'. Text reduced by 60 per cent (*c.* 1583/2654 ll.). Text very condensed: some lines are omitted, others are reversed; it is more a revision with lines omitted than a paraphrase. No titles. Occasional interlinear additions. V (begins imperfectly at l. 4892): 1; VI: 17; VII: 27v.

5. Derbyshire.

6. *IMEV* 3428.63.
   E. Calvert, 'Extracts from a Fifteenth Century MS.', *Transactions of the Shropshire Archaeological and Natural History Society*, 2nd Series, 6 (1894), 99-106; J. A. Herbert, 'Catalogue of the Early Manuscripts of Shrewsbury School', *Transactions of the Shropshire Archaeological and Natural History Society*, 2nd Series, 9 (1897), 294.

7. Very little evidence to go on, but probably Group IV; related to MV 21 and 49 in Books VI-VII.

MV 96   Wellesley, Massachusetts, Wellesley College Library, 8, pp. 12-247, s. xv in.

1. Paper, 126 ff., 210 × 150 mm. *PC* written in anglicana. Single columns, 29-35 ll. per page. Catchwords irregularly; signatures.

Original wooden boards covered with sheepskin. MS paginated rather than foliated.

2. *PC* preceded (on pp. 1-12) by the *Stimulus Consciencie Minor* (*IMEV* 244), beginning imperfectly; a Thanksgiving to Christ attributed to Richard Rolle (*IMEV* 1954); and the latter part of 'The Book of Penance' (*IMEV* 694), beginning 'Sex cases þare are owttane.'

3. Title (on p. 12): 'here begynnes þe langer pryck of concience'; colophon (in a later 15th-c. textura hand): 'Explicit liber qui dicitur Stimulus Conscience.' Inc (on p. 13): 'þe myght of þe ffader alle myghty'; expl: 'þat for us vowched safe on rode to hyng Amen'. Text reduced by *c.* 19 per cent (*c.* 6621/8206 ll.), with three omissions: (1) probably three leaves with ll. 1366-565 between pp. 52 and 53; (2) perhaps two quires of eight leaves each with ll. 7421-8572 between pp. 216 and 217; (3) one leaf with ll. 9154-219 between pp. 234 and 235. Latin titles in text to Books I-IV, in margins to Books V-VI; brief running Latin titles throughout. Capitals for subdivisions. Most Latin quotations in margins as far as Book II; Latin quotations omitted from Book III on. Occasional interlinear corrections. Prol: 13; I: 22; II: 39; III: 56; IV: 85; V: 122; VI: 189; VII (begins imperfectly at l. 8573): 217; Epil: 244.

4. On p. 247, in a later 15th-c. textura hand, is 'Iste liber constat Ricardo Gardner'. On p. 248, in a still later hand (16th c.), is the name of another owner, 'Wylliam Hotterbrim' (probably same name again on p. 250), and on p. 252 are the date 1534 and the name 'skeibey' (probably Skeeby near Richmond in the North Riding of Yorkshire).

5. Fully northern.

6. *IMEV* 3428.86, 3428.90; Hope Emily Allen Additional MS V (*Writings*, p. 374).
   Census, I, 1068.
   Allen, *Writings*, p. 374; Britton, passim.

7. Group I. Closely related to MV 44.

MV 97 Hatfield House, Hertfordshire, Library of the Marquis of Salisbury, Deeds 59/1, covers, s. xv[1].

1. Deeds 59/1 is a memorandum book containing notes on the ownership of the manor of Rockbourne, Hampshire, 1600–02. The covers consist of a parchment bifolium (the next-to-the-innermost one of a quire of indeterminate length) from a MS of the *PC*; the two leaves vary in size, but 130–38 X 210–18 mm. covers the measurements of both; written in an informal textura; single columns, 36 ll. per page except for the last, which has 37.

3. The leaf that forms the front cover contains ll. 4547–620; the leaf that forms the back cover contains ll. 4776–856. No title and no colophon, text beginning and ending imperfectly. Inc: 'And an half aboven þo erthe opynli'; expl: 'Whan mannus sone schal schewyd be.'

4. Book and covers owned by John Babington in 1602 ('John babingtone his booke' on the recto of the front cover); Babington was one of the owners of the manor of Rockbourne from whom Robert Cecil, first Earl of Salisbury, bought it in 1610. The name 'ambrose babington' is on the recto of the back cover, and the book itself contains the will of Francis Keylweye (died 22 January 1602), of Rockbourne, for which Babington was a witness and his son a beneficiary.

5. Passages too short for adequate assessment, but forms suggest north central Midlands.

6. Not in *IMEV*.
   Unpublished description at Hatfield House.

7. Too little evidence on which to place this MS in one of the four groups.

II
The Southern Recension

SR 1 Beaumont College, Old Windsor, Berkshire, 9, ff. 3–158, s. xiv².

1. Parchment, iii + 158 + iii ff., 286 X 192 mm. *PC* written in anglicana formata. Single columns, 26 ll. per page. Catchwords. Modern pagination begins on f. 3 with p. 3 but continues only to p. 65. MS formerly at Beaumont College but now owned by H. P. Kraus of New York.

2. *PC* the only item in the MS originally, and ff. 1–2v were blank, but ff. 1v–2 now contain a prayer in a hand of the 15th/16th c. beginning 'O gloryous angel'.

3. Title: 'Assit principio sancta maria meo Hic incipit liber qui vocatur stimulus consiencie [*sic*]'; colophon: 'Heere endeþ þis holy bok þe whuch is ycluped þe prikke off consciense.' Inc: 'þe miȝt of þe fader of hevene'; expl: 'þat for mannes love made al þinge Amen'. 8056/9624 ll. English titles in text to all books. Capitals for subdivisions. Prol: 3 (= p. 3); I: 9 (= p. 13); II: 19 (= p. 33); III: 31 (= p. 57); IV: 48; V: 69v; VI: 112; VII: 127; Epil: 156v.

4. The name 'Elyzbeth Strangburn', in a 16th-c. hand, appears at the bottom of f. 63.

5. South east Gloucestershire; very similar in language to SR 13, though the hands are not identical.

6. *IMEV* 3429.12.
   Descriptions circulated by Colin and Charlotte Franklin, Culham, Oxford (*c*. 1976) and H. P. Kraus, New York (1979). Allen, *Writings*, p. 373, n. 1; D'Evelyn, passim; Waters, passim.

7. Group A. Related to SR 10 and 11 in Book V.

SR 2 Cambridge, Pembroke College, 272, ff. 1–143v, s. xv med.

1. Parchment, 144 ff., 187 X 127 mm. Secretary book hand with some anglicana features. Collation: 1^{10} 2^8 (with 12^8 inserted in its centre) 3–5^8 6^8 (lacks 7) 7–8^{10} 9^{10} (lacks 9) 10^{10} 11^{10} (lacks 8–9) 13–17^8. Single columns, 22–28 ll. per page. Catchwords; signatures irregularly, beginning with b (quire a omitted at beginning).

3. No title, text beginning imperfectly at l. 458; no colophon, text ending imperfectly at l. 9552. Inc: 'withynne hys modrys wombe hath non oder fode'; expl: 'for ȝif a man doþ rede and con undurstondyng fele'. c. 7161/9039 ll. MS bound (copied?) incorrectly, with the twelfth quire (containing ll. 5921–table of contents to Book VI) inserted in the centre (between ff. 14 and 23) of the second quire; ff. 23, which would have contained text corresponding to MV ll. 1343–71, and 103v, which would have contained text corresponding to MV ll. 5810–36, are blank. Omissions in remaining text: (1) one leaf between ff. 56 and 57, which would have contained text corresponding to MV ll. 3220–75; (2) one leaf between ff. 85 and 86, though apparently no text is missing at this point; (3) two leaves between ff. 103 and 104, though apparently no text is missing. A table of contents appears at the beginning of each book, beginning with Book II. An English title in text to Book II before the table of contents; no titles thereafter, though space is left for them. Some English subtitles in text to f. 10. No Latin quotations or subtitles in text from f. 11 on, though space is left for them. Capitals for subdivisions. I (begins imperfectly at l. 458): 1; II: 8v; III: 28; IV: 46; V: 70 (but part of V also on ff. 15–22v); VI: 105 (but table of contents on f. 22v); VII: 119v; Epil: 143v.

5. South east Suffolk.

6. *IMEV* 3428.34.
   Pembroke Cat., p. 248.
   Andreae, p. 23; Waters, passim.

7. Group A. Related to SR 4 and 5 in Book V and in its configuration of a table of contents before each book. See also SR 15, Category 7.

SR 3 Cambridge, St John's College, 29 (B.7), ff. 5–119v, s. xv med.

1. Paper, ii + 119 + iv ff., 289 × 203 mm. Text written in anglicana, with Latin quotations in bastard anglicana. Single columns, 38–39 ll. per page. Catchwords irregularly; signatures b–k.

2. *PC* preceded by part of *Ipotis* (*IMEV* 220).

3. Title: 'Stimulus Consciencie'; colophon: 'Explicit Stimulus Consciencie.' Inc: 'The myght of the fadir of heven'; expl: 'That for oure love made al thynge Amen quod A.' *c.* 8604/9384 ll. Perhaps three leaves omitted between ff. 5 and 6 that would have contained text corresponding to MV ll. 77–316. Latin titles in margin to Books II–V; English titles in text to all books but III; running Latin titles cconsistently into IV but only occasionally and irregularly thereafter. Prol: 5; I: 6v; II: 13v; III: 23; IV: 33; V: 49v; VI: 79v; VII: 93v; Epil: 117.

4. 15th-c. inscription on end flyleaf ii verso: 'I pray yow pray for me your owne sarvaunt Margery Carew god amend þat ys ames quod M C MARGERY CAREW'; on f. 57 some names of Chaloners, probably in a 16th-c. hand. See also SR 12.

5. Perhaps Surrey or Sussex; very similar in language to SR 12.

6. *IMEV* 3429.4.
   St John's Cat., pp. 38–39.
   D'Evelyn, passim; Waters, passim.

7. Group A. Closely related to SR 12 in Book V.

SR 4 Cambridge, University Library, Ee.4.35.2, ff. 1–96v, s. xiv².

1. Parchment, 89 ff. (ff. 24–25, 33, 41–44 lost), 279 × 184 mm. Written in anglicana formata. Collation: 1^{12} 2^{12} (lacks 12) 3^{12} (lacks 1, 9) 4^{12} (lacks 5–8) $5–8^{12}$. Single columns, 34–47 ll. per page, with the number increasing as the text progresses. Catchwords.

3. Title: 'Here bigynneþ the book þe whiche ys ycleped þe [erasure]'; no colophon, text ending imperfectly at l. 9596. Inc (f. 1v): 'þe miȝt of þe holi fadur In hevene'; expl: 'þe whiche mi defaute amende kan', plus catchwords 'and In letture'. c. 7094/8990 ll., with three omissions: (1) ff. 24-25, which would have contained text corresponding to MV ll. 2064-245; (2) f. 33, which would have contained text corresponding to MV ll. 2821-901; (3) ff. 41-44, which would have contained text corresponding to MV ll. 3467-809. A table of contents (in double columns) to the whole poem, like the one in Morris, p. xxxiv, appears on f. 1 after the title; a table of contents (in double columns) appears at the beginning of each book, with the table for Book I appearing before the Prologue. English titles in text to all books; some English subtitles in text. Capitals for sub-divisions. Prol: 1v; I: 5v; II: 11v; III: 19; IV: 31; V: 46v; VI: 74v; VII: 82v; Epil: 96.

5. South east Gloucestershire, not far from SR 1 and SR 13.

6. *IMEV* 3429.3; formerly Moore 97.
   CUL Cat., II, 167-69; Pink.
   Bülbring, *ES*, pp. 6-11 et passim; D'Evelyn, passim; Tanner, p. 375, n. q; Waters, passim.

7. Group A. Related to SR 2 and 5 in Book V and in its configuration of a table of contents before each book. See also SR 15, Category 7.

SR 5 Dublin, Trinity College, 69 (A.4.4), ff. 65a-72vb, 83va-123va, s. xiv/xv.

1. Parchment, i + 124 ff., 255 × 185 mm. Two hands in the MS, the second of which, in textura, writes *PC*. Double columns, 53-55 ll. per column on ff. 83v-88v, 45 ll. per column for the rest of *PC*. Catchwords irregularly.

2. *PC* the last of the six principal items in the MS; the others are prose: the Psalter in Latin and English, the Apocalypse with Wyclif's exposition in English, *A Tale of Charity*, an exposition

of the ten commandments, and a Latin description of Jerusalem.
On f. 124v is *IMEV* 2631.5.

3. Title: 'Here bygynneþ þe bok þe wich is cleped þe pricke of
conciense' (f. 83va); no colophon. Inc: 'þe myȝt of þe fader of
hevene'; expl: 'þat for mannes love made alle þinge amen'.
c. 8397/9624 ll. The part of the MS containing *PC* is bound
incorrectly: one quire of eight (ff. 65-72v) containing text cor-
responding to MV ll. 4071-5525 displaced from its proper place
between ff. 104 and 105. A table of contents to the whole
poem, like the one in Morris's edition, p. xxxiv, appears on
f. 83va between the title and the incipit; a table of contents
appears at the beginning of each book, with the table for both
the Prologue and Book I appearing before the Prologue. English
titles in text to all books, both before and after the tables of
contents for Books II-VII. Capitals for subdivisions. Prol: 83va;
I: 84vb; II: 87b; III: 90va; IV: 96a; V: 103b (this book also
appears on ff. 65a-72vb); VI: 109va; VII: 114b; Epil: 123a.

4. The MS is probably of ecclesiastical origin, though it belonged
to a layman later in the 15th c.; the name of an earlier owner,
John Hyde, appears at the end of the Psalter.

5. South Sussex.

6. *IMEV* 3428.37 but corrected to 3429.15 in the Supplement;
formerly Savile 237.
Abbott, p. 9; see also Karl L. Bülbring, ed., *The Earliest Com-
plete English Prose Psalter*, EETS os 97 (London: Kegan
Paul, Trench, Trübner & Co., Ltd., 1891), pp. vii-viii, x;
for provenance see Doyle, 'Survey', I, 106, 123; II, 66.
Allen, *Writings*, p. 385; Andreae, p. 23; Britton, p. 332, n.
14; Bülbring, *ES*, passim; Bülbring, *Trans.*, passim; D'Eve-
lyn, passim; David Diringer, *The Hand-Produced Book*
(New York: Philosophical Library, 1953), p. 526, Figure
X-26, lower portion (facsimile of the upper portion of
f. 83v); Waters, passim.

7. Group A. Related to SR 2 and 4 in Book V and in its con-
figuration of a table of contents before each book. See also SR
15, Category 7.

SR 6 Lichfield, Cathedral, 16, ff. 35–189v, s. xv in.

1. Parchment, ii + 246 + ii (foliated i–ii, 1–225, 227–47, 248–49), 258 X 185 mm. Two textura hands at work in *PC*: (1) ff. 35–82v, 92–189v; (2) ff. 83–91v. Quires m and s missing in text of *PC*. Single columns, 22 ll. per page. Catchwords; signatures usually visible.

2. In addition to *PC*, two versions (Latin and English) of Book II, Chap. 2 of the *Horologium Sapiencie* by Henry Suso and three versions (Latin, English, and French) of the *Dicta Anselmi*, Chap. 5, by Alexander of Canterbury.

3. No title; colophon: 'Here endeþ þe bok þat ys cleped þe pryk of concyens.' Inc: 'The mghte [*sic*] of þe fader al myȝtty'; expl: 'þat for oure love made al þynge AMEN'. 6801/8514 ll. One quire of eight leaves that would have contained text corresponding to MV ll. 4537–913 omitted between ff. 123 and 124; one quire of eight leaves that would have contained text corresponding to MV ll. 7123–856 omitted between ff. 163 and 164. English titles in text to all remaining books but II. Occasional capitals for subdivisions. Some additions to the text, both between lines and in margins. Prol: 35; I: 43; II: 54; III: 68; IV: 86; V: 112; VI: 152v; VII (begins imperfectly at l. 7857): 164; Epil: 187v.

4. Owned by William Seymour, Duke of Somerset (1588–1660).

5. Hand 1 in a strong southwestern dialect, probably Somerset-shire, south Gloucestershire, or Wiltshire; Hand 2 has additionally a strong East Anglian ingredient which links it with SR 7.

6. *IMEV* 3429.13; formerly Lichfield 6.
   Benedikz, pp. 9–10; Ker.
   Bülbring, *ES*, passim; Bülbring, *Trans.*, pp. 279–83; D'Evelyn, passim; Waters, passim.

7. Conflated MS: a MV text to l. 463; a SR text thereafter, where it is Group B. Related to SR 8, 13, and 16 in Book V.

SR 7 Lichfield, Cathedral, 50, ff. 1–109v, s. xiv².

1. Parchment, ii + 109 + iii ff., 180 X 130 mm. 'f. 110 is a waste leaf retained as a flyleaf' (Ker), containing lines corresponding to MV ll. 9272–431, ending abruptly at l. 13 of the verso; these lines have already appeared on f. 105r–v. Bastard anglicana, perhaps in two hands, with the change at f. 59. Single columns, 28 ll. per page from ff. 1–40, 32–39 ll. per page from f. 40v–end. Catchwords irregularly.

3. No title; no colophon, text ending imperfectly at the bottom of f. 109v (the last leaf of the text has been torn out, but remains of it can be seen). Inc: 'The myth of þe fader of hevene'; expl: 'And to drede out to do aȝeins godes wille' (the fifth line of a six-line expansion of MV ll. 9573–74). c. 7071/9574 ll.; Book VII considerably rearranged. English titles in text to all books except V, where it is in the margin; frequent English subtitles, usually in text but occasionally in the margins. Capitals for subdivisions. Most Latin quotations are omitted; when they do appear, they usually appear in the margins, in the same hand as that of the text. Occasional corrections in text in the early part of the MS. Prol: 1; I: 6v; II: 14v; III: 24v; IV: 37; V: 54; VI: 84; VII: 92v; Epil: 109v.

4. Owned by Galfridus Glasier, Chapter Clerk, who died in 1668 (from a note at the bottom of f. 1).

5. Norfolk.

6. *IMEV* 3429.14; formerly Lichfield 18.
   Benedikz, p. 28; Ker.
   Bülbring, *ES*, passim; Bülbring, *Trans.*, pp. 279–83; D'Evelyn, passim; Waters, passim.

7. Group B. Related to SR 15 and 17 in Book V.

SR 8 London, British Library, Harley 1731, ff. 1–133v, s. xv¹.

1. Paper, i + 149 ff. (with beginning flyleaf containing scraps from the end flyleaf of an earlier binding and a second f. 133,

138 THE SOUTHERN RECENSION

foliated 133*, containing scribbles and four lines of English verse in a 16th-c. hand), 215 × 140-45 mm. Text of *PC* written in anglicana, with titles and Latin quotations in anglicana formata. Single columns, 28-29 ll. per page. Signatures visible from beginning of quire ii (f. 11) to end of quire viii (f. 94v).

2. *PC* followed by the *Speculum Gy de Warewyke* (*IMEV* 1101) in another hand, ending imperfectly.

3. No title, text beginning imperfectly at l. 59; colophon: 'Here endeþ þe Book þat ys yclepud Prykke of conscyence Explicit tractatus [erasure of three words] Willelmus [probable erasure]'. Inc: 'þan ouȝt a man þat haþ skyle and fey'; expl: 'That for oure love made al þynge Amen.' 7405/9498 ll., with two omissions: (1) one leaf at beginning containing text corresponding to MV ll. 1-58; (2) one leaf between ff. 10 and 11 containing text corresponding to MV ll. 715-82. Latin titles in text to all books; Latin colophons in text to all books except VII. English title in text to Book II; English subtitles in text in all books except III. Source and other notes, primarily in Latin, in margins. Many interlinear corrections. Prol (begins imperfectly at l. 59): 1; I: 5v; II: 13; III: 24v; IV: 38; V: 58; VI: 98; VII: 110; Epil: 132.

4. A note on the beginning flyleaf indicates that a former owner, Richard Reder of Petersfield, Hampshire, on 5 July 1473 surrendered this MS along with two others to the Commissary General of the Diocese of Winchester, perhaps because he was suspected of heresy.

5. North east Wiltshire.

6. *IMEV* 3429.6; formerly Worsley.
   Harley Cat., II, 191b; Wright, p. 284.
   Allen, *Writings*, pp. 387-88 and 387, n. 2; Andreae, passim; Bülbring, *ES*, passim; Bülbring, *Trans.*, passim; D'Evelyn, passim; Morris, pp. i-ii and ii, n. 2; Ritson, p. 34; Tanner, p. 375, n. q; Waters, passim; Yates, p. 335.

7. Group B. Related to SR 6, 13, and 16 in Book V. According to Waters, ll. 5060-441 are borrowed from a MV text.

SR 9 London, British Library, Harley 2281, ff. 1-64v, s. xv in.

1. Parchment, 64 ff., 225 X 145-50 mm. Written in anglicana formata. Single columns, 32-38 ll. per page. Catchwords; signatures.

3. No title; no colophon, text ending imperfectly with a subtitle corresponding to MV ll. 5764-65. Inc: 'The myght of þe fader of hevene'; expl: 'seven werkes of mercy þat hi did noȝt here by hire lyf', plus catchwords 'et bihovet'. c. 4309/5037 ll., with one omission in remaining text: one quire of eight leaves between ff. 24 and 25 that would have contained text corresponding to MV ll. 1931-2658. English titles in text to all remaining books; Latin titles in margins to III. Subtitles in text throughout. Capitals or spaces for capitals for subdivisions to f. 43v. Prol: 1; I: 5v; II: 12v; III: 21v; IV: 25; V: 41.

5. South west Herefordshire.

6. *IMEV* 3429.7.
   Harley Cat., II, 641a.
   Andreae, passim; Bülbring, *ES*, pp. 18-23 passim; Bülbring, *Trans.*, passim; D'Evelyn, passim; Morris, pp. i-ii and ii, n. 2; Warton-Hazlitt, p. 240, n. 1; Waters, passim.

7. Group B. Related to SR 14 and 18 in Book V.

SR 10 London, British Library, Royal 18 A.v, ff. 2-126, s. xv[1].

1. Parchment, iii + 128 + iii ff. (with third beginning flyleaf foliated 1; the text foliated 2-128, with an unfoliated leaf after 128; and the three end flyleaves foliated 129-31), 229 X 159 mm. Written in anglicana. Single columns, 30-35 ll. per page. Catchwords; signatures.

3. No title and no colophon. Inc: 'The might of the fader of hevene'; expl: 'That for mannes love made alle thinge.' c. 8082/9624 ll. English titles in text to all books except I; English subtitle in text and space for capital at beginning of I; many English

subtitles in text. Prol: 2; I: 7; II: 16; III: 26v; IV: 41; V: 59v; VI: 92v; VII: 104v; Epil: 125.

4. Belonged to an Elyot family in the late 15th or early 16th c., as indicated by a note of ownership on f. 130 and a number of Elyot names on ff. 127v–28v and 129v.

5. South east Midlands.

6. *IME V* 3429.10; King's MS.
Royal Cat., II, 263b–64a.
Andreae, passim; Britton, p. 332, n. 14; Bülbring, *ES*, pp. 6–11 passim; Bülbring, *Trans.*, passim; D'Evelyn, passim; Warton-Hazlitt, p. 240, n. 1; Warton-Price, p. 99, n. z; Waters, passim.

7. Group A. Related to SR 1 and 11 in Book V.

SR 11 London, British Library, Additional 11305, ff. 3–126v, s. xv².

1. Parchment, ii + 124 + ii ff. (with beginning flyleaves foliated 1–2), *c.* 270 X *c.* 175 mm. Beginning flyleaf ii (f. 2) is post-medieval (18th c.?) and has the incipit, explicit, and colophon on its recto and the table of contents from the end of the Prologue on its verso. Written in anglicana formata. Single columns, 31 ll. per page on ff. 11–50v, 32 ll. per page elsewhere. Catchwords; signatures.

3. No title; colophon: 'Here endith now this good boke atte this tyme / Called the pricke of Conscience drawen þus in ryme' ('The floure of conscience' at l. 9551). Inc: 'The might of the fader in hevene'; expl: 'That for oure love maked alle thinge Amen.' 7831/9624 ll. English titles in text to all books except I; English subtitle in text and capital at the beginning of I; many English subtitles in text; Latin running titles throughout. Capitals and paragraph marks for subdivisions. Latin subtitles and topical notes in margins, especially in Book VII; occasional corrections in text. Prol: 3; I: 8v; II: 17; III: 28; IV: 43; V: 60v; VI: 95v; VII: 106; Epil: 125.

4. Text written by Stephen Doddesham, monk of the Charter-house of Sheen. Many names in 16th- and 17th-c. hands, the most important of which is John Sharrock, who certainly owned the MS in 1651 (see ff. 86v, 108, 122v) and who lent it to a Robert Hesketh (f. 16); another possible owner is John Semmer-ton from Rustorbe (Rufford?) in Lancashire, which is also the home of a John Hesketh (see ff. 12, 19v).

5. Middlesex.

6. *IMEV* 3429.11.
   List, 1838, p. 2.
   Allen, *Writings*, pp. 386 and 386, n. 2; Andreae, passim; Bül-bring, *ES*, passim; Bülbring, *Trans.*, passim; D'Evelyn, pas-sim; Morris, pp. i–iii, ii, n. 2, and variants passim; Warton-Hazlitt, pp. 240, n. 1, and 241, n. 1; Waters, passim.

7. Group A. Related to SR 1 and 10, though appears to shift SR exemplars, in Book V. Also related to SR 14 later in the text because of the alternate title 'The floure of conscience' at l. 9551.

SR 12   Oxford, Bodleian Library, Bodley 423, ff. 244–351, s. xv¹.

1. Paper, i + 415 + i ff., 272 × 195 mm. Text of *PC* written in anglicana, with Latin quotations and titles in a highly calligraphic anglicana formata. Five MSS bound together by Sir Thomas Bodley, the fourth of which (D), containing *PC*, occupies ff. 244–354v; it is bound incorrectly between ff. 262 and 267: the correct order should be: ff. 262, 264, 263, 266, 265, 267. *PC* in single columns, 36–45 ll. per page (with the number increas-ing as the text progresses). Catchwords; signatures occasionally visible.

2. *PC* followed in MS D by a series of short pieces, mainly in Latin, including notes on the numbers of various items in Eng-land, a commentary on the Decalogue, and the poem 'Vado Mori'.

3. No medieval title, text beginning imperfectly at ll. 311–12; colophon: 'Explicit Stimulus consciencie quod Johannes Appilton.' Inc: 'Quia ad tempus credit et in tempore temptacionis recedunt'; expl: 'That for oure love made alle thynge Amen quod A.' *c.* 8358/9238 ll., with two omissions: (1) probably four leaves before f. 244 containing text corresponding to MV ll. 1–310; (2) one leaf between ff. 350 and 351 containing text corresponding to MV ll. 9465–608. English titles in text to all books except III; running titles irregularly; frequent English subtitles in text. Capitals for subdivisions. Prol (begins imperfectly at ll. 311–12): 244; I: 244v; II: 251v; III: 261; IV: 271; V: 287v; VI: 315v; VII: 329; Epil: 351.

4. On f. 351, just below the colophon containing Appilton's name, is 'Iste liber Constat Domino Johanni B[. . .] Canonico ecclesie beate marie de Suthwerke' (= Southwark, Augustinian Priory of St Mary Overy). See also SR 3.

5. Perhaps Surrey or Sussex; very similar in language to SR 3.

6. *IMEV* 3429.2; *SC* 2322.
   SC, II, Part I, 308–10; for provenance see *MLGB*, pp. 180, 306.
   D'Evelyn, passim; Ritson, p. 34; Waters, passim.

7. Group A. Closely related to SR 3 in Book V.

SR 13 Oxford, Bodleian Library, Laud Miscellaneous 601, ff. 1–115v, s. xiv ex.

1. Parchment, i + 116 ff., 315 × 210 mm. *PC* written in anglicana formata. Single columns, 31 ll. per page. Catchwords. Medieval binding.

2. *PC* the only item originally in the MS; a late 15th-c. hand has added a Litany by the Cross and Blood on f. 115v (*IMEV* 3075).

3. No title; colophon: 'Heere endeþ þe bok þat is ycleped þe prikke of concience', followed by 'Scriptor qui scripcit causa

Christo uniore possit.' Inc: 'The miȝt of þe fader off hevene'; expl: 'þat for oure love made al þing Amen.' 7102/9217 ll. One omission: six leaves between ff. 49 and 50 containing text corresponding to MV ll. 3677–4083. English titles in text to all books except V, which begins imperfectly; frequent English subtitles in text. Capitals for subdivisions. Prol: 1; I: 6; II: 13v; III: 23v; IV: 36; V (begins imperfectly at l. 4083): 50; VI: 83v; VII: 94; Epil: 114.

4. On f. 116 is the name 'John Morgan' in a hand of the late 15th or early 16th c.

5. South east Gloucestershire; very similar in language to SR 1.

6. *IMEV* 3429.1; *SC* 1491; formerly Laud K.65.
Laud Cat., fasc. 1, col. 428.
Allen, *Writings*, p. 377; D'Evelyn, passim; Ritson, p. 34; Tanner, p. 375, n. q; Warton-Price, pp. 96–99 and 96, n. y; Waters, passim.

7. Group B. Related to SR 6, 8, and 16 in Book V.

SR 14 Oxford, Bodleian Library, Lyell empt. 6, ff. 1–116v, s. xv in.

1. Parchment, iii + 117 + ii ff. (end flyleaves foliated 118–19), *c.* 228 × 148 mm. Two hands, both anglicana, with Latin quotations sometimes in anglicana formata: (1) ff. 1–99, 110–15v; (2) ff. 99v–109v. Single columns, 33 ll. per page. Occasional signatures.

2. *PC* the only item in the MS except for a 15th-c. charm against the fever (eight lines of Latin prose) added on f. 117v.

3. No title; colophon: 'Here endith the tretys þat is Callyd þþe Prykke off Conciens' ('flour of conciens' at l. 9551). Inc: 'The myȝt of þe fadir of hevene'; expl: 'þþat ffor oure love made alle þynge Amen'. 7390/9546 ll. One leaf missing between ff. 5 and 6 which would have contained text corresponding to MV ll.

386–463. English titles in text to all books; a blank space intervenes between the title and the beginning of the text in each book except I. Prol: 1; I: 5v; II: 12 (text begins 12v); III: 22 (text begins 22v); IV: 34v (text begins 35); V: 52 (text begins 53); VI: 85 (text begins 86); VII: 95v (text begins 96v); Epil: 115v.

4. Many notes by former owners, of which the following are in 15th-c. hands: 'Liber iste pertinet Johanni Crosby capellano plegit pro iii s iiii d' (f. 118); 'Johannes Graunge' (ff. iii, 118); 'T plegges ffor stemulus conciencie In latyn a sequenciarie a lytyl book of a treteys of John of Burdews and a Rolle of al þe cete of Rome et aliis' (f. 118v).

5. Hand 1 is probably north west Gloucestershire; Hand 2 is too short to assess adequately but probably south central Midlands.

6. *IMEV* 3428.91, 3429.16; formerly Phillipps 2734; then Strong.

Albinia de la Mare, *Catalogue of the Collection of Medieval Manuscripts Bequeathed to the Bodleian Library Oxford by James P. R. Lyell* (Oxford: Clarendon Press, 1971), pp. 287–88.

Allen, *Writings*, pp. 385–86 and 386, n. 2; D'Evelyn, passim; M.R., p. 386a, note; Waters, passim.

7. Group B. Related to SR 9 and 18 in Book V. Also related to SR 11 later in the text because of the alternate title 'flour of conciens' at l. 9551.

SR 15   Princeton, New Jersey, Princeton University Library, Garrett 138, ff. 1–130v, s. xv in.

1. Parchment, 130 ff., 280 × 190 mm. Written in anglicana formata. Collation: 1^6 $2–16^8$ 17^4. Single columns, 30 ll. per page in text (except f. 7, which has 28). Catchwords; signatures a–q (with two sets of a's).

3. Title: 'Here bigynneþ þe boke whiche is iclepid þe prick of conscience þe whiche ys dyvised in vii parties'; colophon: 'Qui

scripsit carmen sit benedictus Amen.' Inc (at the top of f. 7): 'The myght of þe fader almy3tty'; expl: 'þat for oure love made al thyng Amen'. 7414/9624 ll. Some pages must have been out of order in the scribe's exemplar, for the text on f. 63 jumps from l. 3921 to l. 4047, continues from there to l. 4616 on f. 72 and then jumps back to l. 3922, continues from there to l. 4046 on f. 73v and then jumps ahead to l. 4619, from which point it continues as usual. English titles in text to all books; frequent English subtitles in text. Capitals for subdivisions. Occasional marginal notes, both Latin and English, especially in the first half of the MS. Some correction in text. Table of contents, for which see Morris, pp. xxxiv-xli: 1-6v; Prol: 7; I: 13; II: 21v; III: 31v; IV: 44v (text continues on f. 72r-v); V: 63 (though the beginning of the book is on f. 72v); VI: 99v; VII: 110v; Epil: 129.

5. Herefordshire.

6. *IMEV* 3429.19 ; formerly Yates; then Yates Thompson. *Census*, I, 892.
   Allen, 'Authorship', pp. 115, n. 2, and 120; Allen, *Writings*, p. 373, n. 1 ; Bülbring, *ES*, pp. 18-23 et passim; D'Evelyn, passim; Hood, p. 218; Morris, pp. ii-iii, ii-iii, n. 3, xxxiv-xli (Table of Contents), 265, and variants on 106, 139, 144, 164; Yates, pp. 314-35, esp. 319-34.

7. Conflated MS: a MV text to *c.* l. 715; a SR text thereafter, where it is Group B. Related to SR 7 and 17 in Book V. Because of its table of contents, SR 15 may be related to a subgroup of Group A (SR 2, 4, and 5), perhaps combining the individual tables of contents before books in that subgroup into a single one for the whole poem and adding it later at the beginning of the text.

SR 16 San Marino , California, Huntington Library, HM 125, ff. 1-100, s. xiv/xv.

1. Parchment, ii + 100 ff., 238 × 170 mm. Written in anglicana formata. Collation : 1^8 $2^{?8}$ (with 8 excised) 3-4^8 5^{10} 6-12^8

13$^{?6}$ (1-2 and 6 lack). Single columns, 37 ll. per page. Catch-words. f. 100 mutilated.

3. No title, and no space for one; colophon : 'Here endeþ þe pricke of concie [mutilated]', followed, in a different but con-temporary (anglicana) hand, by 'ffinem composui penite [muti-lated]'. Inc: 'þe my3t of þe fader of hevene'; expl: þat for oure love made alle þ[mutilated]'. 7338/9462 ll., with one omission: probably two leaves containing text corresponding to MV ll. 8964-9125 between ff. 97 and 98. English titles in text to all books except II; occasional running English titles and subtitles. Capitals for subdivisions. Prol: 1; I: 5; II: 11v ; III: 20; IV: 30v; V: 45v; VI: 74v; VII: 83v; Epil: 98v.

4. Possible 16th-c. owners: 'Chrystefer Byrkheade' (f. 95v), 'Thomas Jhone' (f. 73v), and 'Rycharde mynstrelley' (f. 98v).

5. Gloucestershire/Worcestershire border.

6. *IMEV* 3429.17; formerly Groves.
   Census, I, 53.
   Allen, *Writings*, pp. 539-40; Schulz, *HLQ*, p. 332; Schulz, *Library*, pp. 138-39; Waters, passim.

7. Group B. Related to SR 6, 8, and 13 in Book V. The base MS for Waters's edition of Book V of *PC*.

SR 17   San Marino, California, Huntington Library, HM 128, ff. 1-94, s. xv in.

1. Parchment, i + 219 + i ff., 240 X 168 mm. One anglicana hand in *PC* (same hand writes the first eight leaves of *Piers Plowman* and the first twenty-two lines of the *Piers Plowman* fragment), with Latin quotations in anglicana formata. One quire of eight leaves is incorrectly bound : the correct order should be ff. 1-16v, 25-32v, 17-24v, 33-94v. Single columns, 40 ll. per page. MS considerably trimmed in binding.

2. *PC* followed by a B-text of *Piers Plowman* (ff. 95-96v, 113-205) (*IMEV* 1459), Latin sequences, the alliterative *Sege of*

Jerusalem (*IMEV* 1583), and 'How the Good Wiif Tauȝte Hir Douȝtir' (*IMEV* 671, with introduction).

3. Title: 'Here bygynneþ þe prologe on the Prikke of consciencie þat ferst telleþ of goddes power'; colophon: 'Here endet þe prikke of conscience.' Inc: 'The myght of the fadur of hevene'; expl: 'that for our love maked alle þynge Amen'. 7530/9624 ll. English titles in text to all books; many subtitles in text in all books. Running Latin titles throughout. Capitals for subdivisions. Marginal rubrics in Prologue. Occasional corrections in text. Prol: 1; I: 4v; II: 10v; III: 26v; IV: 20v; V: 42v; VI: 69v; VII: 77v; Epil: 93.

4. Names of possible early owners: 'betoun brygges' and 'Maude' (ff. 149 and 153 respectively, both in same 15th-c. hand), 'Alleksander London' (f. 101, 15th/16th c.), and 'Richard Rychard' (beginning flyleaf, 16th c.).

5. South west Warwickshire.

6. *IMEV* 3429.18; formerly Ashburnham Appendix 130 (in spite of 129 on spine of MS).
Census, I, 54; see also R. B. Haselden, 'The Fragment of *Piers Plowman* in Ashburnham No. CXXX', *Modern Philology*, 29 (1932), 391-94.
Allen, *Writings*, pp. 373, n. 1, and 539-40; Schulz, *Library*, pp. 138-39; Waters, passim.

7. Group B. Related to SR 7 and 15 in Book V.

SR 18 San Marino, California, Huntington Library, HM 130, pp. 1-240, s. xiv/xv.

1. Parchment, 120 ff., 240 X 160 mm. Written in anglicana formata. Single columns, 28-35 ll. per page. Catchwords; signatures visible to p. 69. MS paginated at the bottom of every recto; foliated irregularly.

3. No title, text beginning imperfectly at l. 77 (one leaf missing, as the signature indicates); no colophon. Inc: 'Ever to knowe

boþe gode and ille'; expl: 'þat for oure love makede al þinge
Amen par charite'. *c.* 7365/9548 ll. English titles in text and
brief Latin titles in margins to all books. Capitals for sub-
divisions. Occasional source and topical notes in the margins;
some correction in text (mainly scrapings, with new readings
written over). 16th-c. printer's marks in the margins. Prol
(begins imperfectly at l. 77): 1 (f. 1); I: 8 (f. 4v); II: 22 (f.
11v); III: 42 (f. 21v); IV: 66 (f. 33v); V: 103; VI: 179; VII:
200; Epil: 237.

4. A note of ownership (*c.* 1500?) on p. 240: 'Iste liber parti-
net Willelmo Smart'; the surname appears three more times on
the same page in the same hand, once as 'W Smart groser'.
Smart became a freeman of the Company of Grocers of London
in 1495 and warden of the Company in 1509.

5. Monmouthshire.

6. *IMEV* 3428.83; formerly Phillipps 3126.
   Census, I, 54-55; see also Schulz, *HLQ,* and Schulz, *Library.*
   Allen, *Writings,* pp. 373, n. 1, and 539-40; Jean F. Preston,
   'The Pricke of Conscience Parts I-III and Its First Appear-
   ance in Print' (unpublished paper, forthcoming); Schulz,
   HLQ, passim; Schulz, *Library,* passim; Waters, passim.

7. Group B. Related to SR 9 and 14 in Book V, though cor-
rected from a manuscript of a different tradition. The first 103
pages of SR 18 were used as printer's copy for *A Newe Treatyse*
attributed to Myles Hogarde and printed by Robert Wyer *c.*
1542-43 (Books I-III of *PC*) and the anonymous *Boke of Pur-
gatorye* printed by Robert Wyer *c.* 1532-33 (Book IV of *PC*).
See, respectively, items 24228 and 3360 in A. W. Pollard and
G. R. Redgrave, *A Short-Title Catalogue of Books Printed in
England, Scotland, & Ireland and of English Books Printed
Abroad 1475-1640,* II, 2nd ed. (London: The Bibliographical
Society, 1976) and I (London: The Bibliographical Society,
1926).

III
Extracts

E 1   Cambridge, Trinity College, 0.2.40 (1144), ff. 104–05, 119r–v, s. xv ex.

1. Paper and parchment, i + 170 ff., *c.* 209 × 114 mm. Same anglicana hand for all three extracts.

2. Extracts from *PC* appear as part of a series of miscellaneous items in both English and Latin, including astronomical tables, diagrams, and extracts; the MS also contains Sacrobosco's *De Sphera Mundi, Secreta Philosophorum*, and other items, primarily astronomical.

3. Extract 1: f. 104r–v contains ll. 3446–99 (with no lines missing) entitled 'Sepcies in die cadit justus [= *PC* 3423] Perab 24° Augustinus de peccatis venialibus'; no colophon. Inc: 'Fyrst whan a man or a woman drynkes more'; expl: 'And yche a syn ys worthy payn.' The extract begins at the very top of f. 104 and ends at the very bottom of f. 104v. 27 ll. (including the Latin title) on f. 104, 28 ll. on f. 104v.
Extract 2: f. 105 contains ll. 3398–423 (with no lines missing) entitled 'Decem remedia contra peccata venialia ut patebit inferus'; no colophon. Inc: 'We fynde wryttyn X thynges sere'; expl: 'May make a dedly syn alle.' The extract begins at the very top of f. 105 and ends at the very bottom, with an entirely different piece at the top of f. 105v entitled 'De primo domo dicit Tholomeus.' 26 ll. (including the Latin title).
Extract 3: f. 119r–v contains ll. 7625–734 (with much condensation and rearrangement of lines); no title and no colophon. Inc: 'Phylysores and clarkes of planetes alle'; expl: 'For in here circul abowte thay go.' The extract begins at the very top of f. 119 and continues to the bottom of the page (25 ll.); it begins again at the very top of f. 119v and ends approximately four fifths of the way down the page (22 ll.). The rest of the page is blank; an extra leaf has been inserted between ff. 119 and 120 with some Latin on both recto and verso; f. 120 is blank, but some astronomical tables appear on f. 120v.

4. Apparently belonged to William Wymondham, Canon of the Augustinian Priory of St Peter at Kirby Bellars, Leicestershire; his name often appears in the MS, including f. 105v. The date on ff. 147v–48 and 159v–60 is 1482/3.

5. North east Leicestershire.

6. *IMEV* 806, 3866, 2753 respectively for the three extracts. Derek Britton, 'Manuscripts Associated with Kirby Bellars Priory', *Transactions of the Cambridge Bibliographical Society*, 6 (1976), 267-70, 277-81; M. R. James, *The Western Manuscripts in the Library of Trinity College, Cambridge: A Descriptive Catalogue*, III (Cambridge: Cambridge University Press, 1902), 142-44.
Britton (as above), pp. 279, 280; Britton, passim; Lewis, 'Editorial', n. 16; Henry Axel Person, ed., *Cambridge Middle English Lyrics*, rev. ed. (Seattle: University of Washington Press, 1962), pp. 22-23 (Extract 1) and 23-24 (Extract 2).

7. MV Group II for Extracts 1 and 2, which are most closely related to MV 42 and 69; MV Group I for Extract 3, perhaps related to MV 34. Extract 3 is on the same subject as *IMEV* 1907.5 and 2794, the latter of which has some of the same lines from *PC*.

E 2 Cambridge, University Library, Dd.5.55, f. 101v, *c.* 1400.

1. Parchment, iv + 93 (out of 102; 81-89 lost) + ii ff., 210 X 140 mm. Extract written in textura. Single columns, 28 ll. per page. Catchwords; signatures usually visible.

2. In addition to the extract from *PC*, the MS contains Walter Hilton's *Scale of Perfection* (Book I), Richard Rolle's *Commandment*, 'Propyr wille þat is forsakyn', Hilton's *Treatise of the Song of Angels*, a *Treatise on Deadly Sin* (also in E 3), and sentences from Bonaventure, Bernard, and Rolle printed in Horstman, I, 129-31 (also in E 8).

3. An extract of 28 ll. identical to that in E 3 and 8, containing the following: 6071-74, 6077-78, 6081-82, 6085-88, 6097-99

(+ 1 line), 6100-5, 6108-13, with two lines of verse written consecutively as a single line. No title and no colophon. Inc: 'þay þat withouten lawe dos synne' (l. 6071); expl: 'þe day of parthynge fra god for aye' (l. 6113). There is a space of approximately two lines between the end of the preceding item and the beginning of the extract, which itself begins with a three-line capital þ.

5. Fully northern.

6. *IMEV* 3561.2.
   CUL Cat., I, 275-76; Pink.
   Doyle, 'Survey', II, 116-17; Horstman, I, 129; Lewis, 'Editorial', p. 52.

7. Taken from a MV text. Probably copied from E 8 (or its exemplar).

E 3 Cambridge, University Library, Ff.5.40, ff. 113v-114, s. xv¹.

1. Parchment, i + 130 (out of 146; 1-16 lost) + v ff., c. 222 X c. 152 mm. Extract written in anglicana formata. Single columns, 29-30 ll. per page. Catchwords and signatures.

2. In addition to the extract from *PC*, the MS contains Walter Hilton's *Epistle on the Mixed Life*, Richard Rolle's *Emendatio Vite*, Hilton's *Scale of Perfection* (Book I), 'Propyr wyl þat is forsaken', Hilton's *Treatise of the Song of Angels*, a *Treatise on Deadly Sin* (also in E 2), Rolle's *Form of Living*, and a series of short prose treatises printed in Horstman, I, 104-28 (also in E 8).

3. An extract of 28 ll. identical to that in E 2 and 8, with two lines of verse written consecutively as a single line. No title and no colophon. Inc: 'þei þat wiþoute lawe don synne' (l. 6071); expl: 'þe day of partyng from god for ay' (l. 6113), followed by 'Mortis vel vite brevis est vox venite / Aspera vox ite vox est jocunda venite' (as in E 8), for which see Hans Walther, *Carmina Medii Aevi Posterioris Latina*, II: *Proverbia Sententiaeque Latinitatis Medii Aevi*, 2 (Göttingen: Vandenhoeck & Ruprecht, 1964),

item 15266, a very popular proverb in the Middle Ages, with many variations. The extract begins with a two-line capital *þ*, but is not set off by spaces from either the preceding or the following item.

5. Norfolk.

6. *IMEV* 3561.3.
   CUL Cat., II, 498–500; Pink.
   Doyle, 'Survey', II, 116–17; Lewis, 'Editorial', p. 52.

7. Taken from a MV text. Probably copied from E 8 (or its exemplar).

E 4 Lincoln, Cathedral, 91 (A.5.2), ff. 276va–277a, *c.* 1430–50

1. Paper, 321 ff. (out of *c.* 335 ff. originally), *c.* 291 × *c.* 210 mm. A carelessly formed anglicana script. Double columns on f. 276v (40 ll. in the first, 43 in the second); a single column of 28 ll. on f. 277. Catchwords.

2. Sixty-four separate items in the MS, in English, including a number of romances—the prose *Life of Alexander*, the alliterative *Morte Arthure* (*IMEV* 2322), *Octavian* (*IMEV* 1918), *Sir Isumbras* (*IMEV* 1184), *Sir Degrevant* (*IMEV* 1953), *Syr Egyllamore of Artas* (*IMEV* 1725), etc.; various religious pieces; a number of Richard Rolle's works; Edmund of Abingdon's *Speculum Ecclesie*; the *Abbey of the Holy Ghost*; and the *Liber de Diversis Medicinis*.

3. An extract of 111 ll. corresponding to ll. 438–551. No title and no colophon. Inc: 'The begynnyng es of thre' (l. 438); expl: 'ffulle of caytefte and of care' (l. 551). The extract begins at the very top of. f. 276va with a four-line capital *T*, continues on f. 276vb, and ends two thirds of the way down f. 277a; the rest of f. 277 is blank except for an alphabet running down the centre. The text is quite different from that in Morris in wording and rhymes, but only three lines are omitted: 472–73 and 501.

4. The MS was written and owned by a Robert Thornton who probably lived in East Newton in the North Riding of Yorkshire, was lord of the manor there in 1418, was still alive in 1456 but dead by 1465. Many other Thornton names in the MS as well as the placenames Ryedale and Oswaldkirk, both in the North Riding.

5. Fully northern.

6. *IMEV* 3428 Extra Passage F; the Thornton MS.

The *Thornton Manuscript (Lincoln Cathedral MS. 91)*, 2nd ed. (London: The Scolar Press, 1977), pp. vii-xx (superseding the description published in 1927 by Reginald Maxwell Woolley).

Allen, 'Authorship', pp. 119, n. 3, and 137, n. 1; Allen, *Writings*, p. 384; Britton, p. 334, n. 18; George R. Keiser, 'Lincoln Cathedral Library MS. 91: Life and Milieu of the Scribe', *Studies in Bibliography*, 32 (1979), 170; Lewis, 'Editorial', p. 52 and n. 16; *The Thornton Manuscript* (as above), ff. 276va-77a (facsimile).

7. Text similar to that in MV 21.

E 5 London, British Library, Royal 17 C.xvii, ff. 117-124, s. xv in.

1. Paper, iii + 159 + iv ff. (with MS proper foliated 4-162 and 10th-c. parchment flyleaves foliated 1-3 and 163-66), 210 X 140 mm. Text of *PC* extract written in anglicana formata, with Latin quotations in textura (though tending towards bastard anglicana as the extract progresses); double columns, 33-42 ll. per column. Catchwords.

2. Twenty-four separate items in the MS, primarily grammatical pieces and religious verse and prose in Middle English (with some Latin), including Myrc's *Instructions for Parish Priests*, Richard Maydestone's version of the Seven Penitential Psalms (*IMEV* 1961), lives of St Mary Magdalene (*IMEV* 2994) and St Anthony, and The Legend of the Blood of Hayles (*IMEV* 3153).

3. An extract containing nearly the whole of Book IV, lacking only the last 158 ll., with 1106 out of a possible 1116 ll. No title and no colophon. Inc: 'Many speke in bokys and redes' (l. 2692); expl: 'þat as bene purchesyd here worthely' (l. 3807), followed at the very bottom of f. 124 by 'And so mot it be Amen for charite.' The extract begins with a three-line capital *M* at the very top of f. 117. Capitals for subdivisions.

4. From the contents the MS would appear to be a priest's handbook, and because it contains a unique copy of The Legend of the Blood of Hayles, it may have connections with Hailes Abbey in Gloucestershire. On f. 1 are two 16th-c. names: 'Samuell Compton' and 'Ch Kirten'.

5. North west Lincolnshire.

6. *IMEV* 3428 Extra Passage A.
   Royal Cat., II, 243a–45b.

7. Probably taken from a MS of MV Group III.

E 6 London, British Library, Additional 36983, ff. 159–174v, s. xv[1].

1. Paper, iii + 305 + i ff., 286 × 216 mm. ff. 3–178v in one anglicana hand, with influence from secretary. Double columns in *PC* except on f. 174v, which has a single column; 31–37 ll. per column. Catchwords. The date 1442 appears in a colophon on f. 215v, but the hand is probably later than that on ff. 3–178v.

2. Nineteen separate items in the MS, all in English verse except two (the *Abbey of the Holy Ghost* and the *Charter of the Abbey of the Holy Ghost*), including the *Cursor Mundi* (*IMEV* 2153), *Ipotis* (*IMEV* 220), the *Speculum Gy de Warewyke* (*IMEV* 1101), William Lychefelde's 'Complaint of God' (*IMEV* 2714), and 'The Myrrour of Mankind' (*IMEV* 1259).

3. An extract containing nearly the whole of Book V inserted (without indication except for a paragraph mark at the first

line) into the *Cursor Mundi* between l. 22004 and a ten-line epi-
logue, with 2095 out of a possible 2323 ll. No title and no colo-
phon. Inc: 'Some clerkis Say þat one schal come' (l. 4085);
expl: 'Afftir þe Dome now mad schalle be' (l. 6407). Capitals
and paragraph marks for subdivisions.

5. Probably Bedfordshire.

6. *IMEV* 3428 Extra Passage B.
Additional Cat. 1907, pp. 265-69.
Allen, 'Authorship', p. 123, n. 4.

**E 7 London, British Library, Additional 37049, ff. 36, 69, 72,
s. xv[1].**

1. Paper and parchment (ff. 1-2 only), i + 96 + i ff., 273 × 203
mm. Many hands (at least four) in the MS; the extracts from *PC*
perhaps in two different hands: (1) f. 36, anglicana formata; (2)
ff. 69 and 72, anglicana. Single columns for the three extracts.
Vivid illustrations throughout.

2. Seventy-one separate items in the MS, including *Mandeville's
Travels*, extracts from English prose chronicles, 'The Desert of
Religion' (*IMEV* 672), and many short religious pieces, of a
miscellaneous nature, in both verse and prose (primarily English,
with a bit of Latin). One of the most important extant Middle
English religious miscellanies.

3. Extract 1: f. 36 contains 47 ll. from *PC* in the following
order: 1370-73, 1090-95, 1096-98 (?), 1178-81 (?), 1532-39,
1542-49, 1592-93, 1598-1603, 1584-85, 1632-34 (?), 1586-
87. No title and no colophon. Inc: 'Apostolus dicit Civitatem
hic manentem non habemus sed futuram inquirimus'; expl:
'þat þai go not to payne withouten ende.' In the margin is the
Vado Mori device, with three figures (a king, an archbishop, and
a knight) each talking to Death.
  Extract 2: f. 69 contains 47 ll. from *PC* in the following
order: 2656-67, 1818-29, 1930-31, 1934-40, 2668-81. No
title and no colophon. Inc: 'In omnibus operibus tuis memorare

novissima tua et in eternum non peccabis'; expl: 'Where ever is day and never nyght.' In the margin the prophet (?) of l. 1930, Jesus son of Sirach from Ecclesiasticus, is standing on Death's neck.

Extract 3: f. 72 contains 56 ll., the first 48 of which are from *PC* in the following order: 933–41, 954–59, paraphrase of 940–47 (?), paraphrase of 978–79 (?), 1213–44; it is uncertain from what part of *PC* ll. 49–56 come, if in fact they come from *PC* at all. No title and no colophon. Inc: 'Alle þe warld wyde and brade'; expl (l. 55, since only the tops of the letters in l. 56 remain): 'In to þis wretchyd warld [. . .] se.'

4. Hope Emily Allen (*Writings*, p. 307) was apparently the first to suggest that the scribe of the MS was a Carthusian, probably from a house in the north of England, perhaps Mount Grace in Yorkshire, and others have followed her in the Carthusian attribution.

5. East Nottinghamshire.

6. *IMEV* 3428 Extra Passages C, D, and E.

> *Additional Cat. 1907*, pp. 324–32; Allen, *Writings*, pp. 306–11; James Hogg, 'Unpublished Texts in the Carthusian Northern Middle English Religious Miscellany British Library MS. Add. 37049', in *Essays in Honour of Erwin Stürzl on His Sixtieth Birthday*, ed. James Hogg, Salzburger Studien zur Anglistik und Amerikanistik (Salsburg: Institut für englische Sprache und Literatur Universität Salzburg, 1980), I, 241–58; Thomas W. Ross, 'Five Fifteenth-Century "Emblem" Verses from Brit. Mus. Addit. MS. 37049', *Speculum*, 32 (1957), 274–75.

> Hogg (as above), pp. 266–67 (Extract 2) and 271–72 (Extract 3); James Hogg, ed., *An Illustrated Yorkshire Carthusian Religious Miscellany British Library London Additional MS. 37049*, Volume 3: *The Illustrations*, Analecta Carthusiana, 95 (Salzburg: Institüt für Anglistik und Amerikanistik Universität Salzburg, 1981), 49, 109 (facsimiles of ff. 36, 69); Lewis, 'Editorial', n. 16.

7. Extracts 2 and 3 are almost certainly taken from a MV text; Extract 1 is much more paraphrastic, but it too is probably taken from a MV text.

E 8 Oxford, Bodleian Library, Rawlinson C.285, f. 39, s. xv[1].

1. Parchment, i (fragment) + 118 ff., 217 X 155 mm. Extract from *PC* written in anglicana, in double columns, 14 ll. per column. Original medieval binding.

2. In addition to the extract from *PC*, the MS contains Walter Hilton's *Scale of Perfection* (Books I and II), sentences from Bonaventure, Bernard, and Rolle (also in E 2), Rolle's *Form of Living*, various meditations, and other religious pieces.

3. An extract of 28 ll. identical to that in E 2 and 3, with two lines of verse written consecutively across the two columns. No title and no colophon. Inc: 'þai þat withoutene lawe dos syne' (l. 6071); expl: 'þe day of partyng fra god for ay' (l. 6113), followed in column a by 'Mortis vel vite brevis est vox ite venite / Aspera vox ite vox est jocunda venite' (as in E 3) and in column b by 'Deo gracias Jesus maria Johannes.' There is a space of approximately two lines between the end of the preceding item and the beginning of the extract, which itself begins with a two-line capital þ.

4. Probably from Yorkshire because of the inscription '[O]biit dominus jo*h*annes marchal' on f. i verso; this was a common name among secular priests in Yorkshire in the 15th c.

5. Fully northern.

6. *IMEV* 3561.1; *SC* 12143.
   Rawlinson Cat., fasc. 2, cols. 123–24; see also Doyle, 'Survey', II, 115.
   Doyle, 'Survey', II, 116–17; Horstman, I, 129; Lewis, 'Editorial', p. 52.

7. Taken from a MV text. E 2 and 3 probably copied from E 8 (or its exemplar).

IV
The *Speculum Huius Vite*

S 1 Dublin, Trinity College, 155 (C.5.7), pp. 149-238, s. xv in.

1. Parchment, 119 ff., 156 X 120 mm. MS written in several early 15th-c. hands; *Speculum* written in textura throughout. Single columns, 24-31 ll. per page in the *Speculum*, with the number decreasing as the poem progresses. MS paginated rather than foliated. Probably two lines cut off from the tops of pp. 237-38.

2. In addition to the *Speculum*, the MS contains works by Richard Rolle (*Ego Dormio, Form of Living, Oleum Effusum* in English), religious verse (*IMEV* 1700, 1717, 1743, 3238, 4056), two English treatises on charity, Thomas de Wilton's *Tractatus de Oratione Dominica*, an English *Commentary on the Two Commandments of the New Law*, and Thomas Wimbledon's sermon *Redde Racionem*.

3. Title: 'speculum huius vite'; no colophon, text ending imperfectly at l. 6966. Inc: 'Byfore þat any creature was wrouȝt'; expl: '[. . .] ignem et vermes in [. . .]'. *c.* 2542 ll. in the extant text. Latin titles in text to Books II, III, and IV; English titles in text to V and VII. Capitals for subdivisions. Some source and other notes in margins; some corrections, both marginal and interlinear. Prol: 149; I: 156; II: 170; III: 179; IV: 188; V: 199; VI: 229.

4. Belonged to John Mascy in the 15th c. (see especially pp. 28-29); other names in late 15th-c. or early 16th-c. hands: John Heghseed, John Thomas.

5. South west Derbyshire.

6. *IMEV* 484.2.
   Abbott, p. 20; E. P. Wilson, 'A Critical Text, with Commentary,

of MS. English Theology f. 39 in the Bodleian Library'
(B.Litt. Thesis, University of Oxford, 1968), II, 59-60.
Allen, 'Authorship', p. 126; Allen, *Writings*, pp. 386-87 and
387, n. 1; Andreae, p. 23; Bülbring, *ES*, pp. 2-6 passim;
Bülbring, *Trans*., passim.

7. The *Speculum* is closely related to, and probably made from,
the version contained in, MV 11 and 14.

S 2 Oxford, Bodleian Library, Additional A. 268, ff. 117a-139b,
s. xv in.

1. Paper, ii + 162 + ii ff., *c.* 205 X 150 mm. Three manuscripts
bound together, the third of which contains the *Speculum*. Text
of the *Speculum* written in anglicana, with Latin quotations in
textura; double columns, 31-39 ll. per column. Catchwords.

2. Contents of the third MS, in addition to the *Speculum*: The
Virtues of the Mass (*IMEV* 3268), an Invocation to the Creator
(*IMEV* 256), and a prayer to the Blessed Virgin (*IMEV* 2104),
with some English medical receipts at the end.

3. Title: 'Speculum huius vite'; colophon: 'Explicit.' Inc: '[B]E
fore þat any creature wos wroȝt'; expl: 'To þe quych joy he us
bryng / þat made heven and erth and alle thyng amen' (prob-
ably a version of ll. 9531-32 because of what immediately pre-
cedes, but cf. the last two lines of the SR). *c.* 3096 ll. in the
text. Latin titles in margins to Books II and IV, in text to V and
VI; English titles in top margins to III and V, in text to VII.
Paragraph marks for subdivisions. Some Latin source and occa-
sional other notes in the margins. Prol: 117a; I: 118vb; II:
121vb; III: 123vb; IV: 125vb; V: 128a; VI: 133vb; VII: 136b.

4. A late 15th-c. hand on f. 36v notes that a Gylbart Barton
bought the MS from a bookseller named Thomas for twenty
denarii.

5. South Lancashire.

6. *IME V* 484.1; *SC* 29387.
   SC, V, 610-11.
   Allen, *Writings*, pp. 386-87 and 387, n. 1.

7. The *Speculum* is closely related to, and probably made from, the version contained in MV 11 and 14.

V

The Latin Translation

L 1 Cambridge, Magdalene College, F.4.14 (14), ff. 14–31v, s. xv[1].

1. Parchment, 129 ff., 249 × 178 mm. Four MSS bound together, the· first of which contains the *Stimulus Consciencie*, which is written in anglicana with some secretary features. Single columns, 35–38 ll. per page in *Stimulus*. Catchwords; signatures occasionally visible.

2. Contents ·(all in Latin) of the first MS, in addition to the *Stimulus*: a *cartula* containing fourteen articles to be observed by lay people, Pseudo-Bernard's *Meditaciones*, and the *Visio de Spiritu Guidonis*.

3. No title; colophon: 'Explicit tractatus qui vocatur stimulus consciencie qui ab anglico translatus est in latinum Si quis ergo sapiens in illo aliquos repereat defectus deprecor ut eos corrigat et translatori imponat et cetera.' Inc: 'Ab eterno et ante tempora fuit deus semper trinus in personis et unus in substancia et essencia'; expl: 'plenum est prorsus omnis suavitatis videre hominem hominis conditorem propter cohabitacionem tam jocunde societatis ad quam societatem nos perducat qui sine fine vivit et regnat Amen'. Titles in text to all books; subtitles in text in Book IV. Paragraph marks for subdivisions throughout; capitals for subdivisions in Books III and IV. Occasional corrections in text. Prol: 14; I: 14v; II: 16; III: 18; IV: 21; V: 24v; VI: 30v; VII: 31.

6. Not in *IME V*.
   Magdalene Cat., pp. 37–40.
   Allen, 'Two', pp. 744–45; Allen, *Writings*, p. 376.

L 2 Cambridge, Pembroke College, 273, ff. 1a–29vb, s. xiv ex.

1. Parchment, iv + 86 ff., 208 × 152 mm. Written basically in anglicana formata. Double columns, 36–38 ll. per column in *Stimulus*. Catchwords.

2. *Stimulus* followed by Gregory's *Cura Pastoralis*.

3. Title: 'Iste tractatus vocatur stimulus consciencie qui ab Anglico in latinum a minus sciolo est translatus Si quis igitur sapiens in illo aliquos reperiat defectus deprecor ut eos corrigat mente pia et tnsactori [*sic*] imponat'; colophon: 'cum Christus apparuit / explicit finis libri'. *Inc*: 'Ab eterno et ante tempora fuit deus semper domini trinus in personis et unus in substancia et essencia'; expl: 'Ecce quam jocundum habitare fratres in unum ipso prestante qui vivit et regnat in secula seculorum amen.' Titles in text to Prologue and all books except III; also titles in margins to V–VII; colophon in text to II. Running titles to all books. Subtitles in text to Book IV; capitals for subdivisions in Books IV and VII. Both source and topical notes in margins throughout, primarily in the hand of the text but also in a later but still medieval hand; occasional corrections, both in text and in margin. Prol: 1a; I: 1vb; II: 3vb; III: 6vb; IV: 10vb; V: 15va; VI: 23va; VII: 25b.

6. Not in *IMEV*; Pembroke Hall.
   Pembroke Cat., pp. 248–49.
   Allen, 'Authorship', p. 116, n. 2 from p. 115; Allen, 'Two',
   pp. 744–45; Allen, *Writings*, p. 376; Ritson, p. 37, Waters,
   p. 4.

L 3 Cambridge, University Library, Dd.4.50, ff. 57–99, s. xv[1].

1. Paper, 136 ff. (out of 142; 33, 113, 116, 130, 133, 139 lost), *c.* 220 × *c.* 148 mm. Written in anglicana. Single columns, 26–35 ll. per page in *Stimulus*. Catchwords irregularly.

2. In addition to the *Stimulus*, the MS contains a number of sermons, a treatise on confession and absolution, *De Officio Sacer-*

dotis, two works by Richard Rolle (*Super Orationem Domini-cam* and *Super Symbolum Apostolorum*), and miscellaneous notes on various topics perhaps for the use of a preacher.

3. Title: 'Iste tractatus vocatur stimulus consciencie qui ab anglico in latinum a minus sciolo est translatus si quis igitur sapiens in illo aliquos repereat defectus deprecor ut eos corigat mente pia et transactori imponat'; colophon: 'Explicit finis cuiusdam libelli qui vocatur stimulus consciencie.' Inc: '[A]b eterno et ante tempora fuit deus semper domini trinus in personis et unus in substancia et essencia'; expl: 'Ecce quam jocundum fratres in unum ipso prestante qui vivit et regnat in secula seculorum amen.' Titles in text to Prologue and all books except III; also titles in margins to II, V, and VI; colophon in text to II. Subtitles in both text and margins to Book IV; spaces left for capitals in Books IV and VII. Source and other notes in margins, including some long ones in the bottom margins; occasional corrections in text. f. 74r-v appears not to be part of the *Stimulus*: a new hand begins writing about priests in the bottom margin of f. 73v and continues to f. 74v; the text of the *Stimulus* that leaves off at the bottom of f. 73v continues at the top of f. 75. Prol: 57; I: 58; II: 60v; III: 65; IV: 70v; V: 78v; VI: 91; VII: 93v.

6. Not in *IMEV*.
   CUL Cat., I, 243-5; unpublished description by M. R. James at the Cambridge University Library.
   Allen, 'Authorship', p. 116, n. 2 from p. 115; Allen, *Writings*, p. 376; Horstman, II, xli, n. 1.

L 4 London, British Library, Harley 106, ff. 138va-vb, 344 vb, s. xv[1].

1. Parchment, i + 374 ff. (foliated 1*-5*, 1-369), 260-70 × 180-90 mm. Same anglicana hand for both extracts.

2. 157 items in all, primarily extracts, in Latin, from a variety of religious writings, including ones by Augustine, Gregory, Anselm, Bernard, Bonaventure, Hugh of St Victor, Edmund of

Abingdon, Robert Grosseteste, Robert Holkot, Richard Rolle, and John Bromyard.

3. Extract 1: f. 138va–vb contains 62 ll. (19 in column a, 43 in column b) entitled 'In tractatu qui intitulatur stimulus consciencie'; no colophon. Inc: 'Timenda est mors propter quatuor primo propter amaritudinem pene unde Christus naturaliter secundum suam humilitatem tamen timuet mortem'; expl: 'sensibilitas et passibilitas est ex parte anime unde anime penam sencient quesito in corporibus'. A condensation and paraphrase of passages from Book III of the *Stimulus Consciencie* as found in the other Latin MSS (cf. the English text in Morris's edition, ll. 1818–2681).

Extract 2: f. 344vb contains 6 ll. entitled 'Stimulus consciencie' (inserted in the middle of the first line of text); no colophon. Inc: 'Nota quod sicut aurem quod clare splendet et purum apparet si in ignem ponatur'; expl: 'ignis in eis aliam reperiet maculum peccati quam pugnabit'. A passage from Book IV of the *Stimulus* as found in the other Latin MSS (cf. the English text in Morris's edition, ll. 3336–48). This passage is followed by a paragraph of 23 ll. that may be a paraphrase of passages from Books V and VI of the *Stimulus* as found in the other Latin MSS (cf. the English text in Morris's edition, ll. 5064–240 and 7117–18).

4. Owned by Sir Simonds D'Ewes (1602–50).

6. Not in *IME V.*
   Harley Cat., I, 31b–34a.
   Allen, 'Authorship', pp. 120, 125; Allen, *Writings*, p. 376; Andreae, p. 5; Morris, pp. i, ii, and ii, n. 2 (the last a mistake for either Harley 1205 or Harley 2281?); Yates, p. 335.

L 5 Oxford, Bodleian Library, Bodley 159, ff. 161a–179a, s. xv in.

1. Parchment, vi + 312 ff., *c.* 310 × *c.* 220 mm. Four MSS bound together, the first of which (of the early 15th c.) contains the *Stimulus*, in anglicana with some secretary features. Double

columns, 43–54 ll. per column for the *Stimulus*. Catchwords and signatures in the first MS. 15th-c. English binding.

2. Contents of the first MS, in addition to the *Stimulus*: sermons by or attributed to Augustine, the treatise *De Salutaribus Documentis* probably by Paulinus the Patriarch of Aquileia, an extract from one of Seneca's letters, *De Tribus Habitaculis*, extracts from Jerome's letters, and an extract from the same author's *Rescriptio de Cessatione Legalium*.

3. Title: 'Incipit prohemium libri nuncupati stimulus consciencie / Quantum deus dilexit naturam humanam et que beneficia dedit ei'; colophon: 'Explicit tractatus qui dicitur stimulus consciencie.' Inc: 'Ab eterno et ante tempora fuit deus semper trinus in personis et unus in substancia et essencia'; expl: 'Ecce quam bonum et quam jocundum habitare fratres in unum ipso prestante qui vivit et regnat in secula seculorum Amen.' Titles in text to all books; subtitles in text and chapter numbers and subtitles in margins to all books. Running titles at tops of rectos throughout. Capitals for subdivisions. All books are divided into chapters, unlike the other Latin MSS, and each book (except the Prologue) has a table of contents preceding it. Source and topical notes in margins; some corrections, both in text and in margins. Prol: 161a; I: 161va; II: 162va; III: 164va; IV: 167a; V: 170a; VI: 175b; VII: 176b.

4. Owned by a John Lyndon in the 15th c. (ff. i verso, 257), and earlier by a Master Richard (f. 257, bottom, under ultraviolet light). Lyndon, who also wrote the table of contents to the MS on f. i verso, was Dean of the Collegiate Church of Holy Cross at Crediton in Devon (f. 257, bottom).

6. Not in *IMEV*; *SC* 2009; formerly NE B. 4. 2.
   SC, II, Part I, 160–61; for provenance see *The Bodleian Library Record*, 2, no. 22 (April 1944), 91–92, and *MLGB*, pp. 55, 250.
   Allen, *Writings*, p. 376; Tanner, p. 375, n. q.

7. Because of omissions at the beginnings of Books IV and V, L 5 cannot be the exemplar of L 1, 2, 3, or 6.

168

L 6 Oxford, Merton College, 68, ff. 74vb–88va, s. xv med.

1. Parchment, vii + 302 + iv ff. (beginning flyleaves v–vii are medieval), 360 × 270 mm. *Stimulus* written in a university book hand (a blend of anglicana and secretary). Double columns, 47–51 ll. per column. Catchword on f. 84v in *Stimulus.*

2. Twenty-four separate items in the MS, in Latin, on a variety of topics, primarily religious, including works by Bonaventure, Thomas Palmer, Robert Alyngton, Thomas Aquinas, Robert Grosseteste, Richard Rolle, John Eyton, William Butler, and John Waldby.

3. No title, though 'Stimulus conscience hampole' is in the table of contents on f. v verso and 'Hampole' is in the top margin of f. 74vb; colophon: 'Explicit tractatus qui vocatur stimulus consciencie secundum hampole.' Inc: 'Ab eterno et ante tempora fuit deus semper idem trinus in personis et unus in substancia et essencia'; expl: 'Ad quod gaudium nos pervenire concedat qui sine fine vivit et regnat in secula seculorum Amen.' Titles in text to all books; subtitles in text to chapters in Book IV. Paragraph marks for subdivisions throughout; capitals for subdivisions in Book IV. Occasional notes in margins; many corrections in margins. Prol: 74va; I: 75a; II: 76a; III: 77b; IV: 79b; V: 81vb; VI: 86a; VII: 87a.

4. MS given to Merton in 1468 by Robert Wyght, fellow of Merton (inscription of ownership barely visible at top of f. v verso).

6. Not in *IMEV*.
   Coxe, I, Part 3, 41–43; F. M. Powicke, *The Medieval Books of Merton College* (Oxford: Clarendon Press, 1931), pp. 206–07, item 971.
   Allen, 'Authorship', p. 121; Allen, *Writings*, p. 376; Bale, p. 348; Oudin, col. 928; Pits, p. 466; Tanner, p. 375, n. q; Waters, p. 2.

7. Because of an omission at the beginning of Book VII, L 6 cannot be the exemplar of L 1, 2, 3, or 5.

APPENDIX

Maps Showing the Dialectal Distribution of the Scribes of the English Texts

General

(a) Counties are presented and named as they were before the Local Government Act of 1974. The Isle of Ely, which was already part of Cambridgeshire, is named separately.

(b) The small number following the main guide number in some entries (e.g., 5_3) refers to the particular hand (of a given text) in question. The small letter following the main number in some entries (e.g., 65b) refers to the kind of language encountered in the part of the text in question; the letters carry no implication of the text being in two or more hands. The details of such variations within single texts are given in the guide itself.

(c) For some remarks on the degree of accuracy implied by the position of the entries, see the introduction (section ii), pp. 21-22.

Map i

(a) This attempts to indicate the distribution of a large number of Main Version texts (designated simply by numbers), of the two texts of the *Speculum Huius Vite* (numbers preceded by S), and of the eight extracts (numbers preceded by E). The S and E texts are presented on the same map as those of the MV because the *Speculum* appears to have been derived from MV Group I and the extracts are all clearly from the MV.

(b) When two entries on the map are enclosed within a single rectangle, as in 70 (and) 40 or 5_1 (and) 5_2, the texts referred to are believed to have the same provenance.

(c) The line through Yorkshire separates the 'fully northern' area from the rest of the country. The sixteen texts believed to belong north of this line are inset in a single group: no attempt has been made to place them more narrowly than 'from somewhere within the fully northern area'. The same procedure has been adopted for the three texts of Irish provenance. The five texts from in or near Lichfield have been similarly inset for reasons of space.

(d) Not entered on the map, for reasons given in the introduction (section ii), pp. 20-21, are MV 1, 2, 10, 13, 14, 17, 26, 32, 39_1, 51, 52, 55, 58, 68, 69a, 74, 77, 78_1, 78_2, 79, 80, 84, 87, 97.

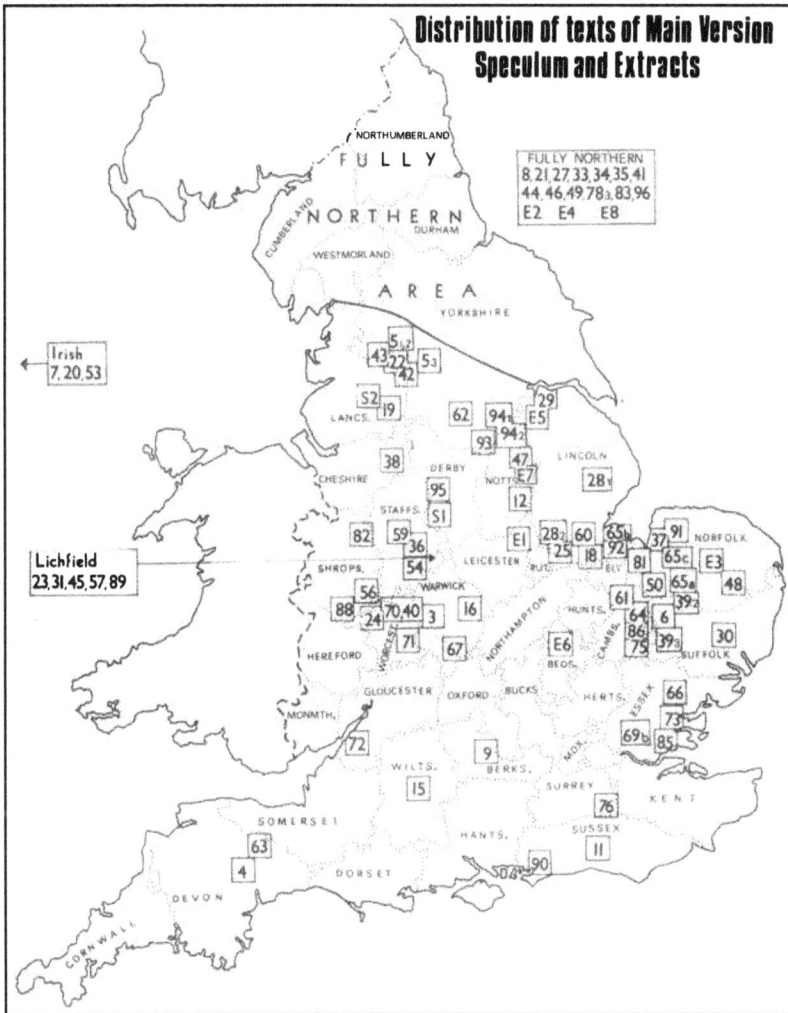

Distribution of texts of Main Version Speculum and Extracts

NORTHUMBERLAND

FULLY

NORTHERN
DURHAM

CUMBERLAND

WESTMORLAND

AREA
YORKSHIRE

FULLY NORTHERN
8, 21, 27, 33, 34, 35, 41
44, 46, 49, 78₃, 83, 96
E2   E4   E8

Irish
7, 20, 53

Lichfield
23, 31, 45, 57, 89

Map i

Map ii

(a) This attempts to indicate the distribution of Southern Recension texts only.
(b) The line marks the limits of the area within which fourteen of these texts fall. The remainder, less easy to localize, have nevertheless characteristics which suggest that they too fall within the same area; see introduction (section ii), p. 22.
(c) The linked circles for 1 and 13 imply that these two texts are believed to have the same provenance.
(d) Not entered on the map are SR 3, 6, 10, 12, 14_2.

Distribution of texts of the
Southern Recension

Map ii

www.ingramcontent.com/pod-product-compliance
Lightning Source LLC
Chambersburg PA
CBHW021144090426
42740CB00008B/927